# Hip Hop and Philosophy

# Popular Culture and Philosophy™
## Series Editor: William Irwin

"**TRUE** ʜɪᴘ-ʜᴏᴘ that hip hop's fifth element—the oft-forgotten element of knowledge or consciousness—is the most critical aspect of this thing we call hip-hop culture. This fact was not lost on Derrick Darby and Tommie Shelby, who dare to support the claim that hip hop is a legitimate worldview, primed to redefine what it means to be one with the world."

> — Mᴀʀᴋ Aɴᴛʜᴏɴʏ Nᴇᴀʟ,
> author of *New Black Man*

"**Sᴛᴇᴘ ᴀsɪᴅᴇ Sᴏᴄʀᴀᴛᴇs, Kᴀɴᴛ, ᴀɴᴅ Sᴀʀᴛʀᴇ—** new seekers of philosophical wisdom are on the scene, and they're giving us the word about sexuality, violence, language, politics, and other problems of philosophy. Ear to ground and mic in hand, this posse of philosophers are pondering the truths of inner-city life through hip-hop lenses, and broadcasting to the 'hood and the 'burbs. Big props to Derrick Darby, Tommie Shelby, and their philosophical crew for maintaining existential and ontological authenticity, aka keeping it real, in bringing us their message. Word up!"

> — Cʜᴀʀʟᴇs W. Mɪʟʟs,
> author of *The Racial Contract*

"**HIP HOP AND PHILOSOPHY** CONTRIBUTES
immeasurably to the rich traditions of both
philosophy and hip hop. Derrick Darby and Tommie
Shelby have dropped the needle on some slamming
tracks, merging the considered flow of the academy
with the funk and fury of the urban beat. The
range of concepts under analysis here is vast and
impressive. The level of philosophical inquiry is
consistently high and the spirit of hip hop is
carefully, lovingly evoked in ways that enrich our
understanding of the contemporary human condition."

— MURRAY FORMAN,
author of *The 'Hood Comes First*

"**PROFOUND, PROVOCATIVE, AND EVEN PLAYFUL,**
*Hip Hop and Philosophy* is a must read for anyone
interested in the philosophical questions raised by
American popular culture or the African American
experience. These hip-hop scholars put aside the
divide between high and low culture and just hit you
with depth and realness. *Hip Hop and Philosophy*
is a brilliant pedagogical tool and a wonderfully
insightful journey into a music form that has
captivated the globe. Big Up!"

— IMANI PERRY,
author of *Prophets of the Hood*

Popular Culture and Philosophy™

# Hip Hop and Philosophy

## Rhyme 2 Reason

Edited by
**DERRICK DARBY**
and
**TOMMIE SHELBY**

OPEN COURT
Chicago and La Salle, Illinois

*Volume 16 in the series, Popular Culture and Philosophy*™

Track 5 draws upon "Pragmatism, Art, and Violence," by Richard
Shusterman, in Tetsuji Yamamoto, ed., *Philosophical Designs for a
Socio-Cultural Transformation*, pp. 667–674, used by permission of
Rowman and Littlefield. Track 13 is a revised version of the article
by Bill E. Lawson which appeared in T.L. Lott and J.P. Pittman, eds.,
*A Companion to African American Philosophy*, reproduced here by
permission of Basil Blackwell.

**To order books from Open Court, call toll-free 1-800-815-2280,
or visit www.opencourtbooks.com.**

Open Court Publishing Company is a division of Carus Publishing
Company.

**Library of Congress Cataloging-in-Publication Data**

Hip hop and philosophy : rhyme 2 reason / edited by Derrick Darby
and Tommie Shelby.
     p. cm. — (Popular culture and philosophy ; v. 16)
    Includes bibliographical references and index.
    ISBN-13: 978-0-8126-9589-2 (trade pbk. : alk. paper)
    ISBN-10: 0-8126-9589-5 (trade pbk. : alk. paper)
    1. Rap (Music)—Social aspects. 2. Music and philosophy.
  3. Hip-hop. I. Darby, Derrick, 1967- II. Shelby, Tommie, 1967- III.
Series.
ML3918.R37H55 2005
782.421649'01—dc22

                             2005019833

*This book is dedicated to the memory of Christopher L. Shelby, a loving brother, committed teacher, and true hip-hop head, and to two beloved daughters, Nastassia and Tatiana Darby, the future of hip hop.*

# Contents

# Foreword

This pioneering and provocative book connects philosophy as a way of life to contemporary black creative forms of meaning and feeling. *Philo-sophia* (love of wisdom) was established in the West by Plato's world-historical enactment of the Socratic literary genre—a genre of cross-examination and artistic depiction that wrestles with the universal issues of life and death, joy and sorrow, justice and injustice, courage and cowardice, love and heartbreak. Plato's magnificent invention was indebted to the mimes of Sophron and his son Xenarchus and the comedies of Aristophanes—both poetic forms that portrayed the realities and lives of ordinary men and women. Plato's fundamental aims were threefold—to immortalize the thoughts and deeds of his mentor Socrates after his earth-shaking death, to dislodge poetry as the paramount authority for wisdom with philosophy, and to put forward a desirable way of life for achieving order for the soul and society in a world of irrational passions and pervasive ignorance.

Hip-hop music was created by talented black urban youth in the United States that fused New World African musical forms and rhetorical styles with new postmodern technologies. Like the spirituals, blues, and jazz—the greatest art forms to emerge from the U.S.A.—hip-hop music expressed and enacted Socratic *parrhesia* (bold, frank, and plain speech in the face of conventional morality and entrenched power). The basic aims of hip-hop music are threefold—to provide playful entertainment and serious art for the rituals of young people, to forge new ways of escaping social misery, and to explore novel responses for meaning and feeling in a market-driven world.

This rich collection of essays—edited by the visionaries Derrick Darby and Tommie Shelby—brings together the work of academic philosophers of all colors on the most influential cultural phenomena in the entertainment industry on the globe. This courageous effort requires not only that one know much across disciplines but also dig deep into African American life and culture.

In other words, one must adopt subtle metaphilosophical views that permit one to relate philosophical inquiry to art and entertainment in an illuminating manner and show how sophisticated forms of *paideia* (deep education), *phronesis* (practical wisdom), and *parrhesia* operate within the works of cultural producers in our contemporary world of free-market fundamentalism, aggressive machismo militarism, and escalating authoritarianism on the streets and in corporate suites. One must grapple with how and why gifted young people—here and abroad—choose hip-hop music as a dominant form of delight and instruction with good and bad effects to resist and reinforce the iron cage of present-day life. One must examine the black roots and global routes of this relatively new cultural genre. And one must evaluate the artistic excellence or histrionic mediocrity of the diverse performances that may result in Socratic awakening or sophistic sleepwalking for those who consume them.

The racial dimension of hip-hop music is inescapable—hence the challenge to examine black cultural expressions as more than mere documentary, political protest, or exotic appeal looms large. This means that philosophers of all stripes must break their relative silence on two pressing topics in their academic discipline—race and music. Just as most philosophers know much about Aristotle, Kant, and Rorty but know little about W.E.B. Du Bois, Alain Locke, or Anna Julia Cooper, most philosophers grasp the significance of Rousseau, Nietzsche, and Adorno but little of Beethoven, Sondheim, or Ellington. And though hip-hop music has yet to produce a figure of the stature of a Mozart, Coltrane, or Aretha Franklin, many towering hip-hop artists deserve our philosophical attention—and the hip-hop phenomena itself warrants examination.

Cicero said Socrates turned our attention from the heavens to earth. William James noted that pragmatism took philosophy from the academy to the streets. This path-blazing book begins and ends with the language and realities of the streets—especially the mean streets of the downtrodden yet creative demos in postmodern America. Does not the love of wisdom require that we interrogate in a Socratic way the voices and views that have emerged from the killing fields and gangsterized hoods of the American empire?

CORNEL WEST

# Shout Outs

Big ups to Bill Irwin, a.k.a. The Bountiful Producer, for being down with this project from the get-go and to Bill Lawson and Eddie Glaude for suggesting we take it on. Much respect to our almighty posse of philosophers for their faith in us, patience, hard work, and amazing creativity in moving from rhyme to reason. Big ups to the Open Court crew, especially to David Ramsay Steele, a.k.a. Da Voice in da Machine, for sage advice and for hyping us to rock the boulevard and the bourgeoisie. Props to Zick Rubin for doing what he does so well. Good lookin' out Z! Props also to Lidet Tilahun for research assistance. We are grateful to our home institutions, Harvard University and Texas A&M University, for their financial support of this project. We learned much from our many friends, colleagues, and students who have talked to us about the pleasures and perils of mixing hip hop and philosophy. Most of all, we want to thank our loving wives, Angela and Jessie, for their unwavering support as we worked on this book and for enduring our many long late night phone conversations about all things hip hop and philosophy. Peace, y'all!

# From Rhyme to Reason: This Shit Ain't Easy

Grandmaster Flash, who perfected the craft of cuttin' n' scratchin' and who united DJ-ing with MC-ing to take hip hop to a higher level, drops this gem on us: "hip hop is the only genre of music that allows us to talk about almost anything . . . It's highly controversial, but that's the way the game is."[1] The same thing can be said about philosophy. It allows us to reflect on and argue about almost anything, and it too is highly controversial. As a matter of fact, philosophy was so controversial in ancient Athens that its most influential philosopher, Socrates, caught a case for "corrupting the youth" with it and was sent to death row for droppin' science on the streets. Socrates's intricate arguments, not unlike the much sweated lyrical technique of Rakim, frustrated his interlocutors, often tying them up in knots before they were able to reach a higher state of enlightenment. And since the haterz couldn't understand him and the young headz couldn't get enough of him, the government smoked the greatest philosopher of his time. Yeah, that's the way the game is!

Philosophy is an ancient discipline devoted to the pursuit of wisdom. But how should we pursue it? Well, like Notorious B.I.G., Supernatural, and Mos Def, Socrates let his knowledge flow straight from his dome in mental battles with lesser minds. He engineered the pursuit of wisdom by asking people about the grounds of their beliefs and then dropped a strategic series of probing questions on them to test the validity of their answers. This Socratic *elenchus*, or cross-examination freestyle as it came to be known, suggests that true wisdom about God, love, virtue, truth, justice, or whatever, is best pursued by modifying one's beliefs in response to interrogation and counterexamples. Fans of hip hop will peep the fact that Socrates's steelo

---

[1] Alan Light, ed., *The Vibe History of Hip Hop* (New York: Vibe Ventures, 1999), p. vii.

is similar to the call-and-response style used by talented MCs puttin' in work to answer life's pressing questions by engaging in epic lyrical battles that sometimes turn into beefs.

Although the release of Sugarhill Gang's "Rapper's Delight" was hip hop's first major commercial hit—introducing hip hop to a broader audience—real students of the rap game know that hip hop was in full effect long before this hit dropped in '79. Students of hip-hop history remember when Boogie Down Productions—on their classic cut "The Bridge is Over"—made it painfully clear to MC Shan and the QB crew that hip-hop music did not start on the streets of Queensbridge. Before the rise of BDP in the South Bronx and Afrika Bambaataa and the mighty Zulu Nation before them, there was DJ Kool Herc in the West Bronx, inventor of the cut n' scratch. Herc rocked the streets of the Boogie Down with two Technics turntables, a mixer and Herculoid speakers with his signature "Apache" mix.

So check it! Putting aside this unforgettable Bronx-Queensbridge beef on the question of where it all got started way back when, this much is clear. From project recreation centers to outdoor street parties fully equipped with DJs, MCs, fat speakers, graffiti artists, and breakdancers, hip hop came from the *streets*. Word up! But so did philosophy. Not from the streets of NYC or Compton but from the streets of ancient Athens—more than 2000 years before hip hop—where Socrates used verbal intercourse to school young headz on how the unexamined life was not worth living and encouraged them to develop their minds and search for the Truth, like KRS-One is still doing today.[2] The bottom line is that hip hop and philosophy are examinations of life on the street and the search for wisdom by those from the street. Word is bond!

But, as we all know, philosophy did not remain on the streets of Athens. It went international, traveling to the far reaches of the globe, and it is now considered one of mankind's most esteemed disciplines. Plato, Socrates's greatest pupil, thought that philosophy was so essential that only philosopher kings were fit to rule the Republic. And as with philosophy, hip hop has not remained on the streets of urban America. In less than three decades, its reach has extended to the entire world,

---

[2] KRS-One, *Ruminations* (New York: Welcome Rain Publishers, 2003).

and it has become synonymous with American popular culture. Back in the day, Kurtis Blow imagined what it would be like if a rapper ruled the world, and after they acquired the knowledge, hip-hop legends, Run-D.M.C., proclaimed themselves Kings of Rock and demanded that Sucker MCs call them sire, which brings us to why we—two duns born and raised in the hood—decided to drop this gem on 'em.

The aim of the Open Court series on Popular Culture and Philosophy is to use popular culture as a medium to introduce philosophy to a general audience. This is all good. But this series wouldn't be complete without a volume that unites hip hop and philosophy, moving seamlessly between the ivory tower and the boulevard, all for the sake of the love of wisdom. No doubt some critics will characterize this mixing of philosophy and hip hop as a perverse union of the sacred and the profane. Yet our intent is to highlight the often suppressed, fifth element of hip hop—knowledge—to represent the funky-ass ways that philosophy is carried out in everyday life, often in unexpected places and using unconventional means.[3] Philosophizing is something we all do, at least some of the time. True that some hip-hop artists have turned the game into a way to get paid, and some philosophers have done the same. But record companies don't own hip hop and universities don't own philosophy. Both belong to whoever understands, loves, and respects them.

The tracks laid down in this volume take this point of view. They show how taking both hip hop and philosophy seriously furthers our quest for knowledge. Rakim and St. Thomas Aquinas school us on the nature of God. Lauryn Hill and Plato reveal the mysteries of love. Lil' Kim and Sartre knowledge us on the objectifying gaze. Ice Cube and Kant ponder the legitimacy of punishment. Nas and Hegel probe the depths of self-consciousness. Missy Elliott and David Hume demonstrate how one can be a feminist and yet love hip hop. Dead Prez and Frantz Fanon identify subtle challenges to living an authentic life. Underground rap and Thomas Hobbes enrich our understanding of what it means to be revolutionary. KRS-One and the pragmatists shed light on the benefits and risks of violence. Hip-hop

---

[3] See "Zulu War Cry," *The Source* 185 (March 2005), p. 64.

cinema and Cornel West help us to avoid confusing race with culture. Dave Chappelle and John Stuart Mill hip us to the ethics of using terms such as "bitch" and "nigga." Common and René Descartes investigate how the mind gains knowledge through perception. And Public Enemy and John Locke teach us how to recognize and respond to injustice.

Raekwon of the Wu-Tang Clan has said of rap: "To flow—that shit is not easy. Rap, to me, is slang poetry. It answers your questions: why young kids is doin' bad, why they turn to drugs to get away from their misery. This is the shit we talk about—and how to escape it."[4] The same is true of philosophy. It answers your questions, but only if you have discipline and patience, like Bambaataa looking for the perfect beat. So, to accomplish our venerable mission we have assembled a Wu-Tang like Clan of highly skilled philosophers who are hip-hop fans *and* have infiltrated the universities of America, Shoalin style, to gangsta doctorates in philosophy. Our Ph.D. Clan is representin' the Boogie Down, Queensbridge, Brooklyn, Philly, the West Coast, Chi-town, the ATL, the Dirty South, Jamaica, and all points in between, with one common aim, namely, to illuminate the philosophical significance of hip hop. Each one, teach one. KRS-One, Rakim, MC Lyte, Pac, Nas, and other great lyricists use rhyme skillz to teach us daily life lessons. Our Clan of philosopher kings and queens will move from rhyme to reason to take up perennial philosophical questions that have perplexed MCs and philosophers alike. And believe us, this shit ain't easy.

---

[4] *The Vibe History of Hip Hop*, p. 98.

# Disk 1

# Da Mysteries: God, Love, and Knowledge

# 1

# Yo! It Ain't No Mystery: Who Is God?

DERRICK DARBY

## Godz N the Hood

"Whad up G?" This is how young *godz* stepped to older godz back in the day in my old hood, Queensbridge. Nas's recital on "Life's a Bitch" (*Illmatic*) and Mobb Deep's chronicles of life from the cradle to the grave on *The Infamous* represent just how much life has changed from when I was a young G growing up in the Bridge on the 41st side of Vernon. As Havoc schools us, beef is settled nowadays not by fists but by blessing sons with iron, loaded with hollow-tips in Gotti clips. And "Whad up G?" is how young and old hood *gangstas* step to one another. Young headz in the old hood—where many men wish death upon one another, as 50 Cent preaches on *Get Rich or Die Tryin'*—are livin' the life of gangstas, straight thuggin', and anticipating the day when death comes around the corner, so that after their downfall they can follow Tupac and the Notorious B.I.G. and be buried as a G.

But back in the day when we rolled up on older godz we weren't seeking beef. We sought the fifth element of hip hop—knowledge. We offered much respect to the older godz who schooled us on the science of the divine mathematics and the divine alphabet. And the older godz were always game for droppin' science. On "Older Gods" (*Wu-Tang Forever*), Ghostface Killah and Raekwon reminisce about the days of old when the older godz put young Gs on and taught us daily life lessons. Back then lyrically gifted godz used rhyme skillz to transcribe the lost and found lessons into a form that made them really real for us—hip hop. Like Mobb Deep represents it on the "Quiet Storm" (*Murda Muzik*), from our perspective the older godz were kickin' "the real shit, shit to make em feel shit . . . drugs to your eardrum, the raw uncut." From their project window pulpit, these poor righteous teachers and lyrically gifted MCs gave their congregations a street side perspective on abiding philosophical questions concerning the nature and existence of God, the problem of evil, and questions concerning how right-eous godz and earthz should be livin'. This perspective was informed by an astute yet realistic appreciation of the project plight, and by a prophetic vision of how the select five percent could enlighten and rescue the lost and misguided eighty-five percent from the devilish ten percent by studying and preach-ing knowledge of self.

Some things have certainly changed in the old hood where many were beginners as Five Percenters before turning to sin-ners, as Nas recalls on "Life's a Bitch." But praise be to Gomars O Dubar that some things have stayed the same. Although many young Gs in the hood now view themselves as young gangstas and not young godz, some of hip hop's divinely inspired rap-pers, the microphone fiend Rakim Allah, Brand Nubian, Nas, and the Wu-Tang Clan, continue the venerable tradition of using rhyme skillz to preach divine wisdom to gangstas and non-gangstas alike. They shepherd the lost sheep in search of what Inspectah Deck and Method Man envision on *Wu-Tang Forever* as a better tomorrow in which godz and earthz attain true knowledge of self and overcome the Devil's trickery, trickery which has lured lost souls in the concrete hell to party, drink, smoke, fuck, dream, and scheme their lives away causing their seeds to grow up the same way. This posse of divine rappers knowledge us on many longstanding questions in the philoso-phy of religion. But on this track I'm gonna rap about just one, the question Rakim Allah explores on his joint "The Mystery" (*The 18th Letter*): Who is God?

## Who Is God?

God, as conceived by traditional Western theism, is an omnipo-tent (all-powerful), wholly benevolent (perfectly good), and supreme creator of the universe. There are other aspects of divine nature, such as omniscience (all-knowing), timelessness (eternal existence), and immutability (incapable of undergoing any change in essence). The great medieval philosophical theologian Saint Thomas Aquinas (1225–1274) is a canonical source for philosophical reflection on all aspects of the presumed nature of God and for classical arguments concerning God's existence. And there are logical connections between how we conceive of God's nature and how we go about showin' and provin' God's existence, though we won't peep them on this track. This track will speak to just one aspect of God's nature, his power. The other aspects of divine nature would need equal billing if we wanted to produce a complete CD on God's essence. But only a fool would give up too many hot tracks before signing with a label. Word up!

## Divine Omnipotence

What can an omnipotent being do? On *The 18th Letter*, the microphone fiend Rakim Allah tells us that by his mental intercourse God created the sun, all planets, and all forms of life including man, as well as one of his best designs, man's mind. God also displayed his awesome power by splitting seas for Moses and making waves for Noah. Peepin' all the great works and powers attributed to God might lead us to conclude that an omnipotent being can do *all* things. You name it. God can do it. This is precisely what it means to say that God is omnipotent, namely, that God is a being who can do all things. But can God really do *all* things?

To be sure, splitting the Red Sea, flooding the entire Earth, and designing and creating the world are impressive works requiring great power. But let's suppose that we can imagine even greater works requiring even greater power. On "Let's Get High" (*2001*), Kurupt invites fellow Gs to get high. And on "Bury Me a G" (*Thug Life Volume I*), Macadoshis raps about how thugged out Gs kick it with homies in the hood, gettin' drunk and hittin' blunts. Under the influence of Cali weed—some serious Cali weed no doubt—one might challenge God to roll a blunt so strong that even he can't hit it. It won't do, of course, to simply say that God don't get high because God is perfectly good. It remains to be shown and proven that a perfectly good being can't get high.

For one thing, weed is legal in other parts of the world, as Young Buck reminds us when he reflects on his trip to Amsterdam.[1] Moreover, as he points out, weed is also legal in the U.S.A. in certain states such as Alaska where weed is deemed necessary for medical purposes. So this rules out the objection that a perfectly good being can't get high because gettin' high is illegal and a perfectly good being can't do what is illegal. No doubt many of us join Young Buck in wondering: "Why you giving it to the person if it's so fucking bad for you?" Furthermore, Young Buck peeps the fact that gettin' high has certain positive consequences: "Weed helps my brain, it relaxes things for me. I love that it eases my mind. I can be mad at the world, smoke me a blunt and kind of like weigh out my problems a little." Somewhat more controversially, he also claims that weed could lower the crime rate if it was legal everywhere: "You could be madder than a muthafucka, like, 'I'ma feel to kill this muthafucka,' Next thing you know, smoke a fat-ass blunt and be like, 'Fuck it. I'll forget about that shit.'" These reflections suggest that being perfectly good and getting high are not necessarily incompatible. It appears, therefore, that God could indeed be challenged to roll a blunt so strong that even he can't hit it.

But for the sake of argument with the weed haterz, suppose that the divine attribute of benevolence prohibits God from actually inhaling the blunt and gettin' high much like Bill (and I don't mean Bushwick Bill) was prevented from inhaling his weed. Still, God's benevolence certainly does not prevent God from merely rolling a blunt so strong that even he can't hit it and showin' and provin' that he really can do all things. This challenge ain't no joke! And it can't be ignored by those who believe that God can do *all* things by virtue of being an omnipotent being.

Here's the dilemma. If God can roll a blunt so strong that even he can't hit it, then there will be at least one thing that God can't do, namely, hit the blunt he just rolled. If God can't roll a blunt so strong that even he can't hit it, then there will be at least one thing that God can't do, namely, roll a blunt so strong that even he can't hit it. In both cases, of course, God is screwed. Either he can't hit the blunt he just rolled or he can't roll the blunt to smoke. So either way God can't accept Kurupt's

---

[1] Young Buck, "Legalize It," *XXL Magazine* (October 2004), p. 68.

invitation to get high—at least not with heavenly-rolled weed. But more to the point, the claim that God can do *all* things by virtue of being omnipotent is shown and proven to be plainly false.

This dilemma, which we can call "the paradox of the blunt," can be generated with other examples. In "U Not Like Me" (*Get Rich or Die Tryin'*), 50 Cent says that when we see him in the hood he got at least two guns; he carries the glock and his "nigga" Tony carries the M-1s holding 50 down against OGs tryin' to rock him. So just as we can generate the paradox of the blunt, we can also generate "the paradox of the glock." Still under the influence of the same chronic that prompted the first dilemma, we can challenge God to create a glock so powerful that even he can't wield it. If God can't create the glock, then there will be at least one thing that God can't do, namely, create a glock so powerful that even he can't wield it. If God can create the glock, then there will be at least one thing that God can't do, namely, wield the glock he just created. So in either case God can't hold 50 down in the hood—at least not with a divinely forged glock—and 50 is better off sticking with Tony and his M-1s for security.

The paradox of the blunt and the paradox of the glock serve the same philosophical purpose, namely, to challenge the claim that God can do all things, which in this context, amounts to challenging the attribution of omnipotence to God. These challenges must be handled with great care by defenders of God's omnipotence. Theists can't simply respond to them by conceding that God is not omnipotent after all, since omnipotence and the other aspects of divine nature are assumed to be a *necessary* aspect of God's essence. Without these attributes God simply would not be God. A more promising response to these challenges would be to follow Saint Thomas Aquinas's strategy in *Summa Theologica*. Aquinas searches for a more bulletproof explanation of what an omnipotent being can do, one that can deflect the blunt and glock paradoxes.

## Aquinas's Solution to the Paradoxes of the Blunt and the Glock

Appreciating the difficulty in explaining in what precisely God's omnipotence consists, Aquinas proposes that we clarify the meaning of the word "all," when we say that God can do *all* things, to arrive at a more satisfactory explanation of God's omnipotence (*Summa Theologica*, I, Q. 25, Art. 3). He contends that God's power extends not to all things but to all things that are possible. Hence the more precise explanation of God's omnipotence is that God can do all things that are logically possible. This is to say that everything that doesn't imply a contradiction in terms is within the scope of God's power. For example, a square circle is a contradiction in terms. So are non-rotating spinning dubs. Therefore, conceding that God can't create a square circle or non-rotating spinning dubs doesn't undermine his omnipotence. Rather than saying that God can't do these things, according to Aquinas, it is more appropriate to say that they can't be done, period!

Is Aquinas's definition of omnipotence bulletproof? Can it deflect the paradox of the blunt and the paradox of the glock? Perhaps. But only if these paradoxes require that God do something that implies a contradiction in terms such as creating a square circle or non-rotating spinning dubs. When we first peep the matter, there appear to be no contradictions involved. After all, we all know Gs capable of rolling blunts too strong to hit (some of us may have committed this sin once upon a time) and it is plainly obvious that guns too powerful to be wielded (with our bare hands) can be created. So what's the problem? If God is truly omnipotent and can do all things that don't imply a contradiction in terms, why can't he roll a blunt so strong that even he can't hit it or why can't he create a glock so powerful that even he can't wield it?

Closer inspection reveals that these paradoxes demand too much of an omnipotent being. Hardly any reflection is needed to see that demanding God create a square circle, or non-rotating spinning dubs, is a contradiction in terms. But we must scope the matter a bit closer to see the contradiction imbedded in the blunt and glock paradoxes.

Consider the blunt case. If we accept Aquinas's definition of omnipotence, then demanding that God roll a blunt so strong that even he can't hit it amounts to demanding that God roll something that is hittable yet can't be hit by a being that has the power to hit anything numbered among the possible things. Herein lies the contradiction in terms, which is not substantively different from demanding that God create a square circle or

non-rotating spinning dubs. Blunts are rolled for hittin'. Unhittable blunts ain't really blunts. A blunt too strong for God to hit ain't really a blunt. Therefore, God's power is not diminished by virtue of not being able to roll something that is rolled for hittin' and yet can't be hit by a being that can hit anything numbered among the possible things. Similar science can be dropped to show and prove that the paradox of the glock also demands too much of a being that can do all things numbered among the possible things.

The bottom line is that the idea of a blunt too strong for God to hit, or a glock too powerful for God to wield, are beyond the realm of the possible. And as Aquinas concludes: "such [things] cannot come under the divine omnipotence; not indeed because of any defect in the power of God, but because it has not the nature of a feasible or possible thing."[2]

Of course not all philosophers agree with this limitation on God's power to the realm of possible things. Some of them will insist that the problem is not with God but with us. Just because our understanding is finite and we cannot imagine a square circle, non-rotating spinning dubs, unhittable blunts, or glocks too powerful to wield, doesn't mean that God's power can't extend to the impossible or contradictory. The great modern philosopher René Descartes (1596–1650), who spent time in Amsterdam and could have smoked weed legally,[3] thought that the problem was with us. Descartes put it this way: "in general we may affirm that God can do everything we comprehend, but not that He cannot do what we cannot comprehend; for it would be rash to think our imagination reaches as far as His power does."[4] From here Descartes infers that God could've made things so that "it should not be true that the three angles of a triangle are equal to two right angles, or in general that it should not be true that contradictories cannot be together."[5] Likewise he could've permitted other contradictions such as squared circles and non-rotating spinning dubs (deuce and a quarter no doubt), though

---

[2] *Summa Theologica*, I, Q. 25, Art. 3.
[3] Props to Bill Irwin for dropping this gem on me.
[4] Letter to Mersenne (15th April, 1630), in *Descartes: Philosophical Writings*, edited by Elizabeth Anscombe and Peter Thomas Geach (Indianapolis: Bobbs-Merrill, 1971), pp. 259–260.
[5] Letter to Mesland (2nd May, 1644), p. 291.

we can't figure out how he could've done these things due to our finite nature.

If we follow Descartes and claim that God's power has no limits and that God can do all things possible and impossible, then we can simply concede that God can indeed roll a blunt too strong for him to hit or create a glock too powerful for him to wield yet deny that these things undermine God's omnipotence. For if God can do the impossible to begin with by rolling a blunt too strong for him to hit, or creating a glock too powerful for him to wield, then he certainly can do other impossible things, such as hit the blunt too strong to smoke and wield the glock too powerful to wield. The point is that if skeptics under the influence of the chronic can generate the paradoxes by requiring—on the sneak tip—that God do the impossible in formulating the paradoxes, then we can certainly dispel them under the influence of the same chronic by supposing that God can do other impossible tasks.[6]

But even if we suppose that Aquinas's restriction of God's power to the logically possible is preferable to Descartes's unrestricted definition of omnipotence, is Aquinas's definition totally bulletproof?

## Divine Omnipotence and Tupac's Jailbreak Paradox

If the above paradoxes fail it is because they demand that God perform tasks that don't fall within the realm of possibility and thus aren't objects of power. Hence the fact that God can't perform them implies no limit on God's power and no defect in the claim that God can do all things that are logically possible. Therefore, they don't imply a contradiction in terms. But there are other tasks that appear to call God's power into question, tasks which are logically possible and don't obviously imply a contradiction in terms.

In a June 1996 interview with the editors of *Vibe*, Tupac pops a cap in Aquinas's supposedly bulletproof definition of omnipotence. In explaining his skepticism about Five Percenters claiming to be God, Tupac recalls his challenge to a Five Percenter

---

[6] For more on this "bullshit," see Harry G. Frankfurt, "The Logic of Omnipotence," *The Philosophical Review* 73 (1964), pp. 262–63.

on lock down with him in the joint: If you God, then pop the fuckin' gate and get me free and up outta here.

Peep the dilemma underlying this challenge. If you God then you can do anything that is not impossible, that doesn't imply a contradiction. Aiding and abetting Pac's escape is possible and doesn't imply a contradiction. Hence God should be able to pop the gate and set Pac free. Yet God can't set Pac free. But if God can't pop the gate then God is even weaker than we thought. With this challenge, Pac has shown and proven that God can't even do certain things that are possible and don't imply a contradiction.

This dilemma, which we can call *the jailbreak paradox*, is similar to a dilemma raised by Aquinas in *Summa Theologica*, which can be called *the paradox of sin*. Sinning isn't a logical impossibility and doesn't imply a contradiction. Gangstas and non-gangstas sin all the time; some non-gangstas and gangstas even get high all the time! If God can do anything that is not impossible or doesn't imply a contradiction, then God should be able to sin. But God can't sin! Hence God can't do some things that are possible *and* don't imply a contradiction.

Although rolling a blunt too strong to hit or creating a glock too powerful to wield are states of affairs that imply a contradiction and prove to be impossible, springing Pac from the joint and sinning are logically possible and don't imply a contradiction, so a God that can do all things that are possible should be able to do these things. If he can't then his omnipotence appears to be a sham!

Tupac's jailbreak paradox and Aquinas's paradox of sin force us to yet another redefinition of God's omnipotence, one that takes into account that divine essence consists of other attributes in addition to omnipotence. As Rakim reminds us on his track, "The 18th Letter," God blesses his flock with dialogue by virtue of being beneficent. Because God has many perfections we must explain the meaning of his omnipotence in relation to other aspects of his divine nature, in particular, we must explain it in relation to God's beneficence.

In his *Discourse Concerning the Being and Attributes of God*, seventeenth-century British philosopher Samuel Clarke (1675–1729) distinguished between *natural* and *moral* contradictions. God creating a glock too powerful to wield is an example of a natural contradiction and is ruled out by the constraint

that God can only do that which is possible. In contrast, God springing Pac from the joint or sinning are examples of moral contradictions. If God were to do these things he would contradict his nature as a perfectly good being. Hence insofar as injustice and sinning are contrary to God's benevolence then his failure to do these things is no diminution of his power.

Socrates (469–399 B.C.), the great ancient Greek philosopher, was arguably as close to being perfectly good as any mortal could be, and he rejected an invitation to be sprung from the joint by his homie, Crito. And Socrates's situation was graver than Tupac's because Socrates was on death row (and I don't mean the label). Socrates dropped several powerful arguments on Crito against popping the gate to set him free. One argument was that a perfectly good person intent on living righteously would never return a wrong for a wrong, and because escaping from the joint would be to return the wrong of being sentenced to death unjustly with the wrong of preventing the state from carrying out its verdict, Socrates was gonna chill and face death. Another argument was that a perfectly good person discharged his obligations, and owing to his debt of gratitude to the state in return for having enjoyed all of the benefits it provided him during his lifetime, Socrates was gonna abide by its ruling that he face death and be buried as a G.

Now I'm not saying that Tupac would have found these arguments compelling, especially coming from a Five Percenter on lock down with him trying to explain why he wasn't going to set Pac free though he could if he wanted to. But if we assume that God is perfectly good, in addition to being all-powerful, with Clarke's distinction between natural and moral contradictions and Socrates's arguments in hand, we can bump off the jailbreak paradox. In one sense, the sense of being able to do that which is possible, God can certainly set Pac free by popping the gate. But in another sense, namely, in the sense of being able to do so given who he is, God can't pop the gate and spring Pac from the joint, since to do so would morally contradict his divine nature as a omnipotent being who is also perfectly good. God simply ain't gonna return injustice with injustice. Now of course one could reply that if God did pop the gate to spring Pac from the joint then Pac's jailbreak must be a good thing since God can do no wrong. But this rap is for another track.

## Ain't No Mystery

On "Ain't No Mystery," Brand Nubian's Lord Jamar speaks to the futility of looking to the sky to find a Mystery God (*In God We Trust*). Instead he implores us to look within self for knowledge of God. For Lord Jamar, this means using his Third Eye to see that the Black Man is God and that it ain't no mystery. From a more general perspective, however, looking within self for knowledge of God means using the light of reason to discern God's essence and the implications of God having this essence. And when we do this, we can conclude with respect to God's omnipotence that the plain truth of the matter is that God can do anything that can be done by God.

Now unlike the microphone fiend, Ra, I don't know how many 7s I got in my head. But I do know that it's gonna take more than a couple of philosophers and professors from the smartest colleges to figure out the science I'm droppin' on this track because it's much deeper than it sounds. Like Nas and Nature, I'm in too deep. I've been exposed to too many arguments for too long and can go on and on, knowhatImsayin'; so I better end it right here. Yo! It ain't no mystery. Word is bond. Peace, God.[7]

---

[7] Much love to my homie, Tommie Shelby, for checking my flow on this track, and to Finnie Coleman. Much love to Professor Richard Gale for cultivating my interest in the philosophy of religion. And much love to my fam, Ahmed Johnson, a.k.a. Ah-Stick, for loving hip hop and Queensbridge from the beginning, and to his mama, my Aunt 'Rain, a.k.a. the unofficial mayor of Da Bridge, for always keeping it real with us ever since we were shorties running the streets of QB.

# 2

# Ain't (Just) 'bout da Booty: Funky Reflections on Love

TOMMIE SHELBY

From blues to country and rock & roll to neo-soul, popular music is replete with love songs. And hip hop is no exception. Although it is generally associated with illegal drugs, vulgar language, gratuitous violence, and raunchy sex, those schooled in the culture know that the music also speaks to the mysteries of the heart. Whether we're talking old school—Whodini's "One Love" (*Back in Black*) and LL's, "I Need Love" (*Bigger and Deffer*)—or new school—Lauryn Hill's *Miseducation of Lauryn Hill* and OutKast's *The Love Below*—there are reflections on love in hip hop. But are any of these funky ruminations on love philosophically profound?

Let's go back, way the hell back, to Plato's *Symposium*, one of the oldest inquiries into the meaning of love in the Western tradition.[1] Plato is to philosophy what Public Enemy is to political rap; he didn't create philosophy, but he perfected the craft, brought it to a wider audience, and deeply influenced future lovers of wisdom. Plato's writings, *Symposium* included, take the form of dialogues between fictional characters, all based on well-known personalities in ancient Athens, and often featuring Socrates, the famous philosopher and Plato's teacher.

The real-life Socrates only freestyled: he never wrote down or recorded his philosophy. Like Supernatural, he kept it all in his dome, letting it flow spontaneously against anyone who

---

[1] Plato, "Symposium," in *Plato: Complete Works* (Indianapolis: Hackett, 1997), pp. 457–505.

14

wanted to engage in a battle of ideas. He was so skilled in his combative, questioning style that the haters just wouldn't let him live, making him pay the ultimate price for staying true to the game. Had he ever put pen to pad, the title of his greatest hits might have been *Get Knowledge or Die Tryin'*. Many, including Plato, have been known to sample—and sometimes bite—his best shit.

*Symposium* is named for its setting: an extravagant drinking party, where duns ain't sippin' on Seagram's and OJ but on Rémy and Möet. Because Socrates and his clique had got so drunk the night before, they decide to chill and not to drink too much. To keep it interesting, though, they form a cipher and take turns rapping about the meaning and value of love, just to see who's got the smoothest flow and illest rhymes. Let's peep the most impressive performances.

## Love Haters: Skepticism about Romantic Love

MC Pausanias keeps it conscious, positive, and, at times, kinda preachy. He claims there are two kinds of love, which we might call *vulgar* and *spiritual*. The vulgar lover seeks only the physical pleasure of another's body—almost anyone's body, as long as they fine—because, to be blunt, he just wanna get his freak on (*Symposium* 181b). Such love is not to be honored or praised, according to Pausanias, because it is unstable and thus unreliable. It is the kind of love associated with young folk. As Andre 3000 says: "I'm too young to be settlin' down, quick to change my mind tomorrow / So now can I borrow your timid torso / More so than your soul, honest me gotta be how I roll."[2]

In contrast, those inspired by spiritual love, while no doubt attracted to beautiful bodies, are primarily interested in another's soul, and not just any soul but one that is righteous. They want to share everything and to spend their lives with their beloved because of the beauty and consistency of their beloved's moral character. This more mature kind of love, Pausanias claims, is truly honorable, for the lover who seeks it aims to become a better person. True love, according to this conception, can't be just about the booty.

---

[2] OutKast, "Spread," *Speakerboxxx/The Love Below* (Arista, 2003).

Looking for traces of Pausanias in hip hop, we find plenty of talk about booty—not to mention booties shakin' in music videos—and a strong tradition of skepticism toward spiritual love. Some deny its very existence. Others regard its pursuit as not worth all the damn trouble. Still others see it as a kind of trap, as a means for the opportunistic to get their hands on your cheddar. Jay-Z expresses this sentiment: "Me give my heart to a woman? / Not for nothin', never happen / I'll be forever mackin' / Heart cold as assassins / I got no passion."[3]

Now these critics of love do value mutually beneficial sexual relationships, either for the pleasures of sex alone or as part of a trade of sex for material goods, power, or money. Lil' Kim suggests that she values these relationships for both reasons. Sometimes she emphasizes the intrinsic satisfaction of good sex, especially the oral variety: "Lick it right the first time or ya gotta do it over / Like it's rehearsal for a Tootsie commercial."[4] At other times, the Queen B@#$h views it as simply a means to stick a nigga for his cream: "That's how many times I wanna cum, twenty-one / And another one, and another one, and another one / 24 karats nigga / That's when I'm fuckin' wit' the average nigga."[5] But these transactions in the sexual marketplace, whatever their value or attraction, should not be confused with love.

Perhaps we need to specify what kind of love we're talking about. As important as they are, we ain't talking about love for friends, family, or God. Snoop and the Dogg Pound got love for all their niggaz and bitches, Eminem got much love for his daughter Hailie, and Nas has love for one God and one love for his homies on lockdown.[6] Our concern, however, is with erotic or romantic love, the kind of love intimately, if not inextricably, linked with sexual desire. So the type of love we're talking about isn't *just* about "that thing," but sex has got to be a part of the equation.

---

[3] Jay-Z, "Big Pimpin'," *Volume 3: Life and Times of S. Carter* (Rock-A-Fella/Def Jam 1999).

[4] Lil' Kim, "How Many Licks?" *The Notorious KIM* (Atlantic, 2000).

[5] Lil' Kim, "Big Momma Thang," *Hard Core* (Undeas/Big Beat, 1996).

[6] See Snoop Dogg, "For All My Niggaz & Bitches," *Doggystyle* (Death Row, 1993); Eminem, "Hailie's Song," *The Eminem Show* (Interscope, 2002); and Nas, "One Love," *Illmatic* (Columbia, 1994); and "One Mic," *Stillmatic* (Columbia, 2001).

Those dubious about romantic love could reply to Pausanias that, to the extent they care about cultivating virtue, they do it by loving, admiring, and learning from their crew, family, and God. And when it comes to sexual desire, well, they're keepin' it strictly vulgar. Following the lead of 3000, we can call persons who deny that they need somebody to love "love haters." Can we find a convincing response to the love haters?

## You're All I Need: Love as Completeness and Eternal Unity

Next on the mic is the funky Aristophanes, whose steelo involves the clever use of myth and vivid allegory. He tells a tale about how, back in the day, each person possessed two heads, both male and female genitalia, and two sets of arms and legs. Consequently, these folks were strong and in no need of love, whether spiritual or vulgar. This made them arrogant and they tried to start beef with the gods. So Zeus quite naturally had to put them in their place. He dropped a thunderbolt on dem asses, cutting each person in two and leaving the halves physically deformed and feeling unfulfilled.

The moral of Aristophanes's odd story is this. Until we find true love, we are incomplete and discontent (*Symposium* 189d–190d). While in this imperfect state, we long for our "other half," desperate to feel whole and at peace. We are in search of that missing part of ourselves, our natural complement. Once a person meets the eyes of that special one "the two are struck from their senses by love, by a sense of belonging to one another, and by desire, and they don't want to be separated from one another, not even for a moment" (*Symposium* 192b–c).

Aristophanes admits that, despite their undying attraction, most lovers can't explain why they desire to be together forever. They regard their love as a mystery, and perhaps no less worthwhile because of it—think here of the "strange love" between Flavor Flav and Brigitte Nielsen. Yet they do know that sex plays a role in erotic love. Sexual intercourse and procreation affirm and symbolize their love. They represent that mutual but inexplicable desire for eternal unity. The couple in love wants to join their bodies in the most intimate way possible and through this to jointly produce a child that will embody their oneness in a single precious soul. With this, Aristophanes thinks he has uncovered the secret of the desire for spiritual love: It is simply the pursuit of wholeness and eternal unity.

This point of view is expressed in Method Man's hit, "I'll Be There For You / You're All I Need To Get By," which features the background vocals of Mary J. Blige.[7] In an uncharacteristic display of sentimentality, our man Johnny Blaze, sometimes known as the Panty Raider, articulates a conception of love through dope rhymes about the utter fulfillment and devotion that comes only with love's bond, a love that has its highest expression in the creation of a child. This vision of love is reinforced through other elements of the track. Blige expresses the idea of "love at first sight" when she invokes the hook from the classic song of the same title, performed originally by Marvin Gaye and Tammi Terrell: "Like sweet morning dew / I took one look at you / And it was plain to see / you were my destiny." And the theme of eternal unity comes in the form of a haunting sample that loops throughout from "Me & My Bitch" by the late Notorious B.I.G.: "Lie together, cry together / I swear to God, I hope we fuckin' die together."

But has Aristophanes really met the challenge of the love hater? Even with the help of Meth, Mary J, Biggie, Marvin and Tammi (and Ashford and Simpson who wrote the original tune), I don't think he has. This conception of love is likely to be compelling only to those who feel incomplete or imperfect to begin with. For individuals who already feel self-sufficient or who value highly their independence, this account gives them no reason to seek spiritual love. As Jay-Z says, because life is already difficult enough, no need to add all the unnecessary drama that love typically brings: "If you havin' girl problems, I feel bad for you, son / I got ninety-nine problems but a bitch ain't one."[8]

But hold up, wait a minute. Perhaps we can preserve Aristophanes's insight—that love is the pursuit of wholeness and eternal unity—by joining friendship with sex. The love hater admits that he needs the love of friends and also needs sex. We could then say that, despite his professed desire to never fall in

---

[7] Method Man featuring Mary J. Blige, "I'll Be There For You / You're All I Need To Get By," *The Hip Hop Box* (Hip-O, 2004).
[8] Jay-Z, "99 Problems," *The Black Album* (Roc-A-Fella, 2003).

love, he is actually in love when he loves a friend with whom he also makes love—kinda in the spirit of the low-crunk ballad "Lovers and Friends" by Lil Jon, Usher, and Ludacris.[9] But is that really what we're after? Nah, we all know the difference. Biggie, no champion of romantic love, does love his "bitch," but he loves her like his "best friend": "Moonlight strolls with the hoes / Oh no, that's not my steelo / I wanna bitch that like to play Celo and Craps / Packin' gats in a Coach bag, steamin' dime bags / A real bitch is all I want, all I ever had."[10] Friendship and sex may be necessary for love, but they're not sufficient.

We might wonder whether it would make a difference if the sex happened to be exclusive? Nah, the sex could just be damn good. As we know from Method Man, there's no need to shop around when you got the good stuff at home. Or perhaps exclusive sex is just a way of showing that you are trustworthy and loyal, down for whatever, as in "you my nigga." Maybe Socrates can help us devise a reply to the love hater.

## A Beautiful Reflection: Love as Spiritual Transcendence

Socrates rocks the mic with heavy doses of logic, irony, and aggression. In his rap on love, he riffs on and samples from both Pausanias and Aristophanes. He gives them their props but doesn't hesitate to let them know when their arguments are wack. Contrary to Aristophanes, Socrates insists that spiritual love is the desire for *beauty*, not wholeness. And he agrees with Pausanias that the lover doesn't desire mere physical beauty but the kind of beauty that includes goodness and wisdom, as when we say a person is beautiful on the outside and inside, in body and soul, like that lovely brown skin lady that Mos Def and Talib Kweli thank God for.[11] Yet, Socrates claims that the desire to love is neither good nor bad in itself (*Symposium* 202a). It is only praiseworthy when the one who is loved is also morally virtuous and therefore *deserves* to be

---

[9] See Lil Jon and the East Side Boyz featuring Usher and Ludacris, "Lovers and Friends," *Crunk Juice* (TVT, 2004).

[10] Notorious B.I.G., "Me & My Bitch," *Ready to Die* (Bad Boy, 1994).

[11] Black Star, "Brown Skin Lady," *Mos Def and Talib Kweli Are Black Star* (Rawkus, 1998).

loved. Sometimes what appears to be love at first sight turns out not to be love at all. Although your beloved may be superbly fine, you could discover that he or she simply lacks virtue. Or as L. Boogie asks rhetorically, "How you gon' win when you ain't right within?"[12]

Socrates continues by pointing out that possessing beauty is necessary for happiness, by which he means a life of flourishing (*Symposium* 202c). In other words, we might imagine that a life in which all of one's desires are fulfilled would be complete, but without a good and wise companion it would be, despite appearances, a deeply impoverished life. He takes this idea and joins it with Aristophanes's insight that love is something we want to possess forever. Socrates therefore concludes: "Love is wanting to possess the good forever" (*Symposium* 206a). So if the love hater wants to be truly happy in life, he or she must trade independence for spiritual love.

Socrates believes that "reproduction" is essential to love too, but not because of a desire to affirm the couple's eternal unity, as Aristophanes and Tical suggest. The true lover desires the immortality of beauty, to give birth to and nurture something beautiful, which will itself bear beautiful fruit, and so on, forever (*Symposium* 206b). It is for the sake of eternal virtue that lovers make great sacrifices for their offspring, knowing that their children embody a beauty that is divine. This point is made in Lauryn Hill's moving tribute to her son Zion: "A beautiful reflection of His grace / For I know that a gift so great / Is only one God could create / And I'm reminded every time I see your face."[13]

But Socrates makes a distinction between two types of "offspring" and thus two types of love. There are those who seek love through giving birth to beautiful children, and then there are those who do so through giving birth to beautiful *ideas*, ideas that will help others to become lovers of wisdom and virtue—that is, philosophers. The second kind of lover is drawn to persons who are beautiful in both body and soul, and with their companionship the lover's knowledge of virtue grows, step

---

[12] Lauryn Hill, "Doo Wop (That Thing)," *The Miseducation of Lauryn Hill* (Ruffhouse, 1998).

[13] Lauryn Hill, "To Zion," *Miseducation of Lauryn Hill.*

by step, culminating in the love of beauty itself, in all its forms. This then is the highest form of love, for the object of love is perfect in every way and never changes. It is love of that which all beautiful things have in common:

> This is what it is to go aright, or be led by another, into the mystery of Love: one goes always upwards for the sake of this Beauty, starting out from beautiful things and using them like rising stairs: from one body to two and from two to all beautiful bodies, then from beautiful bodies to beautiful customs, and from customs to learning beautiful things, and from these lessons he arrives in the end at this lesson, which is learning of this very Beauty, so that in the end he comes to know just what it is to be beautiful. (*Symposium* 211c)

Within this conception of love, Socrates still finds a place for sex without making the badunkadunk the central focus. Sexual attraction to beautiful bodies is a steppingstone to true love, which is love, not of beautiful people, but of the idea of beauty in its purity, without the imperfections of the human form.

Yet, there is something deeply unsatisfying about Socrates's theory of love. According to him, the beloved is merely a means to an end—cultivating moral virtue or knowledge of goodness. The lover values the beloved only insofar as he or she facilitates the quest for absolute beauty. Thus, by this logic, if a more adequate facilitator is found, the beloved should be replaced! Or, perhaps less horrifying, the lover will love other beautiful people just as much as, if not more than, his initial beloved. Either way, we lose two defining features of romantic love—irreplacability and exclusivity. When the lover reflects on the meaning of being in love, he regards his beloved as *unique*; no one can take his or her place. Moreover, he loves *only* his beloved and wants his lover to love only him.

Socrates's conception of love does not really answer the love hater's skepticism. Both see very little in love to recommend. Although the marketplace of beautiful ideas may yield dividends ultimately of higher worth than the marketplace of bling, benjamins, and booty, the love hater could admit this without changing his or her mind about the value of erotic love.

## That's Where the Drama Begins: Love as Possession

After the battle is over and Socrates has been declared the victor, Alcibiades crashes the party with his crew. He arrives from da club, talkin' loud, and drunk as hell. After learning that they've all just been rapping about the meaning of love, he demands an opportunity to display his skillz. Taking control of the mic, Alcibiades moves the crowd with revealing and frank first-person storytelling, full of colorful metaphors and double entendres.[14] Despite his incredible high, his steez is intact and he manages to kick knowledge. In fact, he provides precisely what seems to be missing from the previous accounts, namely, the vicissitudes of erotic desire, the ceaseless struggle between lovers, the drama of love, the funk of love.[15] Folks were tryin' to take the shit out of love. But this is impossible, as Michael Franti reminds us on "Love Is Da Shit": "You were worth every risk so I gave my heart room / And now I'm deep in the doo-doo that makes life bloom."[16]

What Socrates fails to see is that love is a reciprocal relationship. It is not a one-way street between lover and beloved, as if the "love-object" had no will or consciousness of his or her own. We become painfully aware of this when our love is not returned. Alcibiades represents this point of view by offering a personal account of the drama of love between himself and Socrates.

Before reflecting on that drama, we should note that same-sex love relationships were a common and accepted practice in ancient Greek society. In our society, many are intolerant toward persons who express same-sex desire, and some hip-hop artists seem to take perverse pleasure in openly expressing malice toward "fags." Why these artists regard this as adding to their art is another mystery worth exploring, though one I won't take up here.[17] Yet, whatever one thinks about the morality of

---

[14] For an insightful analysis of Alcibiades's rap on love, see Martha Nussbaum, "The Speech of Alcibiades: A Reading of Plato's 'Symposium'," *Philosophy and Literature* 3 (1979), pp. 131–169.

[15] For a rich and original treatment of the drama of love, see Roland Barthes, *A Lover's Discourse: Fragments* (New York: Hill and Wang, 1978).

[16] Spearhead, "Love Is Da Shit," *Home* (Capitol, 1994).

[17] See Track 6 in this volume, pp. 73–74.

homosexuality or the homophobia found in some rap lyrics, I'd challenge anyone who's ever been in love to assert, in all honesty, that the feelings Alcibiades articulates are not universal and authentic sentiments of erotic love.

He first emphasizes the importance of *possession.* For Alcibiades possession is that familiar feeling of being under a spell when in love. Hit by the voo-doo that makes Salt-N-Pepa wanna shoop, the lover is drawn involuntarily to her beloved.[18] Alcibiades claims that Socrates's words have the power to possess in just this way. When that true playa Big Sockratease spits game it hypnotizes those who hear his words: "I swear to you, the moment [Socrates] starts to speak, I am beside myself: my heart starts leaping in my chest, the tears come streaming down my face, . . . and, let me tell you, I am not alone" (*Symposium* 215e).

But Alcibiades thinks of possession in a second sense, that of the powerful pronoun "my," as in *my* nigga or *my* bitch. There's a sense of implied ownership in love, a sense that my beloved "belongs" not just with me but to me. Let's not be misled by economic metaphors, though. The object of one's love should not be regarded as a commodity that can be exchanged for other commodities or for money—unless of course ya pimpin' like Fiddy.[19] Nor can one's "rights" to him or her be transferred to another like a title to a tight ass Hummer. The sense of possession at issue is a desire for *exclusivity,* both sexual and emotional. The fragile bond of love is held together by trust and loyalty. The government cannot protect your "love rights" like it can your property rights. And even if 50 Cent's lover gives the right answer to all twenty-one of his questions, there is no guarantee that she'll follow through on her word. If the lover perceives that someone else is receiving the special affection characteristic of love, the lover becomes jealous, sometimes insanely so. The lover is especially sensitive to any sign that the ties of love might have been broken. As Black Thought from The Roots tells us: "I've seen people caught in love like whirlwinds / Listening to they squads and listening to girlfriends /

---

[18] Salt-N-Pepa, "Shoop," *Very Necessary* (UMG, 1993).

[19] For a philosophical discussion of the similarities between pimping and commerce, see my "Parasites, Pimps, and Capitalists: A Naturalistic Conception of Exploitation," *Social Theory and Practice* 28 (2002), pp. 381–418.

That's exactly the point where they whole world ends / Lies come in, that's where the drama begins."[20]

This brings us to another feature of love's drama. Love can bring one to the brink of madness, making one obsessed and impulsive (*Symposium* 218a–b). As we all know, one does crazy things when in love. Remember when Left Eye burned down her man Andre Risen's crib? Possession can also explain the thin line between love and hate: "Sometimes, believe me, I think I would be happier if [Socrates] were dead. And yet I know that if he dies I'll be even more miserable. I can't live with him, and I can't live without him! What *can* I do about him" (*Symposium* 216c)?" This kind of aggression is often fueled by the implicit knowledge that the beloved can never really be fully possessed, and by the anxiety over being possessed oneself. Since she is an autonomous agent, the beloved is always slightly out of one's grasp, remaining forever elusive. She can, if she so chooses, walk away or withhold affection. One ever fears that the magic could fade, that your beloved could awake from her dream-like state and see you for who you are, with all your flaws. Also, being possessed means accepting a sense of helplessness. It is, as Alcibiades claims, a kind of emotional slavery, which we are both attracted to and naturally repelled by. When the stakes are high and we must make that life-long commitment, we are often overcome with dread, even despite our undying love for our beloved. We are faced with, to reference Andre once more, "Dracula's wedding."

Alcibiades also complains that, in all their private moments together, Socrates never told him any secrets, never revealed anything private. In fact, Socrates, consistent with his philosophy, refused to say anything to Alcibiades that he wouldn't say to any beautiful person who inquired. His relationship with Alcibiades is therefore not special or intimate. It's so impersonal that maybe we shouldn't consider it a "relationship" at all.[21] Socrates doesn't desire Alcibiades in his *particularity*. When Alcibiades offers himself and all that he has to Socrates and makes a desperate plea to the great man, he is flat rejected,

---

[20] The Roots featuring Erykah Badu, "You Got Me," *Things Fall Apart* (MCA, 1999).

[21] See Niko Kolodny, "Love as Valuing a Relationship," *Philosophical Review* 112 (2003), pp. 135–189.

straight dissed. This refusal of exclusivity by Socrates is also a failure of *reciprocity.* When the lover offers himself, an act filled with trepidation, he desires to have that offer reciprocated. Such offers are highly risky ventures, for they make the lover completely vulnerable. Loving takes courage. One is not simply putting one's rep or paper on the line, but one's heart. This is the painful lesson that Lauryn Hill learned when she loved real, real hard once: "That what you want might make you cry / And what you need might pass you by."[22]

Yet despite this rejection, humiliation, and emotional suffering, in the eyes of Alcibiades, Socrates remains perfect in every way. He fully embodies the virtues of modesty, self-control, courage, and philosophical wisdom. Even his vices are regarded as virtues. This kind of *idealization* enables the lover to forgive the flaws of his or her beloved. But the point is not to view the beloved as a mere instance of a universal, such as BEAUTY itself. The point is to see the beloved as one-of-a-kind: "You could say many other marvelous things in praise of Socrates. Perhaps he shares some of his specific accomplishments with others. But, as a whole, he is unique; he is like no one else in the past and no one in the present—this is by far the most amazing thing about him" (*Symposium* 221c).

## The Mysteries of Love Revealed?

There is at least one final thing we can learn from Alcibiades's rap about love. Perhaps to love is not to possess beauty in itself, in its purity, as Socrates claims. Rather, to love is to regard one's beloved as perfectly beautiful *despite* his or her flaws and to forgive these faults when they come from a person with an open and loving heart. But, again, this kind of love requires reciprocity. We only offer it with the expectation that it will be returned, and we should only accept it if we have the honest intention of giving it back. Such a relationship necessarily involves vulnerability—and the drama this brings. We must admit that sometimes relationships get ill. No doubt.

The love hater is not self-deceived about the risks of love. These risks are real, built into the very nature of love. In light of this fact, perhaps no philosophical argument or dope rhyme can

---

[22] Lauryn Hill, "When It Hurts So Bad," *Miseducation of Lauryn Hill.*

convince the love hater to take a chance on love, especially if
he or she fears vulnerability. Romantic love may not be for
everyone. But it's not merely for suckas either. And although we
haven't uncovered all of love's mysteries, it should at least be
clear it ain't just 'bout da booty.[23]

---

[23] For helpful suggestions on earlier drafts of this essay, I thank Derrick Darby,
Bill Irwin, John Pittman, and especially Jessie Scanlon, who has taught me
more than a few things about love.

# 3

# "You Perceive with Your Mind": Knowledge and Perception

MITCHELL S. GREEN

A major theme in rap lyrics is that the only way to survive is to use your head, be aware, and know what's going on around you. That simple idea packs a lot of background. The most obvious ideas about knowledge turn out, if you look at them close up, to be pretty questionable. For example: How do we get knowledge about the world? A natural and ancient answer to this question is that much if not all of our knowledge comes from our senses. So, for example, the nose gives us knowledge of what things smell like, and if all goes well, also indicates whether the thing we smell is healthy, tasty, or noxious. Likewise, the eyes tell us the color and shape of things, and thereby give us information about whether those things are useful, dangerous, and so on. Like everybody else, rappers know all this. Or do they? Maybe some rappers know that this isn't really so.

I'm not talking about Extra-Sensory Perception, channeling, auras, or about what Common calls "The 6th Sense" (*Like Water For Chocolate*). I'm talking about the way that philosophers like to question the most mundane ideas to see if they contain something inside in need of, well, liberation. We're going to discover that philosophers and rappers can find a common cause.

The idea that the senses convey knowledge is so natural, pervasive and ancient that it's part of common sense. According to this idea, what the senses give us is something like what you see on the plasma screen in the pimped out stretch Hummer, or hear on a newly minted Funkmaster Flex track, or smell when having one of OutKast's gasoline dreams. It's what some philosophers who've considered how perception works call *sense data*. The idea is that the senses give your mind a picture, either a visual picture, an auditory picture, or one made up of information from other senses, like olfactory (smell), gustatory (taste), or tactile (touch). What happens then, according to this sense data idea, is that your mind pays attention to this picture, and then gets from it information about how the world is. Then, on the basis of that information you go on to do stuff, like grab the keys to the whip, flip on the beats, pump up the volume, and roll through the hood on the dubs. Like I said, everyone knows this. And like I said, some rappers might know it isn't really true.

Well, isn't that how perception works? Let's keep in mind that just because some idea is part of common sense, that doesn't mean it's true. After all, it was once common sense that the Earth stands still while the Sun and stars revolve around it. And it was once common sense that when someone acts like a freak they're possessed by a devil, spirit, or something of the kind. But now we know that neither of these bits of common sense is true. The Earth doesn't stand still, and people's weird behavior is often the result of mental disease like psychosis, dementia, and so forth. What was common sense to one era often turns out to be a bogus piece of mythology to another. I'm sure that a lot of what we now consider common sense will be scoffed at by some future generation as bogus mythology as well. Might the sense-data idea of perception be one of these?

## Descartes and the Gorillaz on Mental Perception

The Gorillaz think so. Peep the knowledge they drop on their cut, "Clint Eastwood": "I see destruction and demise / Corruption in disguise / But y'all can see me now cos you don't see with your eye / You perceive with your mind / . . . No squealing, remember (that it's all in your head).[1] What could Del tha Funkee Homosapien mean in saying that you don't see with

---

[1] Gorillaz featuring Del tha Funkee Homosapien, "Clint Eastwood," *Gorillaz* (Virgin, 2001).

your eye? After all, what else would you perceive with? Del probably wouldn't be too happy with the suggestion that instead you perceive trees or clouds with your ears, or nose, or tongue. So what could he be trying to say?

Before trying to figure it out let's pause to notice that the philosopher René Descartes said something amazingly like this about four centuries ago. In his *Meditations on First Philosophy*[2] he considers the idea that when he looks out the window he sees people. That seems perfectly obvious, but then Descartes points out that one should never be misled by ordinary ways of talking. Sometimes such ways of talking are confused or misleading, or, as Jay-Z would say, they leave room for "Reasonable Doubt." Descartes also points out that what his eyes really see are Kangols, Rocawear, and Jordans. The conclusion that he sees people outside his window must be something that his mind adds to the sensory information, not something that his eyes give him directly. That's awfully close to saying that one perceives with one's mind, not one's eyes:

> . . . were I perchance to look out my window and observe men crossing the square, I would ordinarily say I see the men themselves just as I say I see the wax. But what do I see aside from hats and clothes, which could conceal automata? Yet I judge them to be men. Thus what I thought I had seen with my eyes, I actually grasped solely with the faculty of judgment, which is my mind.[3]

After denying that we perceive with our eyes (or, apparently, any other senses), the Gorillaz propose instead that we perceive with our minds. Similarly, on *Like Water for Chocolate*, Common tells us that he has seen street dreams deferred, and he has dark spots in his mind where the scene occurred. This also suggests that our minds perceive. On the face of it, that sounds a little crazy. Minds are where we think, reason, and make decisions. But your mind doesn't have eyes, ears, a nose or a tongue. So what might it mean to say that you perceive with your mind?

---

[2] Published in 1641, translated into English by D. Cress and published by Hackett (1993).
[3] *Ibid. Meditations* II.

I think that these rappers might have something interesting to say here as a challenge to the sense-data theory of perception. But it's gonna take a minute to lay it out. First of all, let's go back to the sense-data theory of perception and contemplate it more carefully. For one, think again about that picture of the mind as paying attention to the information that the senses fetch up. How does it know about that information? Does it look? Well, to do that, it would have to use some eyes. But you only have two pairs of eyes, not four. Your mind doesn't have its own private pair. So the mind can't be looking at the picture that the senses give. Does the mind smell? Like with the case of eyes, the mind doesn't have its own nose, separate from the one on your face. You can see the same point goes for all your other senses. So how does the mind get information from what the senses send its way?

Remember that the sense-data idea told us that we learn about the world by having the senses provide information to the mind. The mind then gathers that information, and uses it to deal with the world. But we got all mixed up over the question how the mind really gathers that information. Either it perceives that information, or it gets it in some other way. It definitely doesn't perceive it. After all, the mind doesn't have its own set of senses over and above your one pair of eyes, nose, and so on. So the mind gets that information in some other way. What might that other way be?

Sometimes when an MC has an insight it's a powerful one but might contain more than one idea. That's what's going on here, in the idea that you perceive with your mind. I'm suggesting that there are two ideas here, not one. The first idea is the simpler. It's that "the mind" isn't some special and mysterious place separate from your senses. No, "the mind" is a complex thing that contains senses as its parts. It's also got memory, judgment, intentions, and not everything in it has got to be conscious. (Back to this last part in a moment.) But part of what's going on in the idea that you perceive with your mind is that the senses are part of your mind, not external to it. If you think otherwise it'll be a mystery how the mind ever learns anything about the world.

What's the second idea? It's that the eye always comes ancient to its image.[4] Meaning? Meaning that whenever we per-

---

[4] Ernest Gombrich, *Art and Illusion: A Psychology of the Creative Eye* (London, 1963).

ceive anything at all we always have a huge set of background assumptions about what to look for, what is important, and what is most relevant to our survival. Here's an example known as the Cocktail Party Effect. I'm sure you've been at a large set chillin' when your ears prick up, and you strain all your effort on a conversation two headz away because you're *certain* you just heard your name dropped. Of all the things in the "blooming, buzzing, confusion" of experience, you home in on that one, and of course the reason why is that it probably concerns you. You very much want to know what they're saying about you. The Cocktail Party Effect shows that you can pick out a needle in a haystack of experience. That's because the mind isn't like a piece of wax, which sits passively while the world makes an imprint. Actually the mind is more like a heat-seeking missile. It homes in on the things that matter, whizzing right by all the rest.

So the idea that you perceive with your mind actually contains two ideas inside it. First it's that the senses are really part of the mind, not external to it. Second, it's that all of our perception is driven, colored, and guided by our interests, needs, aims, and sometimes even biases. For better or worse, your mind is there at work all the time when you perceive, not in the backseat receiving information, but guiding, interpreting, coloring and casing your world.

## The New Unconscious

For better or for worse. As a species we wouldn't have had a prayer of surviving if we hadn't been able to detect quickly and accurately things around us that are dangerous, noxious, potentially useful, edible, or sexually attractive. But in some ways these skillz can also be a pitfall because they can create bias. Here are some ways they might do that. First of all, there's a vast ocean of things that your mind does that you might not be aware of. According to a recent convergence of research in experimental psychology, our minds have an enormous unconscious component even though that component doesn't much resemble the one that Sigmund Freud talked about. Maybe there's an ego, an id, and a superego that are forever struggling for control over your actions. Maybe not. In recent years we've started to ask whether there's really evidence for this theory of the mind, and it turns out that such evidence is very hard to find. Maybe Freud was right. No one is saying for sure that he was wrong. But at this point the jury is still out over the question whether he was right, and I won't assume in what follows that he was.

Recent work in psychology gives evidence of a different kind of unconscious. It's the kind that guides us through our everyday dealings with the world. When you look at something you usually figure out in a split second how far away it is, and that judgment is one that you don't make consciously. So you must be making it unconsciously. Again, imagine I tell you that your friend fat Joe has been seeing someone new. You will immediately figure that this is a romantic thing with fat Joe, rather than assume that he's been paying visits to a newborn baby. But this other reading is possible; I didn't *say* that fat Joe has a new flame, and a newborn baby is, after all, a new person. You got my drift, but most likely got it through an unconscious process instead of a conscious one.

The overall picture that emerges of the conscious mind and its relation to the unconscious mind is that of a pilot of a 747 jet to the automatic controls of that jet. Generally, the pilot can fly using only the automatic controls and just needs to make sure that no unusual situations are arising such as turbulence or other weather conditions. Similarly, a huge amount of what enables you to get around in your environment, according to this new theory of the *adaptive unconscious*, is "auto-pilot." You could pay conscious attention to it if you had to, but unless there's some human or environmental turbulence there's generally no need to do that.

But this automatic part of your self, this adaptive unconscious, is not perfect. Sometimes it makes judgments that are shortsighted or ill advised or impulsive, as Public Enemy observes: "Folks don't even own themselves / Payin mental rent / To corporate presidents."[5]

Their point, of course, is that you can't own yourself if you don't know yourself. Let's consider some ways in which we are strangers to ourselves.

---

[5] "He Got Game," *He Got Game* (Def Jam, 1998).

## Strangers to Ourselves

1. Many of us confidently feel that we never forget a face. But we can easily be tricked into thinking that a face we are looking at is a familiar one. Psychologists Heather Kleider and Stephen Goldinger have conducted experiments showing that if you present someone with a photo of a person, she'll be a lot more likely to say that it's someone she's seen before if that photo is clear rather than distorted.[6] But if you think about it, just being clear is no reason to think the photograph is of someone you've seen before. Apparently the clarity of a photo gives us that feeling of familiarity that we mistake for having seen the face before.

2. It's very common to get aroused and then be mistaken about the cause of that arousal. This is shown dramatically in the so-called Love on the Bridge experiment (not the Queensbridge, though it could have taken place there as well). A female experimenter placed herself at the end of a long and treacherous bridge in a state park, and watched for men as they came across. She then interviewed men as they came across the bridge, and at the end of the interview she tore off a piece of paper, wrote down her digits, and told the interviewee that she would be happy to discuss the experiment further if they wanted to holla back at her. The experimenter then did the same thing with men she found relaxing on a park bench. The question: How likely were men from each group to call her later to ask her on a date? It turns out that sixty-five percent of the men on the bridge called and asked her on a date, while only thirty percent of men she found sitting on a park bench called her for a date. The evidence suggests that those men she interviewed at the end of the bridge attributed their arousal to an attraction to her rather than to the fact that they had just completed a physically challenging activity. In most cases, of course, they were probably mistaken about the true source of their arousal.[7]

---

[6] Heather Kleider and Stephen Goldinger, "Illusions of face memory: Clarity breeds familiarity," *Journal of Memory and Language* 50 (2004), pp. 196–211.

[7] See Dolf Zillmann, "Attribution and misattribution of excitatory reaction," in John Harvey, *et al*, eds., *New Directions in Attribution Research*, Volume II (Erlbaum, 1978), pp. 335–368.

3. Can you tell whether someone is faking an emotion in his or her facial expression? Most of us feel sure that we can tell whether, for instance, someone is forcing a smile or making a genuine one. It turns out, though, that the visual difference between a forced and a spontaneous smile is just that the face is slightly symmetrical in the former case but asymmetrical in the latter case. Further, those differences are not readily detectable to most people. There are also auditory differences in their voices, but they too are not readily detectable. Judges, police, and many others whose work depends on telling the difference between liars and others don't actually do better than if they were just guessing.[8] You probably don't either; yet you make a lot of important choices based on whether you think someone is showing their true feelings. 50 Cent says this in "21 Questions":

> If I fell off tomorrow would you still love me?
> If I didn't smell so good would you still hug me?
> If I got locked up and sentenced to a quarter century,
> Could I count on you to be there to support me mentally?[9]

I sure hope he's got a way of knowing whether his girlfriend is sincere other than by looking at her face when she answers.

4. There are still racist people around, though maybe fewer than in the days of Jim Crow. While some racists are consciously so, either due to upbringing or to fear, as Boogie Down Productions edutains us on their cut, "The Racist" (*Edutainment*), there are also unconscious racists, not knowin' that they're racist, even denying their racism, but invading spaces and allowing racism to live on. For example, not long ago some experimenters posed as regular folks looking to rent or purchase a home. They met with real estate agents. Some of these experimenters were black, some white, some Hispanic, but they all just acted like normal folks in the market for a place to live. It was found that the real estate agents on average offered fewer housing options to the black and Hispanic

---

[8] The fun and informative documentary, *The Face: Mask or Mirror?* narrated by John Cleese, discusses some of these experimental findings.
[9] *Get Rich or Die Tryin'* (Interscope 2003).

experimenters, and were less likely to follow up their meetings with phone calls if the "clients" were black or Hispanic than if they were white.[10]

This hate is especially hard to eradicate if it's not even conscious.

5. Finally, I'll bet you think that you'd become an incredibly happy person if you won the lottery. After all, that would enable you to pay all your bills, quit your gig, travel, get nice gear, a pimped out ride, and a house that could be featured on MTV Cribs. Plus you'd still have dough left over for the future. The Notorious B.I.G. and Jay-Z were certainly not shy about confessing their love for dough and the happiness it brought them on *Life after Death*. And it may be that "most of us only care about money makin'," as The Black-Eyed Peas observe on "Where is the Love?" (*Elephunk*). But will all this dough make us happy people? As a matter of fact, most of the time lottery winners end up being euphoric for a little while, and then after the thrill wears off, no happier than before. Besides, many lottery winners report being harassed by friends, relatives, and even strangers for money, and some have had to move to new neighborhoods where they can be anonymous so that people will leave them alone. As Biggie says, "mo money, mo problems." Psychologists who've studied lottery winners find that for the most part they've solved their financial problems but are no happier, and often less happy, than before.[11] So even though for many of us it may be all about the Benjamins, this is not a sure path to happiness.

We're more sure than we deserve to be that we can identify a familiar face, we often mistake the source of our excitement or arousal, we're not very good at telling whether someone is faking an emotion, many people are unconsciously racist while not being racist on the conscious level at all, and most of us are wrong to think that great wealth would make us happy. What should we make of all these details about how we are less aware of our true feelings than we might have thought? From

---

[10] John Yinger, *Closed Doors, Opportunities Lost: The Continuing Costs of Housing Discrimination* (New York: Sage, 1995).

[11] Roy Kaplan, *Lottery Winners: How They Won and How Winning Changed Their Lives* (New York: Harper and Row, 1978).

these examples, and there are plenty more,[12] you can see that while the adaptive unconscious helps us get around in the world efficiently, it's also fallible. Part of knowing your own mind is a matter of knowing the strengths and weaknesses of your unconscious self. That way you might understand the weaknesses well enough so they don't bog you down.

## Proper Use of the Mind

At this point you might be thinking, "Okay, so maybe a lot of people, me included, don't know themselves as well as they think they do. Does this mean I have to go sit for years on a shrink's couch to find out what's in my head?" Not necessarily. Talk therapy has its uses, but psychoanalysis (and other forms of talk therapy) and the experimental study of the unconscious are quite different things. Discussing feelings can help one cope with them better in some cases, but it's doubtful that it's going to help with, for example, the feeling that if only you won the lottery you'd be happy. If you agree that this feeling is not necessarily valid, that maybe you're overrating the ability of great wealth to give you happiness, how can you overcome it other than by talk therapy?

One approach to this problem is to become clearer about what your real values are. Suppose you find enormous satisfaction in writing rap lyrics. Having amazing wealth isn't going to help you much with that. It won't give you inspiration, or help you find an original theme, or enable you to see life in the skewed way that good rap offers us. Sure, if you had a lot of dough your life would be more convenient and you might need to spend less time on mundane pursuits like feeding yourself so that you can spend more time on the verses. But you still won't be happy until you're creating funky lyrics. The same goes for love and friendship: Though it can buy plenty of substitutes, money can't buy either of these things. Reflect for a moment on the things that you value, that give your life worth. These are the things that make happiness; bling is at best decoration on top of that.

---

[12] Timothy Wilson, *Strangers to Ourselves: Discovering the Adaptive Unconscious* (Cambridge, Massachusetts: Harvard University Press, 2003).

I'm suggesting that knowing your own mind sometimes is just a matter of standing back from your own life and coming to appreciate patterns that you might not notice from close up. Do people whose faces seem sincere often trick you? Do you sometimes look back to find that what you thought was love was actually lust, or some other kind of arousal? Do you consistently stay away from socializing with people from other races? These are behavior patterns that can show unconscious inclinations, tendencies, and habits that are not entirely productive. After becoming aware of them, one way to start to modify them is by behaving differently. Make an effort to pursue a friendship with someone from another race, try acting on your feelings for other people without getting carried away into thinking that those feelings must be love. And, in addition to watching people's faces when they talk, think about *why* they might be saying what they are.

My theme has been that your mind is bigger, more complex, and less open to your conscious awareness than you probably realize. In some ways this is a good thing; without our mind's being for the most part on "auto-pilot" we would spend most of each day just getting dressed. But making the most of one's life can depend on understanding how one's unconscious, this adaptive unconscious, can sometimes be shortsighted, impulsive, prejudiced, or overly confident. Maybe that's part of what 2pac was getting when he implores his unborn seed to be an individual, work hard, study, and get his mind straight, on "Letter 2 My Unborn" (*Until the End of Time*). So too, if Common is right on "The 6th Sense," then real hip-hop music, music from the soul, can help us see the relationship between knowledge and perception clearly. But to do this we must heed KRS-One's sage advice on his track, "The Mind" (*The Sneak Attack*): We must make up, clear, and erase doubt and fear from our mind to appreciate the way in which we perceive with our mind.[13]

[13] Research for this paper was supported in part by a Summer Grant from the Office of the Provost at the University of Virginia. That support is here gratefully acknowledged.

# Disk 2

# What's Beef? Ruminations on Violence

# 4

# "Y'all Niggaz Better Recognize": Hip Hop's Dialectical Struggle for Recognition

JOHN P. PITTMAN

> You's a flea, and I'm the big Dogg
> I'll scratch you off my balls with my muthafuckin' paws
> Y'all niggaz better recognize
> And see where I'm comin' from, it's still East Side till I die
> Why ask why? As the world keeps spinning to the D-O-Double-G-Y
>
> —Snoop Doggy Dogg, "Doggy Dogg World"

Do y'all remember Roxanne? Of course you do: the fictional object of the Kangol Kid's affections in UTFO's 1984 hit "Roxanne, Roxanne" will long be remembered as triggering one of the first and most extended "battles" in the history of rap. When Marley Marl and the girl (Lolita Gooden) who came to be known as Roxanne Shanté came out with "Roxanne's Revenge" the following year, the floodgates opened. Around the country, rappers scrambled to get into the action; more than fifty "response records" came out by the time the whole thing was all over. This incident established once and for all the importance of "battles" to the hip-hop industry.[1]

But are battles just a gimmick, a marketing strategy? Or are they an essential part of what hip hop is all about? What, if anything, do battles signify in hip-hop culture? Let's break it down, starting from the top. A bit later on, we'll get some help from

---

[1] An extended account of this episode, and of other battles as well, can be found in the video documentaries *Beef* and *Beef II* (QD3, 2003).

the great nineteenth-century German philosopher Georg Wilhelm Friedrich Hegel.

## "I Ain't No Joke": Rapping and Battling

One of the central forms of hip-hop culture is rapping—rhyming over beats—and one of the most pervasive motifs is a rapper's claim to be superior as a rapper to all others on the scene. This form of rap-sodic competitiveness involves explicit challenges to would-be antagonists and insulting comparisons and put-downs of competing rappers. The imagined context of much rhyming is that of an all-out, every-man-for-himself war for supremacy or mastery. Rhymes of this kind involve boasting or bragging swagger, a combination of self-advertisement, harsh disses of other rappers, and accusations that other MC's try to steal or copy one's style. As Rakim puts it in "I Ain't No Joke," addressing an anonymous MC:

> I wake you up and as I stare in your face you seem stunned
> Remember me? The one you got your idea from
> But soon you start to suffer, the tune'll get rougher
> When you start to stutter, that's when you had enough of biting
> It'll make you choke, you can't provoke
> You can't cope, you shoulda broke, because I ain't no joke.[2]

The battle is a dramatic showdown between two rappers who challenge one another with lyrics such as these and vie to outdo one another in the construction and performance of their raps. Two rappers square off, each claiming to be the best. They can only establish which of their competing claims is valid through a struggle: each is dueling with the other for the status of acknowledged superiority. The winner takes away the glory and the rewards, while the loser loses credibility, since his claim to be the "baddest muthafucka on the mic" has been defeated. A classic example of a battle is that staged between Jay-Z and Nas. Here the lyrics are hard-hitting and take on a fully martial imagery. As Jay-Z raps in "Takeover," addressing Nas:

---

[2] Eric B. and Rakim, "I Ain't No Joke," *Paid in Full* (Fourth & Broadway, 1987).

The takeover, the break's over nigga
God MC, me, JayHova
Hey lil' soldier you ain't ready for war
R.O.C. too strong for y'all
It's like bringin' a knife to a gunfight, pen to a test
Your chest in the line of fire witcha thinass vest
You bringin' them Boyz II Men, HOW them boys gon' win?

Later on in the same rap he presents the fantasized result—for his opponent—of their life-and-death struggle: "Get zipped up in plastic when it happens that's it . . . / They'll have to hold a mass, put your body in a hole."[3]

With "Ether" Nas responds in kind, opening the track with the sound of automatic gunfire and several background invocations of "Fuck Jay-Z!" The track is dripping with venom and anger toward Jigga for having dissed "God's son":

You a fan, a phony, a fake, a pussy, a Stan
I still whip your ass, you thirty-six in a karate class?
You Taebo ho, tryin'a' work it out, you tryin'a' get brolic?
Ask me if I'm tryin'a' kick knowledge
Nah, I'm tryin'a' kick the shit you need to learn, though
That ether, that shit that make your soul burn slow.[4]

This example vividly illustrates the vehemence, the emotional charge, and the violence of expression that battles often produce. But all that still leaves open the questions—are these guys for real, or are they only fronting? What do battles have to do with the heart, the spirit of hip hop? To help answer these questions, let's turn to a philosophical treatment of human struggles formulated during the revolutionary storm that swept Europe some two hundred years ago.

## "You're a Sucker MC": The Struggle for Recognition

One of the great themes of the "western" philosophical tradition — some would say an essential item in philosophy's tool-box of

---

[3] Jay-Z, "Takeover," *Blueprint* (Roc-a-Fella, 2001).
4 Nas, "Ether," *Stillmatic* (Sony, 2001).

concepts—is *dialectic*, a pattern of progressive development through opposition and struggle. The O.G. of modern dialectic was George Wilhelm Friedrich Hegel, whose first and greatest work is *The Phenomenology of Spirit* (1807). A key chapter is entitled "Independence and Dependence of Self-Consciousness: Master and Slave." This chapter has two closely connected topics: first, it relates a crucial moment in the growth of human self-consciousness—that is, of human freedom—and second, it is an account of the most basic form of domination—the relation of master and slave.

Self-consciousness is, for Hegel, a primary stage in human development. Self-consciousness is, most simply, consciousness of self, that is, the awareness of oneself *as aware*, or, in other words, reflective self-awareness. This is, indeed, for Hegel and many others, what distinguishes humans from other conscious beings, such as other animals. This idea is explicitly affirmed by Talib Kweli, when he raps in "K.O.S. (Determination)":

> I feel the rage of a million niggaz locked inside a cage
> At exactly which point do you start to realize
> That life without knowledge is death in disguise?
> That's why Knowledge Of Self is like life after death
> Apply it to your life, let destiny manifest.[5]

Hegel claims that self-consciousness becomes certain of itself only through a process he called the "struggle for recognition." There is only one way that any—say my—self-consciousness can prove itself, can show itself that it is true, *accurate* awareness of myself rather than deluded. That can happen only if my self-consciousness is verified by the acknowledgment of another self-consciousness—if I am recognized for what I claim to be by someone else. So the impulse toward self-consciousness gives rise to the demand for recognition. And that demand is made by both parties: my demand that you recognize me is met by your demand that I recognize you. Each party to the struggle puts forward a demand for recognition—a demand for respect from an acknowledged equal. Thus, the demand for recognition gives rise to a struggle between two self-consciousnesses. Hegel says,

---

[5] Black Star, "K.O.S. (Determination)," *Mos Def and Talib Kweli Are Black Star* (Rawkus, 2002).

"[T]he relation of the two self-conscious individuals is such that they prove themselves and each other through a life-and-death struggle. They must engage in this struggle, for they must raise their certainty of being *for themselves* to truth."[6]

But why do the demands give rise to a *struggle*—why can't they both simply accept one another's demands? That's because of the very essence of self-consciousness. For Hegel, self-consciousness is necessarily self-determining, that is, autonomous or free. Why? Well, think of it this way: consciousness is always consciousness of something—an object—on the part of the one who is conscious—a subject. If I'm conscious of my phone ringing the hook from "Hey, Ya!", I am the subject—the one who is conscious—and the phone ringing is the object—the thing outside of me that I am conscious of. The content of my consciousness in this sort of case is determined by something outside of me—whatever the object of consciousness is. But in the case of *self*-consciousness, the object of consciousness isn't outside myself, it *is* myself. The subject of consciousness and its object are one and the same thing—myself. My self-consciousness ought, therefore, to be determined solely by myself, or, as Hegel puts it, *for itself.*

Maybe you're thinking: this all sounds okay, but what does it have to do with hip hop? Well, consider this classic example from Run-D.M.C.:

> You try to bite lines, but rhymes are mine
> You's a sucker MC in a pair of Calvin Kleins
> Comin' from the wackest part of town
> Tryin' to rap up but you can't get down
> You don't even know your English, your verb or noun
> You're just a sucker MC, you sad face clown.[7]

D.J. Run's rap is a series of put-downs, addressing various features of his presumed antagonist's self—not just his style, but his lack of originality, bad taste in clothes, his "wack" neighborhood, his ignorance of English, and his inauthenticity ("you can't get down"). The rap has the effect of raising Run himself to a

---

[6] G.W.F. Hegel, *Phenomenology of Spirit* (New York: Oxford University Press, 1977), pp. 113–14.

[7] Run-D.M.C., "Sucker MC's (Krush-Groove 1)," *Run-D.M.C.* (Arista, 1984).

level of dominance in relation to his antagonist in virtually every respect. Indeed, this superiority is *recognized*: the "sucker M.C." shows himself to be fan by the fact that he bites Run's lines. In short, though this is not a battle rap, and certainly not a "struggle to the death," the pose is unmistakable: "I'm ready to dominate you totally, suckas!" While it's true that a rap battle is not literally a *life-and-death* struggle, it is the closest thing to a cultural—musical—form of a life-and-death struggle, and the stakes of a rap battle have a similar all-or-nothing character to them. Both parties to a hip-hop battle claim the same prize, and only one can walk away with it. And crucially the prize is a matter of recognition, the acknowledgement of technical superiority, and the respect that goes with it.

But why does the struggle for recognition have to be a *life-and-death* struggle? Since my demand for recognition is that you recognize me as a self-consciousness, it must be a demand that I am seen, and recognized, as purely self-determining. Nothing, and no one, can dictate to me. For that to be true, I must be able to eliminate, or dominate, anyone or anything that threatens my self-determination, my control over my situation. In relation to you, from whom I demand recognition, I can only become self-determining if I can impose my terms on you, gain domination over you. For if *you* are in a position to determine the conditions of *my* existence, then I will not be fully self-determining in the way I need to be. But my demand for recognition is matched by an identical demand on your part. And so the struggle is joined, and it is a struggle for domination. What Hegel's account requires, then, is that self-consciousness must involve a struggle for recognition, and that struggle for recognition must become a struggle for domination and, ultimately, a life-and-death struggle. "It is only through staking one's life that freedom is won."[8]

Now a life-and-death struggle ends only when one of the contenders is decisively defeated, and even put to death. In the struggle for recognition, however, the death of one of the parties would represent a loss for the victor: If his antagonist is actually killed, then the crucial goal of the victor—recognition—escapes him. His opponent is no longer able to provide recog-

---

[8] Hegel, *Phenomenology*, p. 114.

nition since he no longer exists.[9] So the only satisfactory resolution of the struggle is the complete domination, but not the destruction, of the vanquished by the victor. That's why Hegel thinks the struggle for recognition must lead to the relation of master and slave. And this situation—that of achieved mastery and enforced subordination—is earnestly depicted in the lyrics of innumerable battle raps.

But this situation, though resolving one phase of struggle, inaugurates a new one. Though it appears to guarantee a kind of freedom and self-determination to the victor at the expense of the vanquished, this, it turns out, is an illusion. The new situation, which at first appears to be a resolution of the original opposition, is in fact only a new stage in the working out of that opposition.

You may have noticed earlier something about the situation of self-consciousness: the demand that I be completely self-determining is already compromised by the very condition that I am demanding that *another* self-consciousness recognize me as such. The demand for recognition is, on the face of it, an admission of a kind of dependence on the other! The entire situation or problem of recognition is one that, in this sense, is unstable or subversive of its own conditions of existence.

In the master-slave dynamic neither party is truly free. The master is not free because he is dependent on the slave for recognition of his mastery,[10] and sometimes for his very existence as well—for the slave typically produces the means of subsistence for her master and is the foundation of his wealth. The slave is not free because he is not recognized as such by the master. And so the very situation of mastery comes to seem a kind of slavery all its own. Here is another example of dialectical "reversal"—of one thing turning into its opposite. As Andre

---

[9] It's true that if there are observers or witnesses of the struggle, they can provide recognition of the victor's achievement even when the other antagonist is slain. But the recognition offered thus is insufficient to the purpose, since in abstaining from the struggle the onlookers have indicated their unworthiness to give recognition.

[10] Notice the interesting implication here, that the slave, if he is to provide recognition of the master's self-consciousness, must be himself recognized as—in some way—the master's equal. Yet the salient feature of the relation between them is its asymmetry and their inequality.

from OutKast puts it on "Liberation": "Can't worry 'bout what a nigga think, now see / That's Liberation and baby I want it / Can't worry 'bout what anotha nigga think / Now that's Liberation and baby I want it."[11]

Unfortunately, liberation cannot come from simply refusing the struggle for recognition. Refusing to seek recognition from those who present themselves as one's peers can easily become a self-defeating attitude that rejects the world altogether. Sometimes this attitude is presented as reciprocating the world's rejection—"fuck ya'll too, then." Here the individual self-consciousness becomes painfully aware of the opposition between its demands for freedom and fulfillment and the resistant surrounding world. This attitude is exemplified by Tupac Shakur in "Me Against the World":

> The question is will I live? No one in the world loves me
> I'm headed for danger, don't trust strangers
> Put one in the chamber whenever I'm feelin' this anger
> Don't wanna make excuses, cause this is how it is
> What's the use unless we're shootin' no one notices the youth
> It's just me against the world baby.[12]

The attempt to opt out of the struggle for recognition becomes, ultimately, suicidal. . . .

## Gangsta and Rap's Struggle for Recognition

The importance of the theme of freedom in hip hop might also suggest part of an explanation for the rise and prominence of gangsta rap. Gangsta was, for a crucial period, the emblematic cutting-edge style of rap, with which the whole of hip-hop culture was sometimes identified. One way of understanding the sub-genre of gangsta rap is as an extreme, exaggerated metaphoric form of the struggle for recognition. Gangsta is an extended metaphor that highlights a violent, no-holds-barred, sudden-death form of the "battle" in stylized, dramatic narratives. Thus, "gangsta" makes sense as a metaphor for the core impulse of the music and the culture—the struggle for recogni-

---

[11] *Aquemini* (La Face, 1998).
[12] 2Pac, *Me Against the World* (Interscope, 1995).

tion and the theme of freedom. As N.W.A puts it in "Gangsta Gangsta":

> Since I was a youth, I smoked weed out
> Now I'm the muthafucka that ya read about
> Takin' a life or two that's what the hell I do,
> You don't like how I'm livin'? Well fuck you!
> This is a gang, and I'm in it
> My man Dre'll fuck you up in a minute
> With a right left, right left you're toothless
> And then you say 'goddamn they ruthless!'[13]

The ruthlessness of the gang is the proof and guarantee of the freedom—in the sense of independence, self-determination—of the rapper who is a member of it. Here the struggle for recognition takes a form that openly acknowledges that the individual's freedom involves dependence on the group—in this case the gang. The recognition of an individual rapper's reality turns out to involve the recognition of the *objective*—that is, real-world—conditions of his or her life. These are, first of all, that the rapper's life takes place within the gang; but also, secondly, that the gang's life is part of the life of society. This new demand is for a socially and historically grounded understanding of one's *social* existence. And this social context gangsta rap points toward, in its own way, as exemplified in Ice Cube's backhanded tribute to the suburbs: "Cock the hammer then crackle, smile / Take me to your house, pal / Got to the house, my pockets got fat, see / Crack the safe, got the money and the jewelry."[14]

Ice Cube's planned trip to the suburbs represents another kind of demand for recognition. This is no longer solely the individual rapper's struggle for recognition as an individual possessed of talent, imagination, and the skills capable of projecting a compelling, distinctive vision. Here that demand is coupled with the demand that those in "the suburbs" recognize the undeniable connection between their mode of life and that imposed upon those in "the cities." Hip hop's struggle for recognition becomes a demand, and sometimes a plea, that America

---

[13] *Straight Outta Compton* (Ruthless, 1988).
[14] Ice Cube, "AmeriKKKa's Most Wanted," *AmeriKKKa's Most Wanted* (Priority, 1990).

open its eyes to the realities under its noses. It's that reality that gives the harshness to hard-core lyrics:

> Lights turned off and it's the third month the rent is late
> Thoughts of being homeless, crying 'til you hyperventilate
> Despair permeates the air then sets in your ear
> The kids play with that one toy they learned how to share
> Coming home don't never seem to be a celebration
> Bills they piled up on the coffee table like they're decorations.[15]

This second level of the cultural struggle for recognition that defines hip hop is the struggle for recognition of the legacies and cultural traditions from which hip hop has sprung. First and foremost this means the legacy of the urban black and latino/a youth who gave birth to this form of cultural creativity. That legacy is one of affirmative creative achievement and remarkable survival in conditions of special oppression and often of desperation. But this struggle for the recognition of the historical experience of the makers of hip hop is a more protracted and difficult struggle for recognition than that of any individual artist. The stakes are higher, and the struggle is a collective or group struggle, not an individual one.

## Hip Hop and "This Makin' Dollars Shit"

But which group identity is most relevant to hip hop's struggle for recognition? The two stories most often given both stem, indirectly, from Hegel. Hegel's philosophy of history is based on the idea of a succession of (world-historic) peoples, or more specifically, nations. Nations wage, among themselves, a sort of life-and-death struggle for recognition; in each era one nation plays a dominant part in the progress of civilization. According to Hegel's account, the pinnacle of world historical development is achieved by—you guessed it—the Prussian state. Here his account of history concludes. Hegel doesn't hesitate to celebrate the achievements of European peoples at the expense of the people and nations of Asia, who he puts on the lowest rung of historical development, and those of Africa,

---

[15] The Coup, "Underdogs," *Steal This Double Album* (Foad, 1998).

who he regards as having no role whatsoever to play in the development of history.[16]

Other philosophers, influenced by Hegel, have provided conceptions of history that bear more directly on the project of accounting for hip hop's social conditions of existence. Near the beginning of his development as twentieth-century theorist of black liberation, W.E.B. Du Bois put forward a version of the Hegelian conception of history according to which "the history of the world is the history, not of individuals, but of groups, not of nations, but of races, and he who ignores or seeks to override the race idea in human history ignores and overrides the central thought of all history."[17] Accordingly, Du Bois identified races as the main parties to the struggle for recognition on a historical scale. The racial conception has its share of adherents among rap's most well-known practitioners, as evidenced by these lyrics from Public Enemy:

> I'm like Garvey
> So you can see B
> It's like that, I'm like Nat
> Leave me the hell alone
> If you don't think I'm a brother
> Then check the chromosomes.[18]

Another, in some ways more drastic, revision of Hegel's account of history was made by Karl Marx. He argued, famously, that in analyzing everything in terms of self-consciousness and spirit, Hegel was missing a most basic truth about human social life, which is organized around doing, and specifically making, rather than thinking. Real human activity is, according to Marx, first of all the production of the means of survival—of food, shelter, clothing, the essentials needed to satisfy the most basic human needs. Humans must eat before they can think. Marx developed a "materialist" conception of history, reshaping the Hegelian dialectic of nations and peoples into a

---

[16] See G.W.F. Hegel, *Lectures on the Philosophy of History* (Cambridge: Cambridge University Press, 1985), p. 190.

[17] W.E.B. Du Bois, "The Conservation of Races," *Writings* (New York: Library of America, 1986), p. 817.

[18] Public Enemy, "Prophets of Rage," *It Takes a Nation of Millions to Hold Us Back* (Def Jam, 1988).

class-based conception of human history. As he and Frederick Engels famously put it in their *Communist Manifesto*, "The history of all hitherto existing societies is the history of class struggles."[19] Even though the goods that societies depend on for survival are produced collectively by virtually the entire population, that production process is controlled by a small powerful elite who therefore control the product—the wealth—as well. And so history is the process of the struggle of opposing classes—the haves and the have-nots, the capitalists and the workers.

Putting hip hop into the context of this history, this struggle, is not much of a stretch. As Ice Cube's fantasized trip to the suburbs indicates, the struggle for recognition often involves the struggle for a "piece of the action," since the demand for recognition is the demand for a kind of freedom, and freedom in a capitalist society is closely related to the ownership of wealth. Since, as Wu-Tang famously put it, "Cash Rules Everything Around Me" in a capitalist society, he who has the cash is in a position to rule others. But then the demand for recognition of a group as oppressed generates a related demand for redistribution of wealth. But the kind of "redistribution" of wealth advocated—if that's the right word—in *AmeriKKKa's Most Wanted* is meaningful at most on an individual level, and doesn't serve to overcome the basic condition most individuals in an "acquisitive society" confront. Indeed, that acquisitiveness is itself identified as a part of the problem when Talib Kweli says:

> Supply and the demand it's all capitalism
> Niggaz don't sell crack cause they like to see blacks smoke
> Niggaz sell crack cause they broke
> My battle lyrics get conscious minds provoked and ghetto passes
>     revoked
> 'Cause we surrounded by the evil, you know that the people's
>     minds is feeble
> They believe in it, even if it don't make sense, this makin' dollars
>     shit
> Don't take a scholar to see what's goin' on around you.[20]

---

[19] Karl Marx and Frederick Engels, *The Communist Manifesto*, in R. Tucker, ed., *The Marx-Engels Reader* (New York: Norton), p. 375.
[20] Talib Kweli, "Manifesto," *Lyricists Lounge* Vol. I (Priority, 1998).

Indeed, this "makin' dollars shit" comes to rule everything in a developed capitalist society, where everything becomes a matter of buying and selling. So, in the development of hip hop, the *practice* of battling, originating, back in the day, in the schoolyard cipher—informal competitive "rap sessions" with rappers taking turns exhibiting their skillz, turns into the institutionalized form of the "beef" once the rule of cash takes over. When that happens, the cipher show-down becomes the beef driven by corporate profit imperatives and exploitative business deals as much as the petty jealousies that are their pretext. As Mos Def puts it in "The Rape Over," explicitly challenging the claims of Jay-Z's "Takeover":

> Old white men is runnin' this rap shit,
> Corporate bosses is runnin' this rap shit . . .
> We poke out our asses for a chance to cash in.[21]

And so we return to the problem, initially posed in a Hegelian framework, of "conscious minds," of how minds become conscious, and how this contributes to passing beyond "the evil" of "this makin' dollars shit." This is where the dialectic has brought us, and where the struggle for freedom, in its full, and fullest sense, now stands.[22]

---

[21] Mos Def, "The Rape Over," *The New Danger* (Geffen, 2004). Notice, finally, how Mos Def characterizes the "masters" of the rap game in both racial and class terms. The question of the relation of race and class, of which (if either) is most basic, of the dynamic between them—the so-called 'Race-Class question'—has provoked an extensive discussion and controversy in twentieth-century philosophy and social theory. Du Bois himself, as well as sociologist Oliver C. Cox and revolutionary theorist C.L.R. James, among many others, have written on it.

[22] My thinking about hip hop has benefitted from discussions with Luan Demirovic and Francois Restrepo. This track has also been much improved by considerable commentary, as well as help of various kinds, from Tommie Shelby.

# 5

# Rap Aesthetics: Violence and the Art of Keeping It Real

RICHARD SHUSTERMAN

Philosophy seems very old, but the art of poetry (which is central to rap's style and self-understanding) is older still. Before philosophers claimed to be the wisest droppers of knowledge, it was the poets who were celebrated for revealing in captivating rhythm and vivid imagery the traditional wisdom, ideals, and deepest religious beliefs that were embodied in the myths and experience of ancient cultures. To establish philosophy as a rival source of wisdom, Socrates was compelled to show its superiority, which is why he (and Plato after him) fiercely criticized the artists and especially the poets.

Art, they argued (in dialogues like the *Apology*, *Ion*, and the *Republic*), did not convey true knowledge; nor did it improve one's character and ethical behavior. Instead, Socrates and Plato insisted that art distorted reality, stirred up dangerously violent passions, corrupted the soul by appealing to its basest elements, and led people ethically astray. (Some of these charges will probably remind readers of hostile criticisms made against rap music). As philosophy was affirmed as the key to good politics, with Plato advocating the ideal of the philosopher-king, so artists and poets were banned from the Utopian Republic he envisaged. In short, using the double-barreled self-promoting, rival-dissin' style that rap MCs have skillfully emulated, philosophy rose to prominence by vehemently claiming to be number #1 while denouncing the competition as wack.

This "ancient quarrel between philosophy and poetry," as Plato called it, may not seem so severe today, because philosophers, since Aristotle, have often sung the praises of art. But disturbing traces of this quarrel still remain to haunt and constrain aesthetics. Perhaps its most important and pervasive residue is the rigid art versus reality contrast that has been so long presumed by philosophy that it has come to seem unquestionable commonsense. This dogmatic dichotomy suggests that art is somehow only fiction and deceit rather than a powerful reality that can purvey the truth and represent the real in ways just as powerful as scientific and philosophical discourse. From the same dichotomy, philosophers have drawn the dangerous political conclusion that art pertains only to a pure aesthetic sphere, entirely apart from the real world of practical and political action.

## Pragmatism, Rap, and Art

One of the most wonderful and deeply revolutionary aspects of hip hop is the challenging of this dualism. Many of the more thoughtful MCs claim not only to be creative artists but also philosophers; and they see their artistic expression of truth as part and parcel of a political struggle to achieve greater economic, social, political, and cultural power for the core hip-hop constituency of African-American society. This undermining of traditional divisions between artistic culture, science, and politics is part of what I regard as rap's deep "philosophy of the mix" which is expressed, of course, also in its aesthetic techniques of sampling and its references to so many aspects of popular and political culture.

The notion that reality is fundamentally mixed and multiple rather than pure and uniform provides a contrast to Plato's view of true reality as pure, ideal, permanent, and changeless Forms. If rap has an underlying metaphysics, it is that reality is a field of change and flow rather than static permanence. This emphasis on the changing and malleable nature of the real (which is highlighted in rap's frequent time tags and its popular idiom of "knowing what time it is") and on the mixed pluralism of reality rap shares with the philosophy of American pragmatism, first made famous by William James and John Dewey, and later embraced in different ways by the great African-American philosophers W.E.B. Du Bois and Alain Locke. Pragmatism also shares with rap the rejection of the rigid divisions of art and reality, body and soul, culture and politics.[1]

Pragmatism and rap understand art not as an ethereal product of supernatural imagination, but as an embodied activity emerging from natural needs and desires, from organic rhythms and satisfactions, and also from the social functions that naturally emerge from and reciprocally influence the biological. From this pragmatic point of view, art is desired and desirable because it enhances life, by making life more meaningful, more pleasurable, more worth living. Art intensifies experience by engaging reality and by giving expression to the most powerful human drives. One of these basic drives that art seeks to satisfy is the quest for meaningful form. But another is the drive to achieve and express power. This second drive clearly relates to the phenomenon of violence, which is undeniably not only a feature of reality but also a particularly prominent and problematic feature in the specific reality and image of hip hop. This track will offer a brief analysis of the concept of violence in terms of its relation to art in general and rap in particular.

## Violence and the Art of Keeping It Real

The most basic "dictionary definition" of violence is simply "swift and intense force or power." By this definition most good works of art commit violence. The sculptor who chisels, the ballet dancer who leaps, the shrieking soprano playing the Queen of the Night in Mozart's *Magic Flute*, all exhibit physical violence, just as do hip-hop artists, whether they are tagging graffiti, whirling and popping in breakdancing, frantically scratching vinyl as DJs, or busting rhymes and moves as MCs. Great art further works through violence not simply by representing it as in *Oedipus, King Lear, Crime and Punishment,* or *The Stranger,* but by effecting it in the flow of our experience:

---

[1] For an extended discussion of rap in terms of pragmatism, see Richard Shusterman, *Pragmatist Aesthetics: Living Beauty, Rethinking Art* (Oxford: Blackwell, 1992; second edition, New York: Rowman and Littlefield, 2000); and *Practicing Philosophy: Pragmatism and the Philosophical Life* (New York: Routledge, 1997). See also my "Rap as Art and Philosophy," in Tommy Lott and John P. Pittman, eds., *A Companion to African-American Philosophy* (Oxford: Blackwell, 2003).

through the swift, enthralling power of aesthetic experience, which even when not pleasant is relished for its explosive intensity. So much of our routine experience of life is humdrum and boring that we relish art for sweeping us away by the power of its intense experiences.

Violence has of course another meaning, that of harm or injury resulting from its force. Art's basic logic in the economy of human life is to gratify the needs and pleasures of violence in the first sense while reducing the damages of the second. Aristotle's theory of catharsis, though focused on pity and fear, presents the standard aesthetic solution: art is valuable because it allows dangerous, yet gratifying emotions to be enjoyed but then exorcised by expressing them in a safe, because fictional world of mimesis, a realm clearly distinguished from the real. Aristotle, though defending art, thus joins Socrates and Plato and the main tradition of aesthetics that opposes art to real life and seeks to keep it in a realm apart.

Pragmatist and rap aesthetics cannot accept this solution, since we insist on art's deep connection to life, its use as a tool for structuring one's ethics and lifestyle, a means of political engagement to raise consciousness and promote greater freedom. Art is a mere distraction if it is separated from life. But if art is deeply violent, if its power cannot be confined to the quarantined white cube of gallery space or the soft padded dungeons of movie theatres, then its violence should emerge in real life—and it does. The problem is when that violence becomes more destructive than life-enhancing.

## Street Violence and Dead Bodies

No contemporary genre demonstrates this danger more than rap music, with which my version of pragmatist aesthetics has been closely linked, for better and for worse.[2] For more than the last

---

[2] Though the study of rap constituted only one chapter of my *Pragmatist Aesthetics* most of the press reviews concentrated on this topic. See for example, C. Delacampagne, "Une Esthétique du Hip-hop," *Le Monde* (31st January, 1992); B. Loupias, "Le Champ du Rap," *Le Nouvel Observateur* (28th March, 1992); D. Soutif, "L'Or du Rap," *Libération* (23rd April, 1992); J. Preston, "The Return of the Repressed," *The Times Higher Education Supplement* (9th July, 1993); J. Fruchtl, "Die Hohe Kunst des Raps," *Suddeutsche Zeitung* (20th

fifteen years, rap has become America's prime cultural symbol of violence, demonized in the menacing figure of unruly young black men from the ghetto, targeted by the media, the police, and even a long list of premier politicians including our recent presidents. The media history of rap is a history defined by violence, stretching from rap's media discovery with the "wildin" of the 1988 Central Park rape, to the 1992 L.A. riots, to the Snoop Doggy Dogg indictment for murder in late 1993, and more recently to the seemingly related drive-by killings of two young rap superstars Tupac Shakur and the Notorious B.I.G., who were famous not only for their music but for the violent feud between them that heightened rap's longstanding East Coast-West Coast rivalry.

First shot in a 1994 New York City incident for which he blamed the Notorious B.I.G., Tupac was murdered on September 7th, 1996, in Las Vegas, while in the car with his manager from Death Row Records. The Notorious B.I.G. (born in Brooklyn as Christopher Wallace) was gunned down only six months later, March 9th, 1997, after a rap party in L.A., where his presence had provoked disapproval. Only twenty-four, he was buried several days later in New York, and even his funeral erupted into street violence in which the police were involved and made several arrests. All this made an eerie introduction to his new double-album long ago planned for release on what turned out to be the very next week after his funeral and uncannily titled *Life After Death*. Its sales were stunningly lively. Snoop Doggy Dogg's murder indictment enabled his debut album to be sold out before it was even issued. In August 2004, while serving a prison sentence for assault, criminal possession of a weapon, and firing shots into a crowd, the rapper Shyne released a new LP *Godfather Buried Alive*, and it proved the highest selling new entry on the week it debuted. For Shyne, it was clear that his criminal "street cred" contributed to sales of his music: "It brings a bit more reality and a bit more truth to

---

September, 1994); C. Romano, "A Temple Philosophy Professor in Rhythm with Hip-hop Culture," *Philadelphia Inquirer* (28th October, 1992). I respond to these discussions and to other critiques of my rap research in "Rap Remix: Pragmatism, Postmodernism, and Other Issues in the House," *Critical Inquiry* 22 (1995), pp. 150–59.

it."[3] Corporate wisdom has long known that violence sells; but this, of course, is not simply a "rap thing," just think of action movies or the arms trade.

## Aesthetic Violence and Consciousness Raising

Long linked to destructive street violence, rap also displays *aesthetic* violence. The swift, intense force of its beat, its very methods of sampling and scratching records, its aggressively loud, confrontational style give rap the aesthetic vigor that raises the energy and consciousness of its listeners. Rap's early motto of "Bring the Noise" was an auditory declaration of violent protest. Violence of some kind was recognized as necessary for breaking the conspiracy of silence and complacency about economic oppression, police violence, and other social ills of the black inner city. Aesthetic violence was needed to take bad records apart so that their tracks could be made into something better.

Ever aware of its violent heritage, rap has also developed a strong tradition devoted to the theme of "overcoming violence." Already in 1987, the rap community launched a "Stop the Violence" movement under the leadership of KRS-One whose hit by that title was inspired by the killing of his rap mentor and partner Scott LaRock, shot while trying to stop a street fight. KRS-One is still actively continuing this tradition today, having been joined by some other East Coast knowledge rappers like Guru, Jeru the Damaja, and Dead Prez. Unsurprisingly, this tradition gets far less attention from the media, since destructive violence makes more sensationalist news, pandering to conditioned consumer interests and expectations.

But the "Stop the Violence" movement in rap is worth our close attention. Not only because it will help us avoid the philosophical habit of speaking in abstract generalities rather than reporting on concrete realities, but also because rap culture knows a lot about violence; and it makes, in its own vernacular way, some very complex and astute points.[4]

---

[3] See www.mtv.com.mews/articles/1490330/20040818/simpson_ashlee .jhtml?headlines=true). For helpful discussions concerning Shyne and the contemporary hip-hop scene, I am grateful to the Brooklyn DJ and hip-hop scholar Mixmaster Josh Karant.

[4] One recent expression of rap's awareness of the complexities of violence is

Since its very aesthetic is based on the positive violence of swift, intense energy, rap's quest to overcome violence must reject the standard, one-sided solution that violence should be altogether abandoned and simply replaced by an ethos of pure sweetness and tender love. Knowledge rap shows that the problem of violence cannot be so simple. Violence cannot simply be viewed and eradicated as an absolute, unnecessary evil; it is deeply entrenched in our evolutionary make-up as a necessary tool for survival and still has its positive expressions and uses. The problem of overcoming violence is not, then, a question of exterminating it altogether but of channeling and managing it, of separating the good violence that improves realities from the violence that does more harm than good; of using good violence to overcome bad violence.

## Stop the (Bad) Violence!

Let me now get down to particulars by citing some lines from KRS-One and other rappers to illustrate these issues. The first point made in the original "Stop the Violence" (*By All Means Necessary*) anthem was that rap violence must be seen in a context of much wider, politically institutionalized, violence in Reagan's "Star Wars" America: "They create missiles, while families eat gristle."

The second point the song makes is that the destructive killing connected with the rap milieu neither expresses true power nor strengthens rap but only weakens it. This violence, KRS-One argues, does not even frighten the white police force who are happy to see black brothers killing each other and thus discrediting their culture instead of directing their rage on their true enemies: establishment society and the rap community's own bad habits:

> We gotta . . . stop the violence,
> When you're in a club you come to chill out,
> Not watch someone's blood just spill out.

---

in its 2004 election year "Vote or Die" campaign, where the symbolic violence of the power of voting to legally overthrow an undesirable leader or policy is both contrasted and linked to the real violence of death, frequently suffered because of the undesirable policies of undesirable leaders.

That's just what these other people want to see
Some wish to destroy the scene called hip hop
Hip hop will surely decay.
If we as a people don't stand up and say
"Stop the Violence!" "Stop the Violence!"

This title phrase is shouted out here (and elsewhere as the song's refrain) with great vocal power to underline its importance through violent intensity, but also to symbolically outshout rappers who tend to glorify black crime. The auditory message is that one has to be violent to overcome violence, at least in a culture where violence is so deeply entrenched—as perhaps it is in all human cultures but certainly in America and its urban ghettoes.

As its lyrics constantly insist, rap is an art that gets its appeal by "keeping it real." This theme of making art true to life is very familiar; what distinguishes rap, making it both attractive and risky, is its implication of the converse idea: that one makes life true to art. This is most attractive to young people looking for an aesthetic model to give style to their lives. Hip hop, as I argue in *Practicing Philosophy*, captures its fans not simply as music, but as a whole philosophy of life, an ethos that involves clothes, a style of talk and walk, a political attitude, and often a philosophical posture of asking hard questions and critically challenging established views and values. For so-called knowledge rappers like KRS-One, this philosophical life includes metaphysics, political protest, vegetarianism, monogamy, and strict self-discipline. For the gangster style—powerfully established by West Coast rapper Ice-T with his 1991 album *OG*, i.e., Original Gangster and linked with rap's street reality as signified in his *Return of the Real*—the rap reality of both art and life instead demands pimping, drug-dealing, high-living, and mobster-like killings. By blurring the boundaries of art and life, rap's stakes are high. The violence cannot be confined to a purely fictional aesthetic realm, quarantined from life. How then is violence to be handled and its dangerous forms overcome?

KRS-One's efforts to resolve this question start with the Darwinian premise that violent struggle is so deep in our human social nature that it cannot be simply uprooted or suppressed; nor can it be confined to the ghetto neighborhoods. Violence can however be channeled into symbolic, artistic forms that are more productive than destructive in their hardcore power, as KRS-One insists, highlighting the forceful reality of his message: "So when I kick the rhyme I represent how I feel / The sacred street art of keeping it real."[5]

Underlying the power of this art is the basic struggle for survival and for social recognition and prestige, converted from brute murderous cannibalism to victories of symbolic glory through artistic prowess:

> With all this technology above and under,
> Humanity still hunts down one another.
> Rappers display artistic cannibalism through lyricism.
> We fight each other over rhythm.
> Through basic animal instincts we think,
> So the battle for mental territory is glory.

KRS-One's premise here is that despite technological advancement and ideologies of peace, humanity retains an instinctual heritage of violence that was (and perhaps still is) necessary for survival. The key is to express this violence in hardcore poetic expression, in symbolic, lyrical, and rhythmic combat which will not destroy bodies but sharpen the mind, animate the spirit, and create a glorious artistic tradition that can help raise the cultural pride, social profile, and economic potential of African Americans. Guru advocates the same strategy of channeling violent impulses into cultural production in his song "Lookin' Through the Darkness" (*Jazzmatazz, Vol. 2: The New Reality*)

> I try to channel my rage,
> As I travel through the city regularly,
> Turning the anger and frustration straight into energy.
> I rock from East New York to the suburbs.
> The light keeper, knowledge seeker.
> I switch the stress that's on my mind
> Into the voice that rocks your speaker.

Such solutions channel violence onto an aesthetic medium in a field of artistic production and rivalry: kicking rhymes, rocking beats, busting moves, and dueling with other rappers over

---

[5] "R.E.A.L.I.T.Y." KRS-ONE (Zomba Recording Corporation, 1995).

the quest for truth and artistic excellence. Rappers know that their struggle for success in life will inevitably involve them in violence of some sort: the only room for choice (as a Guru song-title from *Jazzmatazz, Volume 2* puts it) is the "Choice of Weapons"—a mic or a gun.

## (Positive) Violence of Self-Discipline

There is also another strategy offered by knowledge rappers like KRS-One and Guru for overcoming destructive violence through rap's positive violence: the violence of strict self-discipline and self-knowledge, a violence on oneself that strengthens the self without hurting others. Repeating the Darwinian message that "everythin' in nature rules by kickin' ass," KRS-One's song "Health, Wealth, Self" (*KRS-ONE*) advocates self-realization through hard-core self-control. His track "Breath Control" (*Edutainment*) relates the theme of self-control to the vocal demands of the very art of rapping; while his more recent "Squash All Beef" (*KRS-ONE*) connects his disciplined vegetari-anism to the general theme of stopping violence, urging his lis-teners to be at least "mental vegetarians" by directing one's energy not at attacking others but at forceful self-control and the quest for knowledge: "Violence in society would be minimal / 'Cause the education here would be metaphysical. / Not livin' by laws but livin' by principles." Jeru the Damaja (in "Ain't the Devil Happy?" from his *The Sun Rises in the East*) is even clearer about how the quest for the power of self-knowledge and self-control requires a violent attack on one's destructive desires: "You must discover power of self / Know thyself / Find thyself / Hate in thyself / Kill in thyself."

Here violence is directed not outwards toward harming oth-ers nor even to a separate artistic medium distinct from oneself, but instead directed inwards, with demanding asceticism, on the material of the self—to strengthen its will and kill the destruc-tive violence of hate. By such logic, true peace and love often require a violent strictness rather than soft indulgence. Consider BDP's "Love's Gonna Get'cha" (*Edutainment*) and "Why Is That?" (*Ghetto Music: The Blueprint of Hip Hop*), where KRS-One urges: "The stereotype must be lost / that love and peace and knowledge is soft / for love, peace must attack And attack real strong, Stronger than war!"

Rap's strategies for handling violence do not try to erase it altogether, but only to overcome it by a more benign, constructive form of violence. Is this limitation of strategy due to rap's particular depravity or is it due to the more general problem of the inescapable role of violence in our human condition? It may seem easier to blame only rap, but greater progress will be made in overcoming the many evil varieties of violence, if we recognized its deep pervasiveness and even its useful positivities.

# 6

# "F**k tha Police [State]": Rap, Warfare, and the Leviathan

JOY JAMES

## The Police State

In *Leviathan*, published in 1651, political philosopher Thomas Hobbes asserts that the true social contract is about law and order, and killing. Hobbes is (in)famous for his assertion that life is "nasty, brutish, and short." The life expectancy for the European male in the seventeenth century was thirty-eight years.[1] Although the life expectancy for African American males in the twenty-first century has surpassed that, recent studies noted that one in twelve fifteen-year-old African American males living in Washington, D.C. could expect to be murdered before the age of forty-five.[2] For some, Hobbes was prescient . . . but back to the social contract.

Hobbes asserts that men who "live without a common Power to keep them all in awe . . . are in that condition which is called

---

[1] See Pat Thane, "Social Histories of Old Age and Aging," *Journal of Social History* 37, No. 1 (Fall 2003), pp. 93–111.

[2] Based on 1998 data generated from U.S. death records and compiled by the U.S. Centers for Disease Control, the average 15-year-old U.S. male faces a 1-in-185 probability of being murdered before reaching age 45. Nationally, a similarly aged black male faces an average 1-in-45 probability that he will be murdered before reaching age 45; an average white male faces a 1-in-345 probability of murder before age 45. See Gareth G. Davis and David B. Mulhausen, "Young African-American Males: Continuing Victims of High Homicide Rates in Urban Communities," *Center for Data Analysis Report* #00-05 (2nd May, 2000), http://www.heritage.org/Research/Crime/CDA00-05.cfm (25th August, 2004).

Warre . . . of everyman, against every man."[3] This absence of a
dominant or recognized "legitimate" power, understood as protective and guaranteeing equal treatment to all under its protec-
torate, reduces society to a battlefield:

> To this warre of every man against every man, this also is conse-
> quent; that nothing can be Unjust. The notions of Right and Wrong,
> Justice and Injustice have there no place. Where there is no com-
> mon Power, there is no Law: where no Law, no Injustice. Force,
> and Fraud, are in warre the two cardinall virtues. . . .[4]

For the *Leviathan*, social stability and harmony are found in
emotion and reason: "The Passions that incline men to Peace
[which] are Feare of Death; Desire of such things as are necessary to commodious living; and a Hope by their Industry to
obtain them. And Reason suggesteth convenient articles of
Peace, upon which men may be drawn to agreement."[5]

"Leviathan" is not merely a metaphor; it is also material and
spiritual manifestations of policing, control, and domination. If
indeed the foundation of the social contract is about policing
through the ceding of one's "right" to protect and avenge herself against her predators—the pronoun is a bit incongruous
here given the male domination of rap and within the dominion
of the Leviathan—then granting the state the power and "right"
to serve as arbiter and enforcer—judge, jury, and executioner—
is tantamount to stating that policing, and its legal right or duty
to killing, is not only a function but a *foundation* of the state.
Consequently, some pro-leviathan politicians have argued that it
is police or military power via the police or militaristic state
which assures continued Industry and Harmonious living—for
those not attacked by the police or military—through the main-
tenance of "law and order" as social stability.

Yet this does not add up. Consider the disproportionate
amounts of state-sponsored violence inflicted on the lives of
women, children, the poor, and racially-fashioned peoples, both
"at home" and abroad. (In contemporary warfare the majority of

---

[3] Thomas Hobbes, *Leviathan* (New York: Washington Square Press, 1976), p.
84.
[4] *Ibid.*, p. 86.
[5] *Ibid.*, p. 84.

casualties are civilians.) When members of Wu Tang or E-40 do the "mathematics," they instruct in the elegance of Wittgenstein but with simplicity, sorrow, and rage. Simple math: the Leviathan = a police state for those excluded from the social contract. Those not included in the social contract = legit targets for state violence. Criminalized blacks, black criminals or "gangstas"—historically considered outside of the contract— exist, in their own fashion, as oppositional sites to state powers and targets for state transgression and nasty, brutish, and short lives.

"Originary" gangsta groups, such as N.W.A. with their "F*** Tha Police," had no pretensions toward or vocation for revolutionary politics. Nonetheless they were a point of origin for those who followed and a juxtaposition to radical contemporaries, the most noteworthy being Public Enemy, who produced sophisticated rap against policing and repression. Dead Prez deepens the tradition of Public Enemy in "Police State" with a sample from a speech by longtime civil rights activist Omali Yeshitela (James Waller). Yeshitela, founder of the National People's Democratic Uhuru Movement and Chairman of the African People's Socialist Party, opens "Police State":

> The state is this organized bureaucracy. It is the police department. It is the army, the navy. It is the prison system, the courts. The state is a repressive organization. . . . The police become necessary in human society at the junction in human society where there is a split between those who have and those who ain't got.[6]

As do Dead Prez and Yeshitela, Ice-T, Tupac, Wu-Tang, and The Coup, "hardcore" or underground rappers assert that the police, the NYPD, the LAPD, are the "biggest gang out there" with the requisite hardware and military technology to professionalize state "gangbanging"—which coexists with community service, law enforcement, and upholding of the peace. So, if gang = police = state as a working hypothesis, then the state can function as a criminal enterprise, that is, with criminal capacity and intent.

"Police-as-criminals" finds its literal expression in the rogue elements of law enforcement, for instance LAPD's Rampart

---

[6] Dead Prez, "Police State," *Let's Get Free* (Loud, 2000).

scandal of undercover cops freelancing as drug dealers, extortionists, and murderers (and "protection" for Suge Knight of Death Row Records, Tupac's last imprimatur).[7] It also expresses itself in the NYPD rape of Abner Louima and firing of forty-one shots at an unarmed Amadou Diallo. (According to theorist Frank Wilderson, civil society, and hence state protection, is reserved for those bodies that do not "magnetize bullets.") Most housed inside the Leviathan assert such tortures and killings as aberrations of law enforcement, and not a proven formula revealing state complicity in crimes against the poor and racially-fashioned. Still the hardcore and underground (which encompass both revolutionaries and the criminally inspired alter-egos to cop sociopaths) rap about death emanating from the police state. There is death from police brutality, racially motivated policing and sentencing, and torture, neglect and warfare in penal sites where the Thirteenth Amendment codifies slavery. There is social and political death from state disruption of radical peace and justice organizations. There are the emotional and biological deaths of politicals and apoliticals from terror or assassination. And of course there is the mass killing (also known as operations 'Just Cause', 'Iraqi Freedom', and so forth) that accompanies imperial policing that manufactures Feare through symbols and lies to further expansionist wars for Glory or Gain.

Despite the criminal enterprises of the state (a.k.a. "human rights violations," prisoner abuse and torture, Cointelpro, contra wars, violations of international treaties), some anti-state narratives of hardcore rap remain anti-revolutionary (a political position that is distinct from the state's *counter*-revolutionary

---

[7] In 1999, LAPD Rampart CRASH (Community Resources Against Street Hoodlums) anti-gang officer Rafael Perez plea bargained to charges of theft of drugs from LAPD evidence lockers for his drug sales; and implicated dozens of CRASH officers engaged in systematic violence against residents of Pico-Union, site of the Rampart Division. The investigation into the Rampart Division involved over 3,000 cases and over 100 victims of police brutality and misconduct had their convictions overturned. Several police serving as security for Death Row records at the time of Tupac's and Biggie Smalls's murders were also later implicated in the LAPD Rampart scandal. See "LAPD Rampart Scandal," *Democracy Now!* (22nd December, 1999), www.democracynow .org/article.pl?sid=03/04/07/0415205&mode=thread&tid=5 (1st February, 2005).

politics; in other words, the former rejects revolution, the latter overthrows it). A bit bipolar, posing as both antagonists and alter egos to state criminals, some rappers seem to reduce the police to rival gang formations rather than tentacles of a Leviathan. Hardcore rappers extol the virtues of pimping, sexual battery, drug dealing, and "honor"—in which killing those who disrespect you is part of the game—while aware of the state's (historical) complicity in institutional rape in slavery, lynching, the convict prison lease system, "lockdown" prisons, and drug trafficking to support illegal wars (Iran-Contragate). The police (state) share the values, timocratic culture, and bipolarity of gangstas (recall President Ronald Reagan's "contras" or counter-revolutionary guerrillas in Latin America and Southern Africa, Ft. Benning's School of the Americas training of death squads, the international theft of global resources and lives, all registered internationally as crimes against humanity).[8]

Hobbes could imagine the state of nature with the usual white supremacist rant: indigenous Americans as "red niggas" bearing the mark of savagery (a cant somewhat akin to Hegel's and Kant's rap on the African as the "black nigga" wearing the mark of the beast). Yet this paternal figure of Western political philosophy seems to have under-theorized the possibility of "state criminals," gangstas who would make those most enraged or disavowed romanticize the "state of nature" and lawlessness upon the land. Three centuries after Hobbes wrote his treatise for an omnipotent government, for state as god, genocidal wars dominated the twentieth century. The "hip-hop generation" was conceived in the post-movement era where contemporary police statesmen and stateswomen were polishing their craft in warfare, projecting the Hobbesian state of

---

[8] The largest, most organized, and destructive criminal enterprises are corporate and statist. The bulk of revenues from drug sales are not made at production or distribution sites, that is in agricultural fields or street sales; the vast majority of drug revenues comes from money laundering, which is done by banks (such as American Express and Citibank) censored for criminal activities. Likewise the majority of cocaine, both powder and synthetic, according to a Sentencing Project report, is consumed by suburban whites while the vast majority of those incarcerated for street sale or addiction are poor and working-class blacks and latinos. See The Sentencing Project, "Crack Cocaine Sentencing Policy: Unjustified and Unreasonable," http://www.sentencingproject .org/pubs_04.cfm (10th October, 2004).

nature as trauma in "low-intensity" conflict that they would first create and then later pacify as "peace keepers."[9]

## Capital, Commodities, and Hardcore Communities

A number of artists have noted that hardcore is not inherently "revolutionary." For example, Meshell Ndegeocello raps/sings:

> So tell me are you free?
> While we campaign for every dead nigga blvd.
> So young motherfuckers can drive down it in your fancy cars
> Free. . . .[10]

The underground of marginalized or disenfranchised peoples provides narratives that define the "outlaw." Yet "outlaws" can be marketed and most want to be paid. Given that not all outlaws are *political*, in the sense of being engaged in counter-state activities, some are inspired merely by predation or personal anti-poverty initiatives. The joining of classes, from the so-called lumpen to the bourgeoisie, to celebrate a confrontation with (state) violence mixes divergent political cultures and economic desires that defy any single equation. Anti-police thugs resist state interference with low-level (un)organized crime in theft, drugs, rape, murder, as well as racial profiling and harassment.

---

[9] The government is not above utilizing rap for its own projects. In his nationalist documentary, *Fahrenheit 9/11* (and its "bootleg" copies), Michael Moore provides a glimpse of the top 40 playlist purchased by taxpayers for the military (it is unclear if the Pentagon pays royalties to the artists): A young white man interviewed, with shaved pate, grins sheepishly as he tells how the military gives out headsets and then cranks up the music to high volume to heighten "killer instincts" when U.S. troops work with assault weapons and grenade launchers. Conducting (asymmetrical) fire fights, they kill anything that poses a threat, generally anything—that is, any child, woman, or man— that moves; hence the high "collateral damage" of Iraqi civilian casualties amid the dead insurgents. The military blares into the heads of its largely (post) teen killing machine Bloodhound Gang's "Fire Water Burn," whose refrain the youth chants wolfishly: "The roof, the roof, the roof is on fire. / We don't need no water let the motherfucker burn / Burn, motherfucker, burn."
(Bloodhound Gang, "Fire Water Burn," *One Fierce Beer Coaster* [UMG, 1996].)
[10] Meshell Ndegeocello, "Dead Nigga Blvd. (Part 1)," *Cookie: The Anthropological Mixtape* (Maverick, 2002).

Anti-police state thugs resist racial profiling and harassment and state organized crime in theft, drugs, rape, murder in domestic and foreign wars. Thugs share tenuous political ties untested and undisciplined by radical mass movements.

Political crises center on economics, and the pursuit of material gain demarcates the revolutionary hardcore from the commercial hardcore (whether commerce focuses on above ground or underground economies). The American Leviathan is a corporate state. While disintegrating capitalism breeds militarism and fascism, the mechanistic, corporate state begets cyborg democracy. The legal narratives of the American Leviathan indicate that the machine is the person. The Fourteenth Amendment to the U.S. Constitution renders corporations "persons." Consequently, capitalism is not a symbolic representation of the individual person or collective people; capital or capitalism *is* person and people. Commercial rappers aspire to become cyborgs: The thing ($$) becomes human or the human the thing. This warp re-enacts the enslavement era loop, where, in the interests of white civil society and consumers, black people became property and then "persons" through the three-fifths clause to the U.S. Constitution; then penal slaves through the Thirteenth Amendment; and finally emancipated "persons" whose rights were less enforced than those of corporations aka "persons."

In the absence of political mass movements, we see that revolutionary hardcore is a difficult sell (underground theory that is given freely—at times because the theorist-artist has another job—has nothing to sell; so the performance becomes dependent upon those who pursue rather than purchase it). Capitalism manages the underground as best it can. The drive for capital promotes some and curtails other underground narratives: boasting about breaking women = $$; boasting about reading to your two-year-old = $0; romanticizing killing or dying by the young rebel = $$; celebrating the pursuit of old age as irascible radical = $0. Capital as medium transforms the hardcore into market transactions, that is, into forms of alienation in labor, desire, and politics. Alienated labor is an equal opportunity affair which marks the rhetorical rebel. Consumers and community constitute different constituencies.

For hardcore to be "heavy in the game," capitalism rides the underground up in order to cash in. Given its commercial aspects, hardcore rap generally proves to be a disruptive rather than a revolutionary force in state machinery. For the price of a CD and CD player, consumers can pimp the underground for street credibility and insurgence, an underground fed by revolutionaries with the political credibility of hardcore activists and political prisoners. Performance-based communities that consist of consumer cohort groups may learn lyrics or lecture on raps amid the absence of engagement with political struggles that move off stage. Although hardcore rap functions like a PSA to name public enemies and keep political scores, pop culture's and pop (academic) theory's timidities in confronting the police state seem indifferent to life outside, and overwhelmingly remain in awe of or obedient to the Leviathan.

The underground can, like everyone else, obscure as it reveals. So, the burden rests on the listener or reader to move beyond consumption as she resists becoming missing in political action. Some rap artists provide a bridge. For example, M1 of Dead Prez mobilizes their chosen audience: "We want to create an urgency about freedom. . . . We're here for all the people, not just the political militants, but the people who need to be awakened to become political militants."[11]

Rebellion is not revolution. The former is episodic and sporadic; its gratifications are immediate and individualistic. Such gratifications are compatible with consumerism and criminality in Leviathan culture, a culture where crime is not always illegal if performed in the service of the state. Paradoxically, revolutionaries, designated as "outlaws" by state fiats, may be actually law-abiding in terms of political principles or international law. (On some levels, the distinction between the law-abiding and non-law-abiding outlaw is arbitrary, given that the state criminalizes, intimidates, or prosecutes ostensible legal opposition to it; for example, the U.S.A. Patriot Act permits the expansion of surveillance and arrest warrants by contravening the Bill of Rights.)

Consumers can turn artists into tricks, pimping and playing for a "revolutionary" high without performing dangerous political acts. Hardcore rappers offer subversive surrogates: Rather than embrace the politics of the radical outlaw, it is easier to embrace the icon, and contain the struggle within story-telling

---

[11] Dead Prez, "M1 Interview at Designer Magazine," *Designer Magazine*, 2004, http://designermagazine.tripod.com/DeadPrezINT2.html (15th July, 2004).

and stage performance. Are bad faith performances more prevalent in commercial and mimetic gangsta rap? Gangsters engaged in criminal activity are not performing in bad faith; but they are not performing as revolutionaries either. That's not the role of the underground per se; only the revolutionary, that is, counter-state, underground functions for radical change. The revolutionary underground has no state religion, no machine or capital for which to kill or die. Live and die with mortality unfiltered through symbolism and magic, and without the magnification of the self through money, god-state, or machine means life and death without props. Perhaps the most difficult props to give up are female accessories.

The greatest commodification in hardcore rap circles about female bodies. Hip-hop math fails the gender test given its refusal to adequately analyze misogyny or the commodities trade in sex and sexual minstrels. Rap's warfare against the police is politically coded as radical; yet its warfare against women and queers marks it as anti- and counter-revolutionary. Rap "representing" the black-brown streets and communities, whose majorities consist of females and queers, constructs internal enemies, with gangstas as gladiators in theaters owned by the state.

Here, the legit targets for disciplinary violence, ridicule, and extortion are presumably, in addition to all queers, only "bad" women—as in Ice-T's rap, only bad cops are to be offed—predatory hustlers or "chickenheads." The cathartic release of cursing police, who are feared by considerable numbers of people, is accompanied by the catharsis of being able to curse women and queers, who seem to be feared by sizable numbers of people as well. When rappers police gender, they assign submissive or character roles based in minstrelsy. In drag, hyper-femmes and hyper-masculines sell. Women and queers destabilize gender supremacists whose style(s) many imitate, including transgendered female-to-males or drag kings who dress as streetwise black males. The hardcore black male remains the most demonized and desired in libidinal excess: The man most love to hate or—for some black women—the one most hate to love.

It's facile to note rap's homophobia and misogyny in order to routinely dismiss its narratives of antagonisms against the Leviathan. Rap's narratives are no more abusive than state laws and domestic and foreign policies, and much less enforceable. Still, women and queers who roll with hardcore's hostilities find themselves liberated into public rages against the machine; and imprisoned by the hatreds of outcastes. Pop and hardcore rap, like pop and national culture, embody the odious and sad, suggesting that resistance occurs on multiple fronts and fronts in multiple ways, as rap artists create art to curse external (police, rival gangs) or internal (women, queers) enemies in order to ward off evil, and create new powers.

## Resistance Raps

In 1992, Ice-T with his heavy metal rock group, Body Count, made the controversial "Cop Killer." Tracy Morrow (Ice-T) notes that most overlook that the song is directed against rogue police, those engaged in brutality and extra-judicial killings. The band on tour invited its (significantly, largely white male) audiences to chant "Cop Killer," as it unleashed its refrain:

> Cop killer, fuck police brutality!
> Cop killer, I know your family's grievin'
> (fuck 'em)
> Cop killer, but tonight we get even.[12]

Yet, as an Australian Aboriginal elder noted, in the early 1990s when Ice-T and Chuck D visited him on remnants of his ancestral lands, decimated and stolen by the state: "The police are not the enemy. The law is the enemy."[13]

I make no claims about hardcore rap's efficacy as "revolutionary." I merely note it as a tool of resistance. Global accessibility through commercialization has promoted hardcore and underground rap's popularity but not necessarily their critiques. The revolutionary impulse in hardcore or underground rap and political theory exhibits not merely antipathy to policing but an ability to contextualize struggle within a political and historical framework of radical resistance. For instance, Tupac Shakur's

---

[12] Ice-T with Body Count, "Cop Killer," *Body Count* (Warner Brothers, 1992).
[13] Bobby Jackson, "Interview with Ice-T," *90.3 WCPN Online* (28th November, 1999), http://www.wcpn.org/spotlight/news/2001/1128hiphop-rerun.html (20th July, 2004).

"Dear Mama" video shows news clippings of the Panther 21 arrest and trial in New York City, in which twenty-one activists were framed by the NYPD and Cointelpro—the imprisonment of black leaders for two years proved successful in crippling New York's Black Panther Party. Still, most often, it is the local police rather than the state or global police that most rappers take to task. Although at the intersections of a Leviathan's domestic and foreign policies, the baddest gangs out there on government payroll are not the NYPD, LAPD, or Philly cops.

Thomas Hobbes did not foresee a Leviathan that would be more pernicious to (some) human life and a healthy order than the alleged state of "nature" that he theorized justified the Leviathan as the god-state-machine. If the State *is* the Law, the State is above the Law; and the Leviathan exists as Police (State) where there is no Law, where Justice is Injustice. At full circle, Leviathan tentacles reach back to embrace the Hobbesian state of nature. Leviathans with their repressive legal and police mechanisms do not cohabit with democracy: Leviathans kill democracy. For if indeed the law is the "enemy," then revolutionary hardcore rappers and theorists remain outside of the law, "underground for life." Yet, not "above the law," they work without the immunity from prosecution given those celebrated civilian or military criminals in state employ; hence, the markers of their vulnerability become public record.

When Michael Franti, a hip hop/rap artist-activist, toured Baghdad and the Occupied Territories in 2004, including the Rafa Refugee camp in Gaza, to witness terror against Iraqi and Palestinian communities, he was censored. Although Ice-T was trailed by local police following "Cop Killer"-as-rhetorical retaliation, posing "civilian" violence as an answer to police violence, Franti's band was placed under surveillance by the federal government for advocating state *nonviolence*. For Franti, a political pacifist: "What people are shouting out for today is that human interests need to take priority over the corporate and military powers."[14]

For a political militarist such as slain prison rebel and Black Panther Field Marshall George Jackson, human interests demand that we explain the function of "the prison within the prison

---

[14] Michael Franti, "Michael Franti Interview," *Globalize Resistance*, 2002, www.resist.org.uk/reports/archive/franti/ (14th July, 2004).

state."[15] It is in the prison within the prison state—where most are poor and where racially-fashioned justice mandates that seventy percent of the two million plus incarcerated are black or brown or red or yellow—that early death, spiritual and physical dying, come not from aging into infirmity, but from war and captivity amid social and state violence. An "Act of God"? For Hobbesians who grant the state power over life and death, and rightful control over the technologies of policing and killing, perhaps. Thus some god(s) renders the "state of nature" as the pursuit of international and national political and economic gains through police-military prowess to discipline the captive or defeated.

Yet, rebellions. To *deus ex machina* from resistance rap flow the divergent prophecies of heretics mixing blasphemous chants to forsake or f**k an expanding [police] state. In an irreverent pose rather than obedient genuflect, Franti's "Crime to Be Broke in America" asks the Leviathan's attendants:

> They say they blame it on a song
> When someone kills a cop
> What music did they listen to
> When they bombed Iraq?[16]

---

[15] George Jackson, *Soledad Brother: The Prison Letters of George Jackson* (Chicago: Lawrence Hill, 1994 reprint).

[16] Spearhead, *Home* (Capitol, 1994).

# Disk 3

## That's How I'm Livin': Authenticity, Blackness, and Sexuality

# 7

# Does Hip Hop Belong To Me? The Philosophy of Race and Culture

PAUL C. TAYLOR

### Sidney's Question—and a Follow-up

The film *Brown Sugar* begins with a bit of explanation from a fictional hip-hop journalist named Sidney.[1] She tells us that she starts every interview with the same question: "when did you fall in love with hip hop?" The film then shows a parade of hip-hop stars—real ones, not film characters—answering Sidney's question, fondly recalling their first encounter with some iconic figure, event, or performance. Watching this scene jogs my memory as well. I think back to my first encounter with hip hop, and find that I can still hear "Rapper's Delight" blaring from the puny tape recorder, still see my middle school friends huddling around the single tiny speaker, still feel the exhilaration and excitement of that new sound, those nimble words. But none of those memories come to me as they do to Sidney's interview subjects, as an answer to her opening question. I can't remember falling in love with hip hop because, frankly, I never did.

It's not what you're thinking. I haven't fallen out of love. My once-warm feelings have not simply grown cool, perhaps under the sobering influence of advancing years. And my years aren't so advanced that hip hop never had a chance with me at all. For what it's worth, Jay-Z and Dr. Dre are about my age, and Russell Simmons is older than I am. I like hip hop about as much as I ever did. And I really did, and do, like some of it. It's just that

---

[1] *Brown Sugar*, directed by Rick Famuyiwa (Twentieth Century Fox, 2002).

love was never the dominant emotion for me. It was more like
the admiration and respect you feel for your best friend's best
guy or girl. *I don't have those feelings*, you say. *But I see why
someone else might.*

Some people may be puzzled by all of this. Whatever else it
is, hip hop seems to be part of black culture. And I am a black
American man who grew up in the Seventies and Eighties when
hip hop burst onto the world stage. So how can I not love hip
hop? Or: what does it mean that I don't? If you're not inclined
to ask these questions, don't worry. Fewer people ask them
these days than perhaps ever before, and this track shows why
this is as it should be. Still, many people do take such questions
seriously. Let's figure out why the questions arise and consider
some answers to them, as these exercises will illuminate central
issues in the philosophy of race and culture.

## The Eminem Enigma

Even if you're not baffled or intrigued by my lack of passion for
hip hop, this track will make more sense if you understand why
other people might be. So let's approach the same issues from
a slightly different direction. If you're reading this book, you've
probably heard of Eminem. But in case you haven't, here's half
of what you need to know: Eminem is the white rapper *du jour*,
heir apparent to such luminaries as Young Black Teenagers (all
of whom were white), Vanilla Ice, the dancehall DJ named
'Snow', and the duo called Third Bass (the best of the lot, and
not just because they didn't name themselves after something
white. The world is not breathlessly awaiting the Talcum
Powder Posse). If you've heard of Eminem it may seem unfair
to put him in the same category as Vanilla Ice and YBT. And
that's the other half of what you need to know. Eminem actually seems to have earned the respect of his mostly black peers.

A respected white rapper is certainly a strange and rare phenomenon. Other examples of this kind of strangeness include
black hockey players, Vietnamese Capoeira practitioners,
Chinese Jamaican restaurants, white running backs (in American
football), and Cablinasian golf pros.[2] These labels describe real

---

[2] Tiger Woods once said he was 'Cablinasian'—white, or 'Caucasian', black,
Indian and Asian—in response to a question about his mixed racial background.

people and things, and relatively rare people and things; but, more than that, they describe people and things that seem in some sense out of place and that are therefore difficult to understand. All these things are versions of (what I'm thrilled to call) the Eminem enigma.

So if you can understand that these enigmas might leave some people puzzled, then you've got the idea. You don't have to accept that white people like Eminem are somehow out of place in the hip-hop world, any more than you have to accept the idea that black people like me are somehow out of touch when we're not passionately attached to hip hop. You just need to recognize that the idea appeals to some people, people who believe that forms of life correspond to kinds of people. And this idea ought to be familiar: it's intimately bound up with our idea of culture.

## Hip Hop and Culture

The way most people think of such things nowadays, the word 'culture' refers to a people's whole way of life. It denotes the entire ensemble of attitudes, institutions, and practices that define a coherent way of living. Working to build and maintain this coherence is what communities do, as their members cooperate to satisfy characteristically human aspirations to, for example, meaningfulness, order, and beauty. So culture comprises the foods we eat and the ways we eat them. It resides in the holidays we celebrate, the decorations we string up on those days, and the religious or political narratives that tell us why we bother. These are all dimensions along which a community may fashion its own distinctive way of life. And these expressive practices, and many more besides, are elements of culture.

Hip hop is a culture in this sense, made up, like any other culture, of many different but related social practices. It hasn't always been seen in this way. Hip hop emerged from mostly black and brown urban communities just as mostly white policymakers and pundits were deciding that these communities were pathological reflections of "normal" society. From the perspective of "normalcy," the people in the South Bronx weren't conferring meaning on their experiences and surroundings; they weren't finding joy and significance in their lives by creating new expressive practices. Hip hop's pioneers weren't using the materials at their disposal, materials provided by technological shifts and made necessary by, among other things, shrinking budgets for traditional arts education programs, to make music and art and dance. They weren't creating new forms of poetry and lyricism out of the bawdy forms of "kinetic orality" that we find in Jamaican toasting, in black southern blues lyrics, and in playing the dozens. Since music and art and dance require oboes and easels and tutus, since poetry is what Plath and Berryman produce, these dark peoples couldn't have been making culture. Not real culture.

Luckily, and as I've said, this evaluative, ethnocentric notion of culture moves fewer people than it once did, thanks in part to interdisciplinary researchers in the field of cultural studies. People may still prefer Bach's fugues to Lil Jon's dulcet stylings (for good reason: I'd prefer a stomach cramp to Lil Jon's dulcet stylings). But now we know that we have to critically analyze specific artifacts to make this preference articulate: we can't simply indict entire traditions.

In this track I'll talk mostly about rap music because it's the aspect of hip hop that I know best. I'm not suggesting that hip hop's other defining practices—breakdancing, graffiti art, making music with turntables and sampling devices, and so on—are less important or interesting. Just think of the hip-hop approach to fashion and design: what would rap, and the American culture industries, be without baggy pants, jeeps, rims, and Timberlands?[3] Now let's return to our guiding question: What does it mean that I, a black American man who came of age in the Eighties and Nineties, am not in love with hip-hop culture?

## First Answer, Intro: Dre's Dilemma

If culture is something all communities produce, then my detachment from hip-hop culture means that I'm detached from the hip-hop community. This isn't necessarily cause for concern: I'm detached from the polka community, too, but it doesn't especially worry me. Like everyone else, I need to find meaning and beauty in my world; but I don't have to find those things in hip hop. But worry sets in if hip hop is, used to be, or ought to

---

[3] My thanks to Tommie Shelby for encouraging me to make this point.

be, *home* to me—if it's where I'm *supposed* to find meaning. This is what's at stake in the film *Brown Sugar.* Sidney's best friend and eventual lover, Dre, sells out and suffers for it. He leaves his relationship with hip hop, with real hip hop, for the phony aping of hip-hop styles by no-talent, music industry moneygrubbers. And this departure from his roots helps him sustain a bad marriage and an unnatural separation from his soulmate, the journalist who happens to share his love of hip hop. So Dre's dilemma is whether to sell out or stay true to his roots.

This dilemma shows us what's at stake, morally, psychologically, and philosophically, if we consent to talking about cultural belonging. We can see this better if we put the dilemma in terms that eighteenth- and nineteenth-century European nationalism made popular, terms that proponents of Afrocentrism and communitarianism have kept before us in recent years. Dre's problem—and, by extension, mine, if this analysis is right—is *alienation*: he is no longer living out an *authentic* existence as a member of his community. On this view, human existence gets its meaning, and human individuals get their identities, from social life. Someone who breaks away from his or her roots is . . . well, let's take the organic metaphor seriously: what happens to a tree if it gets separated from its roots?

Of course, there is considerable wisdom in this story about roots and belonging, authenticity and alienation. Our roots confer meaning on our world and help make life worth living. And people who become unwillingly dislocated from their cultural backgrounds are likely to experience considerable psychological distress. We might put the point even more strenuously. As philosopher Charles Taylor argues on behalf of a whole tradition of thought, being connected to other people—in "webs of interlocution," he says in one place—is a precondition of even forming a sense of self.[4]

But we shouldn't forget the aspects of culture that the narrative of authenticity obscures. For example, cultures proliferate and overlap. They emerge from communities of various sizes and types, all of which may lay claim to a single individual's loyalties at the same time. I may participate in the distinctive ways

---

[4] Charles Taylor, *Sources of the Self* (Cambridge, Massachusetts: Harvard University Press, 1989).

of being and doing that define my neighborhood, my company, my ethnic group, and my city, and find none of these commitments contradictory. One result of this is that alienation from any one of these contexts needn't condemn me to total psychological dislocation and distress.

Also, cultures are not as stable as narratives of roots and belonging sometimes suggest. They are, in fact, always in flux. This means in part that individuals continually appropriate and revise the meaning-making resources that their cultures supply. But, as philosophers like Seyla Benhabib and Will Kymlicka remind us, it also means that cultures are occasions for political struggle and social policy. Pluralist states may decide to select some ways of life for promotion and some for repression. Or settler states may decide, as a matter of justice, to help indigenous populations maintain their cultures, perhaps in compensation for centuries of oppression. The cultures selected for promotion may protect unjust internal hierarchies by repressing members who call for democratic debate and cultural change.[5]

These particular dynamics, concerning the politics of multiculturalism or of subjugated internal minority populations, may seem to have little bearing on the hip-hop world. But the broader point has to do with the politics and techniques of cultural preservation. And the steady stream of public inquiries into the state of hip hop—in light of the commercialization of gangsta rap, or the east-west feuds, or the rise of dirty divas like Lil' Kim—shows that cultural preservation is a crucial part of the hip-hop agenda.

And here we can return to Dre's dilemma, or to the question—about my detachment from hip hop—that brought us to Dre. Preserving a culture involves, among other things, getting people to connect their lives and futures to the relevant community. One way to do this is to insist that participation is a natural imperative, like breathing or eating. If this is right, then ignoring a challenge to "our way of life" is like declining to eat, or letting someone hack off a limb. It's unnatural, irrational, and self-destructive. So my detachment from hip hop might be a problem because hip hop and I naturally belong to each other. But how can we make sense of that idea?

---

[5] See Seyla Benhabib, *The Claims of Culture* (Princeton: Princeton University Press, 2002).

# First Answer, Continued: It's a Black Thing . . .

Like this: *You said above that "black and brown" communities produced and produce hip hop. If that's right, then hip hop is part of black culture. And you, as a black person, should embrace it.*

Appealing to race is pretty much the only way to argue that I have some natural tie to hip hop. Any other way of defining the relevant community will leave me out. Just think about how much I differ from Dre, the character from *Brown Sugar*. He is from New York City, which, by most accounts, is where cultural resources from the Americas and the African diaspora coalesced into hip hop. I, by contrast, am from Chattanooga, Tennessee, which is by no account an interesting site for hip-hop innovation. Every day when he was growing up, Dre heard rappers freestyling on the sidewalks and in the parks in his neighborhood. I didn't really follow up that memorable encounter with "Rapper's Delight" until I went away to college. (The first live rap battle I ever heard was in my freshman dorm. Between two guys from New York.)

Surely training, upbringing, place of origin, and many other factors play some role in picking out the communities to which one belongs. And on these grounds, Dre can credibly assert his membership in the hip-hop world in a way I can't. But if hip hop is, more than anything else, a form of black culture, then geography and upbringing don't matter. It's part of me simply because of how I'm built. Following a suggestion from Cornel West, we might call this a form of *racialist reasoning*.[6] Racialist reasoning is seductively, but also deceptively, simple. It requires at least three potentially troubling steps. If you want to demonstrate my racial ties to hip-hop culture, you'll have to show that hip hop counts as black culture in a way that makes some claim on me. This means showing that cultures can correspond to racial groups, and that it is possible to speak coherently of races at all.

## *Step 1: Racialism*

Let's start with the idea of race.[7] We have this idea because sixteenth- and seventeenth-century Europeans found it useful. It

---

[6] Cornel West, *Race Matters* (New York: Vintage, 1994), Chapter 2.
[7] The argument of this section tracks the view that I develop in Paul C. Taylor, *Race* (New York: Blackwell-Polity, 2003).

helped them make sense of the physical and cultural diversity they encountered on their voyages of discovery, and it helped them justify the labor, land, and lives to which they helped themselves during the more, um, entrepreneurial phases of these voyages. They came to think of races as natural human groupings, distinguishable by inheritable clusters of physical, mental, and cultural traits. People who looked a certain way were supposed to have certain prospects for psychological development and cultural achievement. To put it too simply: light peoples with straight hair were intelligent, temperate, and cultured; and all the darker peoples were to one degree or another not those things.

Let's refer to this way of thinking as *classical racialism*, and recognize its substantial virtues. It greatly simplified the task of justifying otherwise objectionable social arrangements. Black, brown, and yellow peoples needed colonial rulers, for example, because they were like children, in need of guidance—especially when it came to their eternal souls, and their economies. And this race-thinking also provided psychic income to people who lacked other grounds for esteeming themselves, like the majority of white people in the U.S. who *didn't* own slaves, and who weren't living the high life on some plantation, and who needed to be dissuaded from joining forces with the slaves to overthrow the wealthy elites.

There's just one big problem with classical racialism. It's false. Neither culture nor intelligence is inherited the way eye color is. And the physical traits that are supposed to define race membership don't hang together or clearly distinguish human groups the way classical race-thinking requires them to. You know what I mean: there are "black" people with lighter skin than "white" people; there are Asian people with wide, flat noses and black people with narrow, aquiline noses; and so on.

Scientists and anti-racist activists of all colors insisted on these and other difficulties, and by the middle of the twentieth century they'd started to replace the classical conception of race with a kind of *critical racialism*. On this approach races are socially defined groups, groups that we create when we assign meaning to human appearance and ancestry. When nineteenth-century Americans said that people who looked like Frederick Douglass couldn't be expected to write, or do philosophy, or exhibit bravery, and that such people ought to be subordinated to their white superiors, they were assigning meaning to dark skin and African features. Similarly, when contemporary sociologists like Thomas Shapiro say that someone who looks like Beyoncé, or who's descended from someone who looks like Beyoncé, is more likely than a white person to suffer police brutality, racial profiling, and job and housing discrimination, and when they say that she's less likely to have a net worth commensurate with her income level, they're also assigning a meaning to her appearance and ancestry.[8] As it happens, classical racialism assigns false and immoral meanings, while critical racialism assigns plausible and diagnostic meanings.

### Step 2: Color and Culture

So we can still talk meaningfully about races—the protests of certain philosophers notwithstanding.[9] But the price of doing so is giving up on them as natural cultural communities. Races are populations of people whose bodies and bloodlines become meaningful in the right social settings. And for critical race theorists, bodies and bloodlines receive their meanings from the mechanisms of social stratification: the bearers of certain bodies and bloodlines are more likely to receive certain social goods and get treated in certain ways. Cultural "membership" might be among the social goods that get distributed along racial lines. But there's nothing natural about this process. And this means that my relative detachment from black culture isn't obviously a sign of deviance or of some error on my part.[10] Of course, to deny that cultural attachments emerge naturally the way coral reefs do isn't to say that they don't emerge at all. Even if there's nothing about how I'm made that naturally draws me to Angie Stone's hip-hop-soaked neo-soul, it and other beneficiaries of

---

[8] Thomas Shapiro, *The Hidden Cost of Being African American* (New York: Oxford University Press, 2004).

[9] See K. Anthony Appiah, *In My Father's House* (New York: Oxford University Press, 1992); Naomi Zack, *Race and Mixed Race* (Philadelphia: Temple University Press, 1993).

[10] In any case, the kind of cultural attachment that comes with race membership will dwindle in significance next to the more local and robust forms of attachment that define ethnic communities. People often conflate race and *ethnicity*, but it is useful to reserve the terms for separate uses. Asians are a race, we think, but Asians don't share a common culture.

the hip-hop influence might still count as black culture, and they might still make some claim on me.

### Step 3: Blackness, Hip Hop, Prudence, and Duties

So how can we define a culture as black without making it a natural accompaniment of racial identity, as skin color's supposed to be? We might appeal to history; perhaps by pointing out that black people played the major roles in creating and developing the practices in question. Or we might appeal to sociological patterns, perhaps by pointing to the fact, if it is a fact, that the average black person is more likely to participate in or know about the practices than your average non-black person. Neither of these arguments will be airtight, but I'll assume that they're plausible enough. The real problems begin when we move from identifying hip hop as black culture to demanding that black people embrace hip hop. There are at least three options here. None are particularly satisfying.

Here's (the major premise of) one argument: *Participating in black culture gives black people the tools to survive an anti-black world*. But even if black culture can play this role, as I think it can, why would *hip-hop* culture be any better at it than jazz, or blues, or African American literature, or capoeira? People were once fond of describing rap as the black CNN. I'm less convinced of this now than I once was; but in any case, it still doesn't give hip hop an advantage over black churches or barber shops. (Think of these as the black "Nightline" and "Daily Show".)

Here's another (partial) argument: *Black people have a duty to support the practices that emerge from black communities*. But we've already deprived ourselves of the most powerful support for this way of thinking. Without the natural cultural attachments that classical racialism imagines, the mere fact of blackness isn't enough to obligate me to black cultures. And even if it were, we'd still have to answer the question we just posed: why hip-hop culture and not capoeira?

Third try: *Cultural communities are naturally occurring complex phenomena: they are the social equivalent of ecosystems. And we should fight to preserve them, the way we do with imperiled ecosystems. The peril in this case is that hip hop has grown estranged from the black communities that gave it its life, purpose, perspective, and style. It has gone over to the corporate world, to the place where music and fashion are commodities rather than aspects of a community's life-world. Consequently, it is in danger of dying out. It will survive only if black people, like you, reclaim it.*

As with the second argument, the best support for this approach is some form of classical racialism. Otherwise, why would anyone think that *I'm* a more promising potential citizen of the hip-hop community than, say, a Chinese-American who's spent his whole life living in Brooklyn, listening to rap music, and breakdancing? If the aim is really to preserve the culture, then it shouldn't matter what the members look like. What matters is that they learn the traditions, master the relevant techniques, and internalize the proper sentiments and values. Unless we go back to the classical racialist idea of physiology determining character and sensibility, there's not much reason to think that a black person would do this any better than anyone else.[11]

## Second Answer: The Decline and Fall of Hip Hop

Finally, one might argue that I'm detached from hip hop because I'm observant, and not too morally and politically obtuse. *Hip hop has been co-opted and commodified,* the argument goes, *and it dramatizes and spreads horrible ideas about black men and about all women. So why would anyone, anyone with any moral convictions, be passionate about something like that?*

We've touched on some of these ideas already, and the others ought to be familiar. Hip hop has become one of the cornerstones of the profit-driven, multinational culture industry. This industry exports its product mainly from the U.S., where it builds into the product certain unfortunate images and myths. Rap videos show us brutish, violent, and sexually voracious black men; they invite viewers with the proper sexual orientation to ogle hypersexual and permanently available black

---

[11] One might think that black people are more likely to take black culture seriously—that we're less likely to treat it as a way of being cool or subversive, or less likely to drop it when it's no longer trendy. But it isn't at all obvious that this is right. Who takes jazz and blues most seriously?

women; they urge us to identify with people of all colors who aspire only to immediate physical gratification or financial gain; and they reinforce misleading conceptions of an apparently pathological black and urban "underclass." Rap stars have given up cultural criticism for multimedia stardom; they've stopped celebrating black power and started hawking clothes and films and deodorant; they've forsaken the model of Malcolm X and embraced the example of Donald Trump.

Like so much else that we've considered, the complaint is too simplistic. For one thing, it relies too heavily on the mainstream or corporate music industry. There are thriving local and underground music scenes in every musical idiom, and these tend to be much more progressive than what we find on MTV and BET. Also, it focuses only on rap, which, as I've said, is all I'm competent to venture any opinion about. Other elements of hip-hop culture may be much more progressive. Finally, it presupposes a romanticized image of rap music, as it were, "before the fall." Contrary to this depiction, even in the good old days rappers like Public Enemy and KRS-One were in the minority. Most were in it to make a buck, and few had anything interesting to say about politics or culture.

Still, there is something to the complaint. Our culture industries do recycle all manner of insulting gender and racial stereotypes. And one of the principal tasks of the philosophy of culture is to interpret expressive practices and their artifacts like texts, to uncover the hidden and not so hidden complexes of meaning that animate them. This means offering "readings" of specific cultural artifacts, something that I don't have space for here. I simply want to indicate that there is work here to do, and that the philosopher of culture may join people like Tricia Rose and Daphne Brooks in doing it.

Another thing this criticism gets right is its insistence on the culture *industry*. Outfits like Viacom—which owns BET, MTV, CBS, and much else besides—have unprecedented access to the U.S. and world populations. This has far-reaching consequences for the idea of the airwaves as a public trust, and for the ideal of a democratic culture accompanied by a diverse marketplace of ideas. Anyone interested in the study of culture ought to be interested in the unprecedented corporate takeover and consolidation of the most powerful resources for communication and expression ever created. I'm suggesting that the philosophy of culture ought to fold the ethics and political economy of media into the more familiar program of cultural criticism. For now, though, and for reasons of space, all I can do is make the suggestion.

## No Love (for Hip Hop), No problem

Here are some of the things I haven't talked about: The news stories I've seen over the last few years, chronicling the rappers and breakdancers from declining post-industrial cities in Eastern Europe, all of whom find hip hop directly relevant to their increasingly difficult lives. The websites I've seen for Malaysian MCs, and the albums I've heard by British dancehall DJs of South Asian descent. The often-overlooked line of Puerto Rican descent in hip-hop culture, as documented by people like Raquel Rivera.[12] And the fact that America is defined by hybrid cultural forms like hip hop, which means, as Albert Murray, Ralph Ellison, and others have argued with regard to jazz and blues, that to be American is to be, in a sense, impure, and gloriously so.

All of this suggests that once we start to attend to the complexities of history, to the details of cultural borrowings and cross-fertilizations, it becomes hard to say when a culture really belongs to any single group. Still, taking seriously the idea that hip hop belongs to a group that I also belong to has, I hope, been fruitful. If I've drawn the right conclusions, we found that it's pretty difficult to condemn my failure to love hip hop without appealing to some kind of outdated race-thinking. We learned that there are more plausible and up-to-date forms of race-thinking but that even these offer no support to the hip-hop proselytizer. We saw that there are non-racist ways of identifying hip hop and other expressive practices as instances of black culture. But we concluded that these more sophisticated racialisms hardly support the command that black people must embrace hip hop.

---

[12] *New York Ricans from the Hip Hop Zone* (New York: Palgrave-Macmillan, 2003).

# 8

# Queen Bees and Big Pimps: Sex and Sexuality in Hip Hop

KATHRYN T. GINES

## Bamboozled: Images from the Idiot Box

Sex and the reduction of women to objects of lust and violence is among the staple themes in feminist thought, particularly Black feminist thought which has exposed the persistent myth of the Black "jezebel" and the unceasing portrayal of Black women as bitches (or angry, emasculating matriarchs), hos, and tricks. Sometimes overt and other times veiled, these images appear in the evening news, television sitcoms, and films. Perhaps they are most explicit in the lyrical and visual content of hip-hop music and videos. So it's no surprise that many male hip-hop stars have been criticized for their negative portrayal of women in their songs and videos or that hip-hop music is often described as sexist, misogynist, masculinist, and reflecting a general disdain for women.[1]

Tupac and Nelly, for example, have been criticized for negative depictions of women in their lyrics and videos. But criticisms of them and other male rappers are often unbalanced insofar as they focus on negative portrayals of women while uncritically embracing the perpetuation of stereotypical perceptions of *Black masculinity*. Furthermore, inadequate attention is

---

[1] I see rap as a sub category of hip-hop music and hip-hop music as a sub category of hip-hop culture. And I recognize that much of my analysis in this track doesn't apply to all of hip-hop culture, in which music is only a part, or even all of hip-hop music, some of which attempts to portray Black male and female sexuality in a positive light.

given to female rappers guilty of upholding destructive sexual ideologies about women *and* men. Lil' Kim, for example, has been demonized for reinforcing negative images and stereotypes about Black women (both through her music and her image), but the way she represents Black men in her lyrics gets less attention.

In this track I'm going to look at the way hip hop contributes to the construction of sexuality through myths and stereotypes. My approach is similar to Spike Lee's film *Bamboozled*, which explores the negative images of blackness produced and reinforced by 'the idiot box'. During this examination we'll contemplate the existentialist philosophical notions of *objectification, the gaze, performativity,* and *authenticity.*[2]

## "Bitches," "Hos," and "Housewives": What's in a Name?

C. Delores Tucker, the first Black woman to serve as a Secretary of State and the founder and chair of the National Congress of Black Women, Inc., is a women's activist and an opponent of what she calls "gangster rap" and "pornographic smut." Describing some hip hop as pornographic is not entirely inaccurate when one considers the uncut versions of music videos that could easily double as pornographic videos. And then there is Snoop Dogg who entered the porn industry with a video titled "Doggystyle."

While rappers like Snoop Dogg are targets of Tucker's criticism, her disdain for Tupac's music is unmatched. In 1997 Tucker and her husband William Tucker sued Tupac's estate accusing the deceased rapper of slander, invasion of privacy, and causing Ms. Tucker emotional stress. They further charged that Mr. Tucker suffered loss of consortium in connection with two songs on *All Eyez on Me* that mentioned C. Tucker by name, "Wonder Why They Call U Bitch" and "How Do U Want It?"

---

[2] I must emphasize that it is not my intention to "preach" or make a moral commentary against hip-hop artists or hip-hop culture. Rather, it is my aim to use examples from hip hop to introduce philosophical concepts while also encouraging critical reflection on the images that we consume from the idiot box.

In the first song Tupac describes the behavior that he claims prompts men to label some women as bitches. This includes women "sleeping around" and going after men for money. According to Tupac, they should be getting educated so that they can be more independent: "Keep your mind on your money / enroll in school /and as the years pass by / you can show them fools." And Tucker's name is dropped at the end of the song when Tupac explains: "Dear Ms. Delores Tucker / keep stressin' me . . . / I figured you wanted to know, you know / why we call them hos bitches / and maybe this might help you understand / it ain't personal." Although Tucker's criticisms of pornographic smut may be valid, Tupac's "Wonder Why They Call U Bitch" doesn't fall into this category. Tucker misunderstands Tupac; he is criticizing the unequal exchange of sex for money, a cycle that sometimes ends in single parenthood, welfare dependency, and HIV. He isn't attempting to reduce all women to bitches and hos.

Yet we should examine other aspects of the song more closely. Tupac's explanation of the use of "bitch" evokes the image of the hypersexual Black welfare mother. Patricia Hill-Collins informs us: "The controlling image of the 'bitch' constitutes one representation that depicts Black women as aggressive, loud, rude, and pushy."[3] It also entails assumptions about Black women's sexual looseness. Collins adds, "Whether she 'fucks men' for pleasure, drugs, revenge, or money, the sexualized bitch constitutes a modern version of the jezebel, repackaged for contemporary mass media."[4] Tupac conjures up this sexual looseness in his explanation of the use of "bitch" in spite of his efforts to discourage women from becoming "bitches." So he reinforces rather than reproaches the image.[5]

The same is true of the connection Tupac makes between Black women's sexuality and welfare dependency, a correlation that government officials (including Republicans and Democrats) have used to justify cuts in welfare programs under the guise of "welfare reform." Collins exposes the myth of the

---

[3] *Black Sexual Politics: African Americans, Gender, and the New Racism* (New York: Routledge, 2004), pp. 123, 126.

[4] *Black Sexual Politics*, p. 127.

[5] In fairness to Tupac, he also has other hits like "Keep Your Head Up" that uplift and encourage Black women.

Black welfare mother as an image that "provides ideological justification for efforts to harness Black women's fertility" insofar as the Black woman is portrayed as a lazy and immoral maternal failure who reproduces these vices in her offspring.[6] This image reinforces the stereotype that Black women are on welfare because they are lazy and promiscuous. And that they have multiple babies by multiple fathers and expect everyone else to pay to support them. But these stereotypes ignore the countless Black mothers, wed and unwed, who work two or three jobs trying to support their families with minimum wages or less.

While many of us are familiar with this inaccurate portrayal of the Black welfare mother, we don't typically conceptualize Black women on welfare as meritorious "stay-at-home" moms like those popularized and celebrated by radio personality Dr. Laura.[7] Rather, the general attitude towards Black women who stay at home with or without welfare, can be summed up by the chorus of Dr. Dre's song "Housewife" (2001): "So what you found you a ho that you like / But you can't make a ho a housewife." Kurupt adds on the same cut, "And bitches ain't shit but hos and tricks." Notwithstanding the growing number of middle-class Black women who have the option of staying home to raise their children, the prevailing idea is that all Black women are hos who don't deserve to be housewives. This includes both urban and suburban Black women who are considered "ladies" in the street and "freaks" in the bedroom. "Housewife" and other songs suggest that Black women can't be trusted because they are constantly using sex, scheming, or "plottin'" on a man, trying to bring him down. Perhaps these aren't rappers' personal views. Still, they are the lyrical content of songs like "Housewife."

In "How Do U Want It," Tupac states: "Delores Tucker, you's a motherfucker / Instead of tryin to help a nigga, you destroy a brother / Worse than the others—Bill Clinton, Mr. Bob Dole / You're too old to understand the way the game is told." Tupac asserts that like Clinton and Dole, Tucker is too old to understand the language he uses to express what unfolds in his life, his world, his situation. Rather than hearing him, Tupac says,

---

[6] *Black Feminist Thought: Knowledge Consciousness, and the Politics of Empowerment* (New York: Routledge, 1991), p. 76.
[7] *Black Sexual Politics*, p. 132.

"They wanna censor me; they'd rather see me in a cell." Here we also see Tupac evoking the image of the *emasculating Black woman* who, despite any merits in her position is always accused of trying to "destroy a brother." This is the old yet enduring idea that Black women are always trying to pull brothers down.

The irony is that the desire to censor Tupac and confine him to a cell is not motivated by the desire to stop him from spreading vicious lies or slander, but to mute the crude and frank way in which he exposed some fundamental truths about oppression. Tupac didn't try to outline a prescriptive ethics that everyone ought to follow. He offered a descriptive analysis which functions as a mirror of our society's attitudes about the sexuality of Black men and women. Thus my point is not to condemn hip hop as "bad" for society or for individuals, but rather to highlight how societal attitudes toward Black men and women are reflected in hip hop.

## Peepin', Pimpin', and Drillin' the T and A

Like Tupac, Nelly came under fire for his negative representations of women. This St. Louis artist known for songs like "Hot in Herre" and "Pimp Juice" (*Nellyville*), has been criticized for his video "Tip Drill," which was protested by students at Historically Black Colleges and Universities (HBCUs) including Spelman (a women's college), Morehouse (a men's college), and Howard (a co-ed university). It was the women at Spelman College who received national attention, some of which was very critical, for their protests. The video is flooded with images of women (of various shades, shapes, and sizes) wearing thong bikinis, or in many cases just thongs and topless. These women are constantly slapping each other's butts or having their butts slapped by men as they gyrate in their thongs just inches away from men's faces. In addition to this, the women are also simulating sex (oral, anal, and vaginal) in multiple positions both with men and with one another. The fact that men are also throwing money at the women in the video (apparently cash or credit is accepted as a credit card is swiped down one woman's butt!) conveys the message that these women are prostitutes or strippers.

Nelly said that he was misunderstood and that he didn't intend to degrade women. He added that he has great respect for his mother and sister, both of whom would let him know if he had crossed the line. But neither his mother nor his sister had the credit card in their butt. While I don't doubt Nelly's sincerity, the real issue is the blatant *objectification* of women in Tip Drill and other music videos. A rapper's respect for certain woman notwithstanding, these videos reduce women *en masse* to mere sex objects. Objectification is the reduction of a person to an object to be dominated, manipulated, constrained, or even ignored (also known as *non-recognition*). Collins tells us that in Black popular culture there has been a shift from *celebration* to "*objectification* of Black women's bodies as part of a commodified Black culture."[8] She adds: "Objectifying Black women's bodies turns them into canvases that can be interchanged for a variety of purposes . . . African American men who star in music videos construct a certain version of manhood against the backdrop of objectified, nameless, quasi naked Black women who populate their stage."[9] By denying their individuality, music videos often allow the male performers to see Black women as sexual objects without being seen by the women, a concept known in existentialist philosophy as the *gaze*.

French philosopher Jean-Paul Sartre examines objectification using the concept of the gaze in *Being and Nothingness*.[10] He presents a scenario in which he peeks through a keyhole and can see people behind the door without being seen by them. In this example, the "peeper" represents the subject. Those seen behind the door are reduced to objects, that is, until the "peeper" hears footsteps and is suddenly confronted with the possibility that someone he can't see is looking at him, reducing him to an object. The subject doing the peeping or gazing always poses the threat of *non-recognition*. He sees without being seen, thereby reducing the other to an object. While this threat of objectification and non-recognition is reciprocal between social, political, or other equals, it becomes more complex in a society (such as ours) of race, class, and gender hierarchy.

In a later book, *Anti-Semite and Jew*,[11] Sartre asserts that this reciprocal objectification (or the threat of non-recognition) is not

---

[8] *Black Sexual Politics*, p. 128.
[9] *Black Sexual Politics*, p. 129.
[10] *Being and Nothingness* (New York: Washington Square Press, 1943).
[11] *Anti-Semite and Jew: An Exploration of the Etiology of Hate* (New York: Sckocken, 1948).

possible in a hierarchical society (the example he uses is the Jew in an anti-Semitic world). We can add that the reciprocal objectification of the gaze is not possible for a person of color in a racist society or a woman in sexist society due to the power dynamics, evident in music videos like "Tip Drill," where women are reduced to sexual objects. They are seen and manipulated yet unable to see or be acknowledged as persons.

To be sure, the "Tip Drill" video is a fitting backdrop for the lyrical content of the song in which the hook is: "I said it must be your ass cause it ain't ya face / I need a tip drill, I need a tip drill." [12] Here, a "tip drill" is a woman with a sexy body or a big butt, but without the pretty face. Focusing on her "ass" or her body renders the woman in question "anonymous." The term "tip drill" is also borrowed from basketball and evokes the image of "running a train" on a woman, or several men having sex with one woman, one after another.[13] The video implies that the women performing these acts are glad to do so for multiple partners and for the money. But a man can also be a tip drill. A woman in the song has a verse in which she asserts: "It must be your money, cause it ain't your face / You's a tip drill, nigga you a tip drill . . . I got you payin' my bills and buyin' automobiles / You's a tip drill, nigga you a tip drill." The "tip drill" here is an unattractive male who may be good in bed, but is primarily used for his money. And so the stereotypical dichotomy between men and women is reinforced: men only want sex, women only want money, and both will do whatever it takes to get it.

## "Suck My D**k": The Gaze Reversed from Tha Beehive

A *dichotomy* or *dichotomous thinking* is a process of dividing or categorizing people, things, or ideas into supposedly mutually exclusive groups. Other terms used to describe a dichotomy include *bifurcation* or *binary thinking*. Examples of such think-

---

[12] Nelly, "E.I. (Tipdrill Remix)," *Da Derrty Versions: The Reinvention* (Universal, 2003).

[13] Tip drill also symbolizes not only the penis (the "tip" doing the "drilling"), but also the man doing the "drilling" and the woman being "drilled." Tip Drill does not have to be full intercourse but might also include, for example, inserting only the tip of the penis into the vagina, oral sex, or a lap dance.

ing are conceptions of black versus white; male versus female, reason versus emotion, and the virgin versus the whore. Challenging these dichotomies requires *acknowledging* and *confronting* the objectification of women and moving towards empowering women as subjects or agents of their sexuality. Take the example of the virgin and the whore, which is used to restrict and police Black women's sexuality. To avoid being labeled a whore, Black women must go to the opposite extreme of becoming "pure" virgins. But the problem is that at both extremes, whether the virgin or the whore, women have no authentic sexual voice. They are forced to be either the *hyper-sexual whore* (which becomes an excuse for the label of "bitch" and "ho") or the *pure virgin* (who is expected to be intimidated by or even fearful of sex, avoiding it altogether).

One way of responding to the virgin-whore paradigm has been to embrace one extreme and redefine it in a more positive or empowering way. Lil' Kim utilizes this strategy in her rap lyrics and music videos in which she comfortably asserts her sexuality. She is arguably the most successful female rapper at taking up and popularizing the image of the *ho* and the *bitch* unapologetically.

Lil' Kim, whose alias is Queen Bee (standing for Queen Bitch), made space for herself in the male dominated world of hard core rap with overt sexuality. Her lyrics graphically expose the double standards of sexuality for men and women. When men sleep around they are players and pimps, but when women do it they are bitches and hos. Consider these lines from "Suck My D**k" (*The Notorious KIM*): "Imagine if I was a dude and hit-tin' cats from the back . . . / Yeah nigga, picture that! / I treat ya'll niggas like ya'll treat us." Then when asked "Why you actin' like a bitch?" The Queen Bee responds: "Cause ya'll niggas ain't shit / and if I was a dude / I'd tell y'all to suck my dick." Lil' Kim is taking phrases that have been used to belittle women or put them "in their place" and she is throwing them back into men's faces. Lil' Kim also "flips the script" on men in the bed-room by demanding oral sex, something it was thought only men could demand. In "Queen Bitch, Part II (*The Notorious KIM*)" she raps: "Niggas want to run up in my pussy like a pap smear / I'mma tell you now, just like I told you last year / Niggas ain't stickin' unless they lick the kitten." In other words, there will be no intercourse without men performing oral sex.

Some may praise Lil' Kim as a Black woman in charge of her sexuality, while others may denounce her as reinforcing the stereotype of Black women as whores. However, critical reflection reveals that Lil' Kim is merely seeking to move men from the subject to the object position where she can manipulate them as sexual objects. But this attempted reversal of sexual status strengthens rather than undermines the prevailing distorted image of Black sexuality. In the end, Black women are still hos and bitches while Black men are players and pimps, and these images reinforce one another. Consequently, we can't evaluate Lil' Kim's image in a vacuum. We have to remember that the image of the sexually loose Black woman has been used to rationalize the ways in which she has been exploited. The sexual exploitation of Black women is a fact that must be investigated from a historical perspective, both through the institution of slavery, as well as through the change in the sexual status of white women during that time. There was a transition in the sexual status of white women from sexual temptress to pure virgin, and a corresponding burden placed on Black women to bear the stereotype of the hypersexual jezebel. This characterization allowed white men to blame Black women for their own sexual addictions and it allowed white women to deceive themselves to believe that Black women, not white men, were to blame for their husbands' sexual offenses. The stereotype of the Black woman as a whore made her sexually available to men because she was said to have wanted or to have initiated these assaults.

In "The Continued Devaluation of Black Womanhood," bell hooks notes that "Black women have always been seen by the white public as sexually permissive, as available and eager for the sexual assaults of any man, Black or white. The designation of all Black women as sexually depraved, immoral, and loose had its roots in the slave system."[14] She adds that this sexual exploitation caused a devaluation of Black womanhood that has not changed over several centuries. A recent example of this public sentiment is the incident with Janet Jackson and Justin Timberlake at the half-time show for the 2004 Super Bowl. During their routine, Timberlake ripped off part of Jackson's

---

[14] *Ain't I a Woman: Black Women and Feminism* (Boston: South End Press, 1981), p. 52.

wardrobe to reveal her right breast. According to *Vibe* magazine, Internet inquiries to catch a glimpse of this flesh even surpassed searches on the September 11th tragedy.[15] Timberlake said it was a wardrobe malfunction. What is interesting is the fact that Janet Jackson, not Justin Timberlake, received the brunt of the criticism about the incident. This Black woman was held responsible for a white man tearing off her shirt and exposing her breast (intentionally or unintentionally) in a public performance.

## "Big Pimpin'" and Gender Performativity

Operating alongside the myth of the Black female jezebel is the myth of Black male rapist and sexual predator. Like the sexualized images of Black women, these perceptions of Black men go back to the institution of slavery and can be traced forward to more contemporary portrayals of Black men in music and the media. Over one hundred years ago Ida B. Wells-Barnett exposed the myth of the Black man as a rapist, which, along with lynching, was a tool, used to prevent Black political agency. This propaganda was also used to prevent consensual relationships between Black men and white women, and to deflect attention away from the reality of the white male rapist. The Black rapist image was used to instill fear in white women of Black men, but it was also used to provide an excuse for lynching, which Wells-Barnett described as "our national crime." Contrary to the popular belief that lynching was only a response to sexual crimes against white women, Wells-Barnett demonstrates that many lynch victims were not even charged with such crimes, and when sex crimes were the charge, these charges were often unsubstantiated. Barnett's issue was not with instances in which interracial rape actually took place, in fact she spoke out against this. Rather, she was concerned with the false accusations of rape, or even more, with consensual interracial relationships labeled as rape.

Today the image of the Black rapist or sexual predator still persists (consider attitudes toward O.J. Simpson or Kobe Bryant), but this image has also morphed into the present day

---

[15] *Vibe* Magazine Online, Lynne d. Johnson, "A Week of Boob Obsession and Media Frenzy," (6th February, 2004), http://www.vibe.com/modules.php?op =modload&name=News&file=article&sid=182.

image of the Black male as a "player" or a "pimp." The pimp is not just the man who solicits customers for prostitutes. Being a pimp is a way of dressing and carrying oneself, and having the general attitude that women are sexual objects to be used and manipulated for one's personal pleasure or gain. As Jay Z put it in "Big Pimpin'" (*Volume 3: Life and Times of S. Carter*): "You know I—thug em, fuck em, love em, leave em / 'Cause I don't fuckin' need em." Nelly's hit "Pimp Juice" and the promotion of his energy beverage that has the same name is also an indicator of the prevalence of this "pimp" image. Buttressing both the image of the rapist and the more contemporary image of the "pimp" is the idea that Black men have an insatiable, even animalistic appetite for sex or sexual perversion. This has been perpetuated by the myth that Black men have larger penises than white men, that it is their sexual appetites that lead them to irresponsibly father multiple children by multiple women, and now, that this drive for sex is so strong that it has led Black men to seek both male and female sexual partners, a phenomenon known as the "down low."

The term "down low" used to denote having a secret heterosexual affair on the side. It now represents Black men who are openly involved in heterosexual relationships, but who also surreptitiously engage in sex with other men and yet don't consider themselves homosexual or bisexual. The hysteria in Black communities about *down low brothers*, particularly among Black women concerned about whether "their men" have a man on the side, is fed by this characterization of Black men as sexual addicts. While it is true that AIDS among Black women is rising at alarming rates, and that this increase has been correlated with down low brothers having unprotected sex with men and then coming home for sexual encounters with unsuspecting women, AIDS is not at the center of this hysteria. Rather the hysteria is driven by both homophobia *and* the idea that Black men are so eager to have a sexual release that they will even engage in anonymous sex with other men to get it.

## The Possibility of Authenticity: The Life We Choose

Everyone, from Nelly and Lil' Kim to you and I, *performs* gender roles and sexuality daily. We chose to conform to or to resist these stereotypes. Feminist theorist, Judith Butler, argues that sex and gender (and it would be appropriate to add race) have been constructed and figuratively inscribed on our bodies.[16] We are all performing socially constructed gender roles, something she calls *gender performativity*. By this she means that gender roles are constantly acted out and acquire meaning when they are "properly" and repeatedly performed. Hence the ideas and ideals of gender are created and maintained through repetitive gender performance.

Hip hop offers us a racialized context for the performance of gender and sexuality. The repetitive processes are the music itself (played repeatedly on the radio), the videos (played repeatedly on television), the consumers (who are inscribed upon in their hearing and seeing), but also—and perhaps most important—the *performers* themselves. The performers present and represent a particular *performativity* of gender, forcing and reinforcing perceptions of Black sexuality (and even Black morality) globally. Collins explains: "Because of its authority to shape perceptions of the world, global mass media circulates images of Black femininity and Black masculinity and, in doing so, ideologies of race, gender, sexuality, and class."[17] The mass media have grown into a colossal gaze and image-producing machine that outlines specific gender roles that we are expected to embrace and embody. Hip hop is used as a tool of mass media to objectify Black men and women under a global gaze, allowing them to be seen without seeing. Despite this overwhelming influence, what is empowering about gender performativity is that we may choose to perform gender and sexuality within or outside of the confines imposed by the media. As Nas put it on his hit "I Can" (*God's Son*): "I know I can be what I wanna be. If I work hard at it, I'll be where I wanna be."

Through hip hop we can create radically different conceptions of gender and sexuality that do not conform to preexisting stereotypes. Once we are conscious of this fact, we are faced with a choice. We have the opportunity to choose whether we will be *authentic* or *inauthentic* in our performance. As Sartre explains: "Authenticity . . . consists in having a true and lucid

---

[16] *Gender Trouble: Feminism and the Subversion of Identity* (New York: Routledge, 1990).

[17] *Black Sexual Politics*, p. 122.

consciousness of the situation, in assuming the responsibilities and risks that it involves, in accepting it in pride or humiliation, sometimes in horror and hate."[18] On the other hand, inauthenticity consists of trying to run away from, deny, or ignore the situation that confronts us. That is, attempting to run away from, deny, or ignore the fact we have been objectified and that Black sexuality has been grossly distorted. Will we choose authenticity or inauthenticity? Will we conform to the role that society wants us to perform? Will we act out the stereotypes that have been prescribed for us? Will we perform in a way that is merely reactive to these stereotypes? Or will we perform in a way that is radically different and new? It is time for us to make a decision. As Nas explains on *Nastradamus* it is, after all, "The Life We Choose."

---

[18] *Anti-Semite and Jew*, p. 90.

# 9
# Grown Folks' Business: The Problem of Maturity in Hip Hop

LEWIS R. GORDON

Conventional wisdom says that hip hop speaks to inner city black and Latino youth and their counterparts in the white suburbs. In the case of the latter, their membership in what is often called "the hip-hop community" is a function of their *performance* of blackness despite their racial and political designations as white. Yet, the blackness they perform, *as hip-hop culture*, is what members of black communities could easily recognize as *black adolescent culture*.

The same conclusion applies to blacks and Latinos. Hip hop has, however, become a primary exemplar of authentic black culture. This development is attested to not only by the multitudes of black adolescents and folks in their twenties and thirties (and even older) who are drawn to it in their quest for an authentic black identity, but also globally as even adolescents in Africa and among black indigenous populations in the South Pacific do the same. We could add performances of blackness in Asian and Latin American countries to this roster of loose membership. We may wonder, however, about the consequence of investing so much of a claim to black authenticity into what is in practice and sentiment black adolescent culture. From a philosophical perspective, there is already a fallacy and a form of decadence at work when part of a community subordinates the whole, when what is in effect a subgroup eliminates the legitimacy of the larger community from which it has sprung.

One effect is that there seems to be more lay-ethnographic interest in black teenagers (and older black folk who behave

like teenagers) as spokespersons for the rest of the black community, or better yet—*communities.* Where else do we find such an approach to the study of a people that is able to avoid the objections of misrepresentation? Even with working-class white youth in 1970s England, from whom the Punk movement was born, there was an effort on the part of those who studied them to distinguish their subcultural behavior from the wider category of working-class white people. One understands that part of being young is behaving in ways that stretch the limits of culture marked by the weight of responsibility. There is, however, a peculiar absence of such caution in popular and many scholarly treatments of hip hop, where black adolescents seem to have become the wellspring of knowledge and creativity, as though tapped by the divine force of the gods—or at least ancestral voices of resistance. And at times, the acknowledgment of such ascriptions fails to translate into an objection but an affirmation: What's wrong with advancing black adolescent communities as exemplars of black authenticity?

## So Many Tears: A Fanonian Riff on Hip Hop

Let me say at the outset that I am not against hip hop as a form of cultural play. Much of hip hop is quite simply fun, and many of the expressions of joy and outrage manifested in activities from rapping over a beat to spray-painting a mural exemplify the Harlem literary critic and philosopher Alain Locke's insight that "Man cannot live in a valueless world."[1] But human beings cannot *live* in a world in which there is no one minding the children. A world without adults is a world without limits, and the consequences of such a world is hardly one in which children could receive the support mechanisms that enable them to be children in the first place. Yet this problem of a children-run world, of Peter Panism, faces more acute problems when the ever-spoiling dynamic of "race" is thrown into the proverbial mix. Consider the reflections of Frantz Fanon in his classic text, *Black Skin, White Masks* (1952).[2]

---

[1] Alain Locke, *The Philosophy of Alain Locke: Harlem Renaissance and Beyond,* edited by Leonard Harris (Philadelphia: Temple University Press, 1989).

[2] Frantz Fanon, *Black Skin, White Masks* (New York: Grove Press, 1967).

Fanon argued that however healthy a black individual might be, he or she would experience the secretion of alienated forces when making contact with the white, antiblack world. That is because that world has waiting for such individuals a sociogenic construction called *the black* but most often signified by *le nègre*—ambiguously "negro" and "nigger." This construction is reflected from the eyes of whites, whose points of view are socio-politically constituted as *the* point of view on reality, as how black individuals "appear" in the social world. Such an appearance stimulates asymmetrical invisibility: The black individual *encounters* such a *notion* of blackness that is not how he or she lives but as how he or she *is supposed to be*. The immediate effect is a doubled reality between the lived and the believed. To appear, then, as what one is not is to encounter the self as always other than the self, which makes the lived-self an invisible reality because of the absence of that self as a source of appearance. The result is, as Fanon observed, a destruction of the self into many fragments—to be torn apart—and thrown out into the world of a journey in search of putting together a dismembered self. Added to the situation is the ability of this soul torn asunder to see how he or she is seen, to become, in other words, the mirror whose reflection is already a distorted one. In the fifth chapter, "The Lived-Experience of the Black,"[3] this search takes Fanon on a course from embracing a neurotic Reason to diving into the depths of rhythmic ecstasy as the waves of Negritude push him ever deeper, and paradoxically ever forward, in a black sea.

To Fanon's chagrin, his moment of rapture is torn away from him as he finds himself in a moment of dry, sober reflection on its escapist status: Negritude, Jean-Paul Sartre showed, was a negative moment in a dialectical struggle for universal humanity. "Robbed," as he announced, of his last chance, Fanon began to weep. The significance of tears, the reintroduction of fluids, of washing, of catharsis, is a familiar aspect of our ongoing struggle with reality. Sometimes, in fact often, reality is difficult to bear. Tears do more than wash our eyes; they wash away, symbolically, psychologically, and existentially, what we have

---

[3] This passage appears in the English translation as "The Fact of Blackness," but the French refers to *L'expérience vécu du Noir*, which is more aptly translated as "The Lived Experience of the Black."

built up as resistance against what we are unwilling to face. Fanon's autobiographical admission of his own efforts at delusion and the tears that washed them away present to us the ironic aspect of any struggle against a suffocating world: our struggles are double-directional—both without and within.

Fanon's tears prepared him for facing the problem of psychopathology and *le nègre*. The difficult truth, Fanon argued, is that Western society has no coherent notion of a black *adult*. Whether it is as the pathetic plight of the assimilation-hungry petit-bourgeois black or the rebellious, illicit economy of the lumpenproletariat black—whom Richard Wright portrayed as Bigger Thomas in *Native Son*—the consequence is of the former not "really" being black and the latter standing as the kind of black to be "controlled." In short, both poles represent displacement, and because of this, neither can stand for the normal. Yet paradoxically both stand as normal *for blacks*, which means that black psychology is entrapped in *abnormal* psychology. To be black is literally to be abnormal. The effect, Fanon observed, is that to be black is never to be a man or a woman. It is to be, under this collapse into pathogenic reality, locked in underdevelopment, frozen, in other words, in perpetual childhood.

Is black liberation possible in a world that denies adulthood to black people? Can black people hope to achieve liberation through adopting an alien reflection of blackness that militates against the possibility of maturity?

## A Nietzschean Perspective on the Black Aesthetic

The question of black adulthood raises questions of the context of our query and the legitimacy of its social aims. When we think of the clothing of hip hop—the sweat suits, the sneakers, the hats, stocking caps, the T-shirts, and even the gold-capped teeth—where but in the contemporary neo-global economies of Western civilization can we find their source? The same applies to the technology of hip-hop aesthetic production from vinyl records on which to scratch to the spray paint through which to make thought and name visual.

The Fanonian question poses, however, an additional problem whose roots are in the thought of the German philosopher and philologist Friedrich Nietzsche and whose modern manifestation is in the blues: The question of social health. In *The Birth of Tragedy from the Spirit of Music*, Nietzsche argued that the ancient Greeks were aware of the suffering that lay at the heart of life itself, and their health was manifested by their response to it, namely, the creation of Attic poetry, drama, and music in tragic plays.[4] For Nietzsche, in other words, health is not a function of the absence of disease and adversity but instead a matter of an organism or community's ability to deal constructively with such challenges. That the underside of life is suffering and death does not negate the value of life itself. In fact, it makes it more precious. Yet, a healthy attitude to life requires its affirmation without the kinds of seriousness that lead to over-attachment and cowardice. This message still speaks to humanity.

Jean-Jacques Rousseau discussed the underside of modern life in his "Discourse on the Sciences and the Arts," where he introduced the problem of the dialectics of enlightenment.[5] Think of the scale of human suffering that accompanies the progress promised by modernity—modern war, conquest, colonization, slavery, racism, genocide; the proliferation of new kinds of disease; and the profound level of alienation of human beings from each other, to name but a few. Modern life has placed a variety of burdens on the aesthetic production of black designated people. On the one hand, there is racist imposition that challenges whether black people have an inner life, which imperils the notion of even a creative life. Black aesthetic production, in this sense, is locked at the level of pure exteriority, of ritual and repetition, the result of which is without diversity and individuation; it is purely unanimistic, locked in sameness of experience and worldviews and devoid of reflection.

Added to problems of individuation are demands of political efficacy. Once black aesthetic productions emerged as *aesthetic productions*, black artists began to receive criticisms premised upon the view that the black artist had a special calling to serve interests of black liberation. Such arguments undergirded the development of the Black Arts Movement of the 1960s, and they

---

[4] Friedrich Nietzsche, *The Birth of Tragedy from the Spirit of Music* (Oxford: Oxford University Press, 2000).

[5] Jean-Jacques Rousseau, "Discourse on the Sciences and the Arts," in Rousseau, *The Basic Political Writings* (Indianapolis: Hackett, 1987).

continue to haunt the work of black artists today. We should be reminded, however, that the claim that art should be more than the creative expression of an artist is not limited to black reflections on the subject. Leo Tolstoy, for instance, was concerned about the moral dimension of art. Karl Marx's thought led to generations of scholars and activists seeking out the revolutionary potential of art. Martin Heidegger worried whether we were losing places in which art can properly "dwell." And Jean-Paul Sartre appreciated the ways in which art suspended seriousness, although he defended the role of the politically "engaged" artist.

What distinguishes black aesthetic production here is the impact of racism and its baggage full of color questions. Black artists may be drawn toward art because of a sheer love of art, but the context in which that love is expressed is a world wrought with many social contradictions. Just as W.E.B. Du Bois argued that black folk encounter ourselves as problem people in a white dominated world, the black artist constantly encounters black art as problematic art in a white dominated art world. Black art becomes, as Fanon observed with black psychology, *abnormal art.* It functions as a disruption of the "normal" scheme of things. The result is expectations that, like the black athletes and large numbers of incarcerated black folk, black art must flow from paradoxically naturalistic, causal forces linked to blackness itself—never hard work, individual talent, and reflection—simply pure causal mechanisms infused by experience. The black artist produces work in a context in which there is already a glass ceiling on the potential of his or her work to transcend socially imposed limits. How, then, could black art be politically effective when its aesthetic efficacy has been stratified, and turned the other way, how could the aesthetic quality of black art be defended in a world of black political impotence?

## We Need a (Postmodern) Hip-Hop Revolution

Complicating matters is the near hegemonic rise of postmodern discourses in the study and interpretation of culture since the 1970s. The interplay of the impact of the studied on the studier and the language of the latter on the former emerged full form in the popularity of postmodern cultural studies in and outside of the academy. There was, and continues to be, a dimension of postmodern cultural studies of hip hop that is right on target and is, perhaps, the best way to approach the study of hip hop, and that is, ironically, a non-postmodern realization of its *accuracy*. This requires the distinction between postmodern *form* and *content*. To say that hip hop is postmodern is hardly supportable by the content of hip hop, since much of what is often endorsed by hip-hop artists is very modern and often, worse, conventional.

Even the more rebellious hip hop often affirms the more negative side of, say, patriarchy on the one hand (a world of only "bitches" and "ho's") or the more stereotyped conceptions of 1960s and early 1970s notions of revolution on the other. For instance, Dead Prez's depictions of being revolutionary Africans in "I'm A African" (*Let's Get Free*) drew much from popular cultural images of black militancy—and beautifully, cleverly, and powerfully so (one of my children's and my favorite cuts for these reasons)—but it leaves me wondering what is revolutionary about conventional and nostalgic images of black revolutionaries: "Nigga, the red is for the blood in my arm / The black is for the gun in my palm / And the green is for the tram that grows natural / Like locks on Africans." Wouldn't a revolutionary development also articulate an image that transcends the present in a forward direction? Yet, the *form* the music takes is unmistakably revolutionary, and in a powerfully postmodern way with an underlying, unexpressed but felt duality: Hip hop may ultimately affirm one set of values, but it also voices the artists' shared irritation with the travails of modern life, especially as it has been dished out to people of color.

This shared irritation has taken aesthetic form in hip-hop innovations. The postmodern aspect of hip-hop music and culture is that it is unruly. Hip hop breaks nearly every modern aesthetic convention. The abstract features of such convention appeal to repetition, harmony, resemblance, and similitude, the violations of which are apparent in hip-hop singing.[6] Consider, for example, that hip-hop music began as "rap." That it involves music with lyrics enables such work to be listed as "songs," yet it would be a mistake to call talking, often in rhymes, over a

---

[6] See my *Her Majesty's Other Children: Sketches of Racism from a Neo-Colonial Age* (Lanham: Rowman and Littlefield, 1997), pp. 240–44.

beat the same thing as singing. Moreover, when rappers do sing, they rarely sing on key. In effect, they defy the conventions of singing and the rules of a song. Even at the level of accompaniment, it is often the beat that prevails over chords and instrumental *obligato*. The human voice echoes and supports the rapper in ways that bring the novice to the fore. It is almost better in hip hop *not* to sound like a talented singer. Think of the wonderful and not-so-wonderful grunts and squawks that mark performances by such artists as Biz Markie (as in "Just a Friend" on *The Biz Never Sleeps*) and Ja Rule ("Mesmerize" on *The Last Temptation*), and even though more polished, Mos Def and Kanye West do, in the end, often sing off key.

By contrast, the impact of rap has been such that talented singers (in the conventional sense) came to hip hop at first as purveyors of the chorus, but eventually as standing up front throughout as we see in music by such artists as Ashanti, D'Angelo, Lauryn Hill, Mary J. Blige, Alicia Keys, and Angie Stone. There may be some debate on whether these artists are properly *hip-hop* artists, versus, say, soul and R&B, but it is clear that they are highly favored among hip-hop fans. The point, however, is that they challenge the rules governing professional singing. Even when they sing on key, it is not out of necessity. In effect, hip-hop singing has a usually communal dimension; it invites the listener to sing along because *however one sings will be fine*. The absence of criteria by which a song can be sung better by some versus others locates this aspect of hip-hop performance as postmodern.

## Maturity and the Philly Sound

An immediate problem raised by the ascent of hip hop as a representative of authentic black culture is, as we have seen, its valorization of adolescence. But not all of hip hop is this way. There are alternative voices in hip hop, which have always maintained a connection with the blues, staying attuned to its dual reality of flesh and thought fused in a conception of the erotic and the mature that, perhaps, could best be characterized as thoughtful flesh.

For example, consider Me'Shell NdegéOcello's *Plantation Lullabies* (1993) and *Bitter* (1999). There's nothing childish about her work, as she brings out the contradictions of contemporary life in ways that are attuned to what it means to bear responsibility for one's actions. She achieves such reflections through exploring themes ranging from listening to music from periods of social resistance on "I'm Diggin You (Like An Old Soul Record)" on *Plantation Lullabies*—"Listen to the 8-track . . . / Remember back in the day / When everyone was black and conscious. And down for the struggle"—to those precious moments of erotic life in which one pays close attention to such features as one's lover's hair on "Dred Lock" (*Plantation Lullabies*)—"Let me run my fingers through your dred locks / Run them all over your body 'til your holler stops"—and on even to theological reflections on race and sexuality, as in "Leviticus: Faggot" (*Bitter*): ". . . See my dear we're all dying for something searchin' and searchin' / Soon mama found out that god would turn his back on her too."

Although all music is ultimately a form of play, of suspending the weight of seriousness on life itself, adult play is in truth different from child's play. Child's play seeks never to end, which means, at its heart, it is a desire for the impossible. Adult play is always aware of an impending end. In the midst of adult play is the lurking underside of life itself, namely, death. Life is lived, from such a perspective, because of a sober realization of the limits of life.

In addition to NdegéOcello, the hip-hop contributors to the Philly music scene also transcend the New York–California construction of hip hop as a battle between two adolescent sensibilities. Although these Philadelphia artists are technically "east coast" artists, there is a difference between their musical style and musical themes. Many of them are influenced by the black nationalist politics of northern and western Philadelphia, some of which, in fashion and interpretation of history, is influenced by Afrocentrism and the multitude of Black Muslim and Christian, and even Black Jewish congregations in the city. There is, as well, the impact of the musical education offered by some of the public schools for the arts and the Quaker Friends schools, which has resulted in a cadre of excellent musicians. Such artists include D'Angelo, Erykah Badu, Jill Scott, Angie Stone, and, of course, the Roots. The connection between them and the spiritual and urban blues laments of John Coltrane and Nina Simone can easily be heard.

Angie Stone, the most recent to ascend in that group,

explores many of life's themes through the lenses of Northern Philly black liberation politics. For example, her 2001 *Mahogany Soul* album is reminiscent of the kinds of critique found in the music of Billie Holiday, Dinah Washington, and Abbie Lincoln. Beginning with "Soul Insurance," in which she invokes the ancestral voice of soul through calling forth the expression, "Hey, sista / soul sista," as a lyric, she then moves on to "Brotha," in which she declares her love for brothas reminding her listener: "You got ya wall street brotha, ya blue collar brotha, / Your down for whatever chillin on the corner brother.../ You know that angie loves ya."

Then in the cut, "Pissed Off," she alerts the listener that her love isn't blind as she explores the dynamics of an abusive, insecure relationship: "Lookin' at life through the glass that you shattered (so pissed off) / Little shit like love doesn't matter anymore. Baby, whassup? . . . / Brotha can I live, can a sister live?" Later on, over the music to the Philadelphia classic R&B group the O'Jay's "Back Stabbers" (1972), she explores the dimension of needing to find a way to get over an ended relationship in "Wish I Didn't Miss you": "I'm sick for ever believing you / Wish you'd bring back the man I knew / Was good to me, oh Lord . . ." All these songs are done with Stone's alto voice atop choruses of rich, soulful harmony over hip-hop beats. And the album exemplifies the spirit of the artists with whom she is associated and the themes she writes and sings about bring the tragic and poignant dimensions of life to the fore.

There are, of course, other artists holding down a conception of hip hop that transcends racist expectations of childish, naive banter, such as New York artists Mos Def, Talib Kweli, MC Lyte, and Chicago's Kanye West. Their lyrics present an image of hip hop that suggests an alliance with intelligence and maturity that is not necessarily a contradiction of terms. Since the focus of hip hop is primarily ultimately entertainment, however, a formulaic route for the mature hip-hop artist seems for the most part to be the avenue of cinema, of which the list of artists here, with the addition of Queen Latifah, Will Smith, and LL Cool J, are clear instances. Their ability to work across many areas of entertainment is a testament to their extraordinary talent, but the serious question is whether such transitions for these artists stand as a form of moving beyond versus affirmation of hip hop. That hip hop works in comedy and violent action films is already evident, but it remains to be seen how it unfolds as drama.[7]

## The Hunger for More Than Serious Play

Hip hop is clearly not *analytically* incapable of taking the drama of life—blues legacies as Angela Y. Davis so aptly put it in her book on female artists—to a level both contemporary and relevant.[8] But herein is the rub. Just as their predecessors, hip-hop artists face the realities of commodification. Much money is made by a version of hip-hop culture that takes the dollar to near levels of idolatry. Such versions will take their inevitable course in the short-term medium of popularity, decay, and death. The enduring capacity of artistic expression that speaks to our *adult* sensibilities is marked, simply, by the fact that we all face the winds of change over time and with it, the reflective force of age and aging. That hip hop is not only its music, not only its visual art, not only its witty proliferation of terms and hip syntax, but also an attitude toward life itself raises the question of what it would mean for grayed hair and wrinkled skin to reflect on life in baggy pants, exposed under-wear, weaves, and a display of diamonds (the *bling!*) and gold.[9] The follies of youth, when collapsed into a resistance against change itself, fall from a leap to the stars to the mire of the ridiculous.

It is easy to exaggerate the role of art in our daily lives. Art does not have to change the world, but it always plays a role in how we live. A human being in a valueless world would suf-

---

[7] A piece of trivia might be informative here: Queen Latifah was originally cast with leading man Robert De Niro to play the role that Halle Barry played with Billy Bob Thornton in *Monster's Ball* (2001). See the website: www.contactmusic.com/new/xmlfeed.nsf/mndwebpages/latifah%20almost%20landed%20monster.s%20ball%20role. On the question of drama, the 1997 movie *Love Jones* might qualify as a hip-hop movie given the place of spoken-word poetry as the context for the film and the place of hip hop in its soundtrack.

[8] Angela Y. Davis, *Blues Legacies and Black Feminism: Gertrude "Ma" Rainey, Bessie Smith, and Billie Holiday* (New York: Vintage, 1999).

[9] This question and description haunt hip-hop and pop culture, for example, in the third season (2004) of VH1's *The Surreal Life*, which featured Public Enemy's Flavor Flav as the only black member of the cast.

fer a profound sense of loneliness. As the existentialists have shown so well, we bring values to the world.[10] Wherever and whenever we encounter art, we find an accompanying human spirit. Hip hop speaks to adolescents for the same reason that artistic expressions of joy and resistance have always spoken to adolescents: such a difficult time of life could be crushing if walked alone. But life must eventually be faced, and our ability to live an adult sensibility of not being alone requires a maturation of mundane life—one that is not escapist but at the same time not devoid of play.[11] We may think of the metaphor behind the dull thump of the bass drum and its repetition, of the message it conveys, in spite of all that is rapped over the beat, in spite of the clever scratches, in spite of the twists and pelvic gyrations that stimulate awe, that life itself marches on toward death in a message always greater than ourselves.

Still, the heart of hip hop—black, brown, and beige inner-city youth—clearly suggests that the *blackness of hip hop* stands in a different relation to its future than the nonblack world that celebrates it. For how can one have an aesthetic relationship to aesthetic production in a world that offers no alternative to such an attitude toward life? How can play be coherent if its participants are consigned to perpetual childhood? Hip hop, in this sense, suffers from an unfortunate circumstance of *serious play.* Paradoxically, it needs a possibility beyond adolescence for even mundane adolescence to emerge, since without it hip hop would simply be another manifestation of black, brown, and beige limits. It would be all that can be in a world in which we crave, hungrily, for more.[12]

---

[10] See, for example, Jean-Paul Sartre, *Being and Nothingness: A Phenomenological Essay on Ontology* (New York: Washington Square Press, 1956); and Simone de Beauvoir, *The Ethics of Ambiguity* (Seacaucus: Citadel Press, 1948).

[11] There is not enough space to develop this thesis here, but I encourage the reader to consult my discussion of the aesthetics of mundane life in revolutionary practice in my *Fanon and the Crisis of European Man: An Essay on Philosophy and the Human Sciences* (New York: Routledge, 1995), Chapters 3–4.

[12] Thanks to Jane Anna Gordon and Doug Ficek for reading early drafts of this chapter, and to Mathieu Gordon for whom hip hop continues to offer so much.

# Disk 4

# Word Up!
# Language, Meaning,
# and Ethics

# 10

# Knowwhatumsayin'?
# How Hip-Hop Lyrics Mean

STEPHEN LESTER THOMPSON

## Thesis: The Lyricist Message

*Rap is the black CNN.* Widely attributed to Public Enemy's Chuck D, this view implies that rap informs the culture at large about ideas current in the black community. It follows that *hip-hop lyrics mean the way messages do.* They are meant to be *true* as they conform to regular patterns of meaning.[1] So there should be a straight line from a fact to an idea about it in the lyricist's mind to the lyric's meaning. This *communicative-message model* of hip-hop lyrical meaning holds that a successful hip-hop lyric must be a genuine testimony about the lyricist's real self, telling the truth from the standpoint of a real person. Ice-T really had scrapes with the law, Lauryn Hill really had scrapes with the wrong kind of man, and Eminem really learned his craft in scrappy Detroit. And the messages their lyrics convey are rooted in these real experiences.

The communicative-message model answers numerous questions arising in hip hop. For instance, rap is so black-identified that the perennial question arises about whether non-blacks (such as Eminem or the Beastie Boys) can create rap music. The dispute isn't about the mere ability to rhyme over beats. It's over whether non-blacks can report truths thought to derive from

---

[1] The philosopher David Lewis develops a similar idea for general communication in his classic 1968 paper "Languages and Language," reprinted in his *Philosophical Papers* (New York: Oxford University Press, 1983), pp. 163–188.

being black. If rap is communicative in the way that messages are, then how can one report on things one hasn't seen or experienced? As a defense, the non-black rap artist can appeal to the "blackness" of their background to show that they have access to the truths their lyrics convey. (Eminem's *8 Mile* attempts this.) Alternatively (as in the Beastie Boys example), they can underscore the way their acts draw from different musical genres, such as punk rock.[2] As such, their role as "reporters" of black life is greatly attenuated, and they can be interpreted as left-field "commentators" drawing from other kinds of experiences.

## Anti-Thesis: The Lyricist Narrative

Rapper Young Buck recently observed: "Rap is weird, man. A muthafucka can say what he wants in they music. But it's just putting words together, so you gotta be your own judge of how real it is."[3] Buck's point is that rap artists entertain and enlighten by creatively expressing their ideas. If they have a burden to testify truthfully, neither that burden nor its satisfaction seems easily settled in the meanings of lyrics. It follows that *hip-hop lyrics mean the way narratives and stories do.* They are meant to be *as-if true* by conforming to the lyricist's adopted persona in their adopted biography.[4] There should be a straight line from an as-if fact to an idea about it in the lyricist's mind to the written lyric's meaning. This *narrative-story model* of hip-hop lyrical meaning holds that a successful hip-hop lyric be enlightening, entertaining, and even poignant in telling the as-if truth from the lyricist's adopted persona. Marshall Mathers tells stories about the "thoughts" and "actions" of a character named "Eminem," Sean Combs tells stories about a character named "Puff Daddy"

---

[2] Compare their tracks "Sabotage," "Root Down," and "Get It Together," for instance, to see how their musical styles vary on a single disc. *Ill Communication* (Capitol, 1994).

[3] Vanessa Satten, "Diamond in the Back," *XXL Magazine* (August 2004), pp. 117–18.

[4] A similar kind of point appears in philosophical discussions of meaning in art. See, for instance, Monroe C. Beardsley, *The Possibility of Criticism* (Detroit: Wayne State University Press, 1970), p. 238; Beardsley, *Aesthetics*, second edition (Indianapolis: Hackett, 1981), pp. 238–242. Judith Grant extends this sort of analysis in her paper "Bring the Noise: Hypermasculinity in Heavy Metal and Rap," *Journal of Social Philosophy* 27 (1996), pp. 5–30.

(aka "P Diddy," aka "Puffy"), Kimberly Jones about a character named "Lil' Kim," and Calvin Broadus about a character named "Snoop Dogg." And the narratives their lyrics convey are rooted in the as-if experiences of these adopted personae.

The narrative-story model addresses numerous concerns that arise in hip hop. For instance, hip-hop artists often reject claims that they are role models for disaffected youth. After all (goes the reasoning) they are artists who are responding to what their art demands of them. And part of what it demands is to sometimes venture into territory society is reluctant to occupy—well-suited to artistic and creative narrative but ill-suited to being a role model for young people.

## Synthesis: Mixin' Messages and Narratives

There are good reasons for trying to synthesize these competing models. How is a listener supposed to "judge" the "realness" of a given lyric, especially since—unlike most other lyrical art forms—rap music attempts to communicate ideas and not merely represent the artistic fantasies of its creators?[5] What beliefs and attitudes can we fairly ascribe to lyricists on the basis of their lyrics?[6] This is closely related to more general aesthetic questions about the integrity and meaning of artworks themselves. After all, rap is an art form presented to listeners in a way that allows for that long kind of listen, the kind where different interpretations emerge and conflict, and lyrics bump into each other, refusing to be easily decoded and figured out. What Jay-Z means by "H to the izz-O" is one level of query; how his use of *izz-O* is related to his (and Snoop's) oft-mimicked *fo' shizzle* is another.[7] The aesthetic interest in rap must include a theory of rap as an artwork that conveys meaning.

Another motivation for a synthesis derives from all-too-familiar moral and political questions about rap music. Some people

---

[5] Richard Shusterman helps sort out this kind of concern in his discussion "Rap as Art and Philosophy," in Tommy L. Lott and John P. Pittman, eds., *A Companion to African-American Philosophy* (Malden: Blackwell, 2003), pp. 419–428.

[6] See Jerrold Levinson, "Messages in Art," *Australasian Journal of Philosophy* 73 (1995), pp. 184–198.

[7] Jay-Z and Linkin Park, *Collision Course* (Warner, 2004).

wonder about the rapper's moral responsibility for the views expressed in their lyrics. Gangsta' rap, big-pimpin' braggadocio, thong songs, gin-and-juice posturing, thug life, and bitches-and-ho's clichés provide the familiar litany of examples, linked by the paired worries about violence in black urban life and negative attitudes toward women. This responsibility gets more complicated in that many of the messages in the lyrics (as well as visuals in the videos) seem to celebrate what many consider pathologies of urban black life. Others are concerned about the political component of hip-hop lyrics and how criticisms of power, authority, and the social order are to be understood.[8] N.W.A.'s "F*** Tha Police" (*Straight Outta Compton*) is an obvious (though dated) example, as is KRS-One's *Keep Right*. Public Enemy's "Fight the Power" (*It Takes a Nation of Millions to Hold Us Back*) is an especially striking example, since one cannot listen to Chuck D on that record without calling to mind Spike Lee's 1989 (famously political) *Do the Right Thing*. Nas's *Street's Disciple* and The Game's *The Documentary* provide more recent social commentaries of sorts.

Other people are interested in the cultural fabric hip-hop artists are crafting—the so-called hip-hop nation—complete with cultural values and markers of all sorts. Wyclef Jean, Lauryn Hill, Mos Def, Q-Tip, and others aren't just artists performing in a certain style, but are seen by many of their fans as part of a larger movement of authenticity. Tupac was very explicit about his notion of "thug life" being both a lyrical trope on his records and a way of authentic living for young people in desperate circumstances, suggesting a broad culture-making role for rap music. He envisioned his lyrics inspiring listeners only seeing hopelessness and violence in their own thug lives.[9] Surely Pac's lyrical meanings include his intention to depict that life with poignancy and subtlety. (Older music fans surely remember punk rock as a style of music, a style of dress, and a social movement all at once.)

Here, then, is an obvious synthesis of the communicative-message and narrative-story models: *hip-hop lyrics are truth telling and authentic messages of the real selves of their authors*

---

[8] See, for instance, Track 13 in this volume.

[9] *Tupac: Resurrection* (New York: MTV Films, 2003).

(borrowing from Chuck D), *though they are so conveyed in sto-ries and narratives of the personae adopted by those lyricists* (borrowing from Young Buck). I will argue against this tempt-ing synthesis by challenging the claim that an idea in a lyric derives from an idea in the mind of a lyricist.[10]

This synthesis runs afoul of hip hop's most notorious prob-lems, the bitch-and-ho problem and the problem of beefs. These problems trade on a fundamental confusion about whether hip-hop lyrics mean communicatively or narratively, whether they aim at genuine truth or merely as-if truth. For instance, are sex-ually explicit lyrics about women—"bitches and ho's" in the ver-nacular—meant to be truth-telling and factual or are they meant depictively, indicating the sort of thing a certain character might say? When traditional roles are reversed, and women utter lyrics that are sexually explicit or demeaning (Lil' Kim comes to mind), are they meant as truth-correcting to prevailing sexual stereo-types or as counter-narrative to those stereotypes? These confu-sions are not restricted to outsiders in the listening culture at large, but often persist even among such privileged audiences as industry insiders. The miscommunications and counter-narrative posturing (which is it?) that typify beefs are cases in point. Some of these problems surface for every lyrical art, but they are espe-cially troubling for hip-hop verbal performances.

## Messages from Kelis's Yard and Lil' Kim's Beehive

If rap lyricists communicate messages that they intend to com-municate to listeners, then what intention-to-communicate is it reasonable to impute to them? For example, what does Kelis intend to say by the lyric: "my milkshake brings all the boys to the yard" (*Tasty*)? It's one thing to know the English meanings of these words. But hip-hop fans know that she intends some-thing over and above that, and makes her money as an artist by *intending* more than that.

---

[10] The idea has a thick philosophical history. See Paul Grice, "Meaning," in *Studies in the Way of Words* (Cambridge, Massachussetts: Harvard University Press, 1989), pp. 213–223. First published in *The Philosophical Review* 66 (1957), pp. 377–388.

The philosopher Jerrold Levinson proposes that, in general, "a work of art says what, on the basis of the work contextually construed, it would be reasonable to impute to its artist as a view that he or she both significantly held and was concerned to convey."[11] Following this proposal, we might say that what Kelis's lyric expresses is that which she can be said to *significantly hold*, provided that she is *concerned to convey* that view in the lyric. (I'm assuming that she wrote the lyric in question.) So for the meaning of "my milkshake brings all the boys to the yard," we should say that the lyric says what Kelis significantly holds—that her body attracts men—and that she is concerned to convey that in the lyric, the art being the metaphoric suggestion that her body attracts like a milkshake. I say *significantly* held, as opposed to just held, since presumably Kelis (like the rest of us) holds many things that are not part of her intending to say something by the lyric. But the *concerned-to-convey* relation is trickier, since for her to be concerned to convey some view she holds, it seems she must do so *with respect to some listener*. So, once we introduce the idea of a conveying relation, we must say something about Kelis's audience.

That audience is neither uniform nor simple. Some listeners will be savvy enough to unpack the lyric's sexual meaning, perhaps even being such "insiders" in the intended audience that they understand something about the children's playground banter she mimics, as well as the way popular black music often straddles that fine line between sexual confrontation and playful teasing. Others will be "outsiders," getting some message from the lyric, certainly, even as they invariably misperceive it to some degree.[12] These two sorts of listeners will have to be accommodated in a general analysis of a lyricist's being concerned to convey something.

This is especially important since lyrical meaning can hinge on this. For instance (as Levinson points out) an insider audience might take lyrics to be "purveying stories or confessionals that simply 'tell it like it is', without moralizing," while to an outsider audience those same lyrics are personified irony, presenting "morality plays that admonish against certain forms of

---

[11] "Messages in Art," p. 188.
[12] *Ibid.*, p. 195.

behavior tempting to those in hard circumstances."[13] A certain sort of listener, for example, might take Lil' Kim's sexually frank lyrics in songs like "Suck My D**k" (*The Notorious KIM*) to be self-demeaning, along the lines of classic feminist criticisms about objectifying women. But another sort of listener could take her to be asserting that sexuality on her own terms, defiantly, in ways generally not deemed acceptable for women.

Hence the most exacting view about lyrical meaning may come to this: a lyric means what a lyricist intends to say, by which we mean that a lyricist significantly holds some view, and is concerned to convey that view in their lyric to an audience of insider and outsider listeners. Levinson argues similarly but he takes the relevant intended message to be higher-order, since in some cases there may be conflicting first-order views being conveyed. As he puts it, a higher-order message "enfolds the ones that are equally suggested by the work but at odds with one another, and which is more plausibly ascribed to the author than either of the first-order messages taken by themselves."[14]

Suppose you knew Lil' Kim personally, and knew for a fact that she believed that women *should* flaunt their sexuality with men in a way that classical feminists (say) would take to be self-demeaning, thereby debunking the self-affirming, Lil'-Kim's-a-feminist-icon meaning that some might suggest. On this scenario, the classical feminist is the outsider audience, given Lil' Kim's intention, and the insiders are (presumably) those that recognize (and perhaps accept) the currency of the sexual-flaunting message. This will be a challenge to any theory that regards lyrics as messages, particularly because of the dual-audience feature just introduced; dual audiences imply dual meanings. So which view is she *really* concerned to convey? Perhaps Lil' Kim's intention is to convey conflicting (first-order) views to her audiences. Nevertheless, it would still be plausible to attribute to her some higher-order message—even if only the (higher-order) intention to intend different messages for different audiences. Isn't that after all what we recognize as subtlety: an outsider gets one message, an insider another, *and we take the lyricist to have intended that?*

---

[13] *Ibid.*, p. 195.
[14] "Messages in Art," p. 196n.

The main idea is that, whatever message we take the lyric in question to be communicating, it is traceable back to the lyricist as a *super-view* that enfolds multiple, potentially conflicting (plain old) messages that can be sorted by their targeted audiences. After all, there is surely a true story about what Lil' Kim intends to convey, mixed messages and all. And the problem doesn't dissipate even if her super-view is that there is *no* message meant to be conveyed. Lil' Kim might be trying to confound philosophical analysts seeking to discern her intended meaning by deliberately writing lyrics that don't reflect any intended meaning. But then *that* would be her super-view, and we'd just have to expose her intentions to discern her real message. Meaning nothing in a lyric is a way of meaning something in a lyric, and the philosopher's task is to explain that.

## Messages in Context: Slim Shady and Stan the Fan

Our task multiplies, since it is trivially true that a target listener is presented with a hip-hop lyric in some context. That context includes the conventions and traditions associated with the art form, "knowledge of which would be presumed in a savvy listener."[15] Familiarity with the ritualized insults of vernacular black speech, for instance, diminishes the relevance to lyrical meaning of the customary meanings of expressions; an astute listener recognizes braggadocio when they hear it, and an astute lyricist will figure that into their intended meaning.

Eminem works such savvy into his song "Stan" (*The Marshall Mathers LP*) as he relates letters from a disturbed fan, and then his own response. Stan writes to Eminem (aka Slim Shady): "Dear Slim, you still ain't called or wrote, I hope you have a chance / I ain't mad—I just think it's fucked up you don't answer fans." Eminem brackets the lyric with standard letter-writing conventions to establish the kind of talk that this is, and uses a number of references and devices to tell the listener— who might themselves be the sort of fan who writes this sort of letter—what kind of communication this is. After subsequent letters (and ultimately a cassette recording of that fan's suicide)

---

[15] *Ibid.*, p. 194.

document Stan's downward emotional spiral, Eminem includes his own belated reply letter to that fan. Its rather pedestrian opening suggests his lack of any alarm, followed by his growing sense that the writer is troubled. He works the context of lyrical-meaning evaluation to get his target listeners to understand the views he is concerned to convey. And the gravity of the lyrical meaning is such that it can convey one thing to a critic who may decry what they regard as rap music's violence and nihilism, another thing to a deranged fan who may be on the same path as "Stan," and still another thing to a listener who is skeptical about Eminem's credibility as a serious rap artist, someone who can tell "the truth" the way such artists are supposed to. That this story is meant as true is not left to chance, as the closing lyric of Eminem's reply to Stan suggests: "I seen this one shit on the news a couple weeks ago that made me sick / Some dude was drunk and drove his car over a bridge . . . / And in the car they found a tape, but they didn't say who it was to / Come to think about, his name was . . . it was you." It all works because the listeners understand the exchange, and the intended meaning comes across.

Of course, the contribution to lyrical meaning by targeted contexts of meaning evaluation is always going to be somewhat slippery. After all, a listener might hear a lyric on a dance floor, from a passing SUV, or through their iPod while running around the Central Park reservoir. The context variables are numerous and ever-shifting. Whether a boast about "bitches and ho's" is meant as a derogation of women, or as an implicit criticism of someone who thinks of women that way, might be alternately grasped by a listener (in part) depending on whether they are being thoughtful and reflective, annoyed and anxious, or driven by adrenaline and sexual energy. Since there is no privileged context of evaluation (the way museums are for paintings, say), a lyricist will always have some trouble targeting a particular audience with an intended meaning.

So now we see one chief problem for the synthesis under consideration. The line from lyricist to lyric cannot be straight because the relevant intentions to mean this or that cannot be transparent. Lil' Kim can always mean one thing to one audience or another, and we'll never know. Eminem can always construct a narrative built around as-if truth, and we'll just have to take his word for it. Hence, if hip-hop lyrics pass Young Buck's test, they will fail Chuck D's test, and vice-versa. That the synthesis acknowledges this doesn't provide a solution for it. Because it isn't fully transparent, the *concerned-to-convey* relation will always plague Chuck D's communicative-message model. If we can identify conventions of truthfulness for hip-hop lyrics, then we could close the problem down. But the synthesis prevents this option, because on Young Buck's narrative-story model, the conventions may be regular, *but they aren't regular in the same way*. As long as a lyricist's intentions are audience-sensitive, we can always ask which audience such-and-such meaning is intended for, a question it seems we cannot reliably answer. To further illuminate this analysis let's consider another problem for hip-hop lyrical meaning: the beef problem.

## Ja Rule v. 50 Cent: Beefs, Personae, and Meaning

Ja Rule explains that his feud with 50 Cent developed after 50 Cent "felt the need to call my name and disrespect what I am doing, which is crazy. . . . So when I come back now and say I don't like him for this, this and this reason, everyone goes, 'Well now, it's getting out of hand.'"[16] Part of the interpretation problem for Ja Rule is that he feels he cannot evaluate 50 Cent's motivation for disrespecting him, and so is confused about the nature of the insults. He is further confused by their reception and so feels hemmed in. It's as if Ja Rule doesn't know which kind of listener he is—since he is surely adept at sorting the multi-level views that lyrics convey—nor does he know whether 50 Cent is speaking "in character," that is, in his customary persona. And because he suspects it to be genuine, and not persona-mediated, he insists (the way any listener would) on a rational accounting for the view expressed. Since he cannot complete that accounting, he takes 50 Cent to be "crazy."

Ja Rule is in a predictable bind given the failure of the synthetic claim under consideration. (Tupac was in a similar bind as he tried to figure out what Biggie and Puff Daddy were saying about him after the first time he got shot; interviews with

---

[16] Ja Rule, interview by Louis Farrakhan, *MTVNews.com* (11th March, 2003), http://www.mtv.com/bands/j/ja_rule/news_feature_031103/.

Biggie before he died suggest that he was confused too.) To get out of this bind, Ja Rule needs *either* to complete the rational accounting (perhaps there is a genuine reason—maybe an unnoticed slight—for 50 Cent to have negative feelings about him), *or* reinstate the mediating persona (so that 50 Cent can be understood as speaking a part, and the interpretations will be of views enfolded by a super-view).

Someone may take this dilemma about beefs to make the case that rap music lyrics are *not* ultimately communicative, but I think this would be mistaken. The reasoning might run like this: if interpreting lyrics is a matter of discerning the super-view in question, so as to ascribe *it* to the lyricist, then what is at issue in how hip-hop lyrics mean is which persona is being adopted. If the persona is the key to (lyrical) meaning intentions, then our interpretive task is to specify what that persona is like (to make sense of what views it is conveying). Presumably this would involve seeing how that "character" shows up on different records, in videos, maybe even in other venues altogether. (Snoop and Puffy, for instance, exemplify acts that are bigger than their records.) But to study the character of a persona is to recognize that it is fictional. That is why beefs are settled the ways they are settled: either by being recognized as persona-driven—and so un-genuine and fictional—or else their persona is seen through to an actual insult made by the *real* person, sometimes with tragic, Biggie-and-Tupac results. But this implies that rap lyrics, to be genuinely interpreted, must be taken apart from the context of a persona. The communicative meaning problem that my analysis is supposed to help solve thus evaporates, leaving only an aesthetic meaning problem, no more difficult than wondering what James Gandolfini's "Tony Soprano" means by such-and-such a line. (Answer: nothing, since he's a fictional persona, not a real person.)

But this objection misunderstands something fundamental about how hip-hop is created. The solutions to beefs may indeed suggest the desirability of separating lyric from persona. But that doesn't imply that personae are not communicative, or else that they are only quasi-communicative in some fictional bracketed way. Why do beefs get started in the first place? Not because of misunderstanding, but because *personae are genuine extensions* of the lived lives of rap artists. And so lyrics are at once the words and (thus) the thoughts of actual lyricists *and* the characters they adopt. That is why Young Buck has the dilemma about judging rap music. It's not because anyone can string together any words they like and mean anything they like by them. It's because there is an implied burden of authenticity. To be a rapper is to speak what is real, and it's the realness that is difficult to authenticate. So the task of discerning the super-views behind the meaning of hip-hop lyrics remains thoroughly communicative, perhaps more so than for lyrics in other styles of music.

## Hip-Hop Lyrics: No Black CNN and No Art of Storytelling

My conclusion, then, is that lyrical meaning cannot but teeter on personae that arise as extensions of lived hip-hop lives, and I remain skeptical about attempts to close lyrical meaning in hip hop down any more tightly than that. While we are surely convinced that we know *in general* the difference between story and report, truth and as-if truth, we cannot be sure which way *lyrics* have been intended. If that is so, the logical impasse between Chuck D and Young Buck seems inevitable in hip hop, and if that is so, then hip hop's claim to be the black CNN is in just as much jeopardy as its claim to be an art form. But this isn't a bad thing. Because, as the following three cases illustrate, gaps in lyrical meaning keep listeners immediately involved in the work the music tries to do.

### *One*

Mario Winans seems caught in a dilemma about meaning with his song "Pretty Girl Bullshit," with its wholly inappropriate title given his deep church background. He realizes it and tries to wriggle himself free in a recent interview: "I never say the word in the song. I don't even think it's spelled out on the record. So that could be bull *shoes* really."[17] Doubtful. He supposes (insincerely, I'm sure) that his famous gospel-singing mother (for instance) is a listener who will uptake the view expressed by the phrase *bull shoes* or some other innocuous term just because she lacks the actual utterance of the full expletive. His intention

---

[17] Mario Winans, interview by Letisha Marrero, *Vibe* (August 2004), p. 117.

to convey the inappropriate expletive, though, is out in the open, given the way any contemporary listener would likely hear the lyric. His lyrical-meaning-intention betrays his explanation. Indeed, he manages to convey the meaning *bullshit* without saying it, his meaning intention see-sawing ever so precariously. The meaning of his lyric remains loose and unsettled so as to protect his gospel-singing persona.

### Two

Freestyling rap seems to present any robust synthetic view of hip-hop lyrical meaning with a difficult challenge. Lil' Flip's free-association style, for instance, is tricky to treat either communicatively or narratively: "Buy the house, I buy the block / Buy the boat, I buy the dock / Sitting sideways at IHOP / Watch the trunk to see it go pop."[18] Some of his critics go so far as to deny that his rhymes should even count as lyrics. "It's because he's country," argues DJ Enuff. "He'll say some slick shit here and there, but he ain't Nas or Black Thought. His style and the way he carries himself make him hot. No one would ever say he's a lyricist."[19] It will have to be enough, I think, to consider freestyling as a borderline case of both communicative and narrative lyrical-meaning-intention in hip hop. Lil' Flip as free-styler is a persona without a narrative or a message, much like jazz scat-singers of another era.

### Three

Lauryn Hill calls her debut solo record *The Miseducation of Lauryn Hill* as a way to both present and critique popular notions of how a woman ought to deal with love and life. After we hear a classroom discussion among young people about love, we hear her sing on "Ex Factor": "It ain't working / And when I try to walk away / You'd hurt yourself to make me stay / This is crazy." It's as if we hear the "miseducation" in grade school, and then fast forward to its irrational aftermath, cataloguing one of its distorting effects. We move from song to song on that album as Lauryn Hill moves from persona to persona: from miseducated

---

[18] Lil' Flip, "Realest Rhyming," *The Leprechaun* (Sony, 2002).
[19] Quoted in Benjamin Meadows-Ingram, "Tongue-Tied," *Vibe* (August 2004), pp. 118–121.

fallen woman; to enlightened re-educated woman on "That Thing"; to biblical West Indian prophet—complete with accent and syntax shifts—on "To Zion," "Lost Ones," and others. Somehow we understand her, finally, as a meta-persona who takes her fate into her own hands in the album's title song: "I made up my mind to define my destiny." The narratives have their impact because these are her *true* lived experiences, while the lived experiences are presented *as if* they happened in just this story arc, so that the listener can grasp their significance. It makes little sense to force the issue of settling the lyrical meaning, since the persona-shuttling is precisely the point.[20]

---

[20] I thank Derrick Darby and Tommie Shelby for helpful comments and supportive suggestions on early drafts of this track.

# 11

# Girl Got 99 Problems: Is Hip Hop One?

SARAH McGRATH and LIDET TILAHUN

Is hip hop bad for women? Well, it's complicated. Many feminists, cultural critics, and politicians often focus on its negative portrayal of women. But anyone who makes the blanket statement that hip hop is bad for women hasn't looked at enough of the culture: it's like someone who sees *American Psycho*, believes the movie is misogynist, and concludes that Hollywood is bad for women. This track will consider several arguments for the conclusion that some hip-hop lyrics—call them "the controversial lyrics" to be clear that we're not talking about all lyrics—are bad for women and ask whether any of these arguments are sound.

## Hatin' on Hip Hop?

But first, we want to give some examples of lyrics that are about women but *don't* seem to be bad for them. Some lyrics protest the situation of poor urban women; others encourage women to talk about sex or to take control of their lives. For example, in "Brenda's Got a Baby," Tupac lets us in on the life of a woman without education and opportunities: "I hear Brenda's got a baby / But, Brenda's barely got a brain / A damn shame / That girl can hardly spell her name."[1] Tupac continues by showing ya "how it affects the whole community." He's just reporting the facts. Far from being an indictment of Brenda, or unwed mothers, this is a protest song.

---

[1] 2Pac, "Brenda's Got a Baby," *2Pacalypse Now* (Interscope, 1991).

Some lyrics seem to encourage women to talk about what they want from their sexual partners. Female hip-hop artists like Lil' Kim and Missy tell women to embrace their own sexuality, and to acknowledge their desires and sexual preferences. In "One Minute Man," Missy talks about wanting sex to last when she says, "I don't want, I don't need, I can't stand no minute man / I don't want no minute man."[2] Some hip-hop music also encourages people to regard black women's bodies as normal, healthy, and desirable. Sir Mix-A-Lot's "Baby Got Back" (*Mack Daddy*) might make some women feel good about the shape of their bodies.

Artists such as MC Lyte, Lauryn Hill, Medusa, and Eve urge women to take charge of their lives. And some female artists critique their male counterparts for objectifying black women and failing to take on real issues. Here's Ms. Dynamite from the song "It Takes More": "The shit that you promote: Fighting, fuckin' / Like you don't want to grow / You're talking so much sex / But you not tell the youth 'bout AIDS."[3]

In addition to challenging the agendas of male rappers, female rappers challenge conceptions of what women are or can do. Queen Latifah rhymes in "Ladies First":

> Sloppy slouching is something I won't do
> Some think that we can't flow (can't flow)
> Stereotypes, they got to go (got to go)
> I'm a mess around and flip the scene into reverse.[4]

This idea of flipping the scene into reverse suggests appropriating a situation so that women come out on top—or at least not on the bottom.

But on the face of it, some rappers endorse violence against women. The N.W.A. song "One Less Bitch" tells the story of a "perfect ho" who got out of line and so had to go:

> Now listen up and lemme tell you how I did it, yo. I tied her to the bed
> I was thinking the worst but yo I had to let my niggaz fuck her first
> Yeah, loaded up the 44, yo, then I straight smoked the ho

---

[2] Missy Elliott, *Miss E . . . So Addictive* (Goldmind/Elektra, 2001).

[3] Ms. Dynamite, *A Little Deeper* (Polydor, 2002).

[4] Queen Latifah, *All Hail the Queen* (Tommy Boy, 1989).

'Cause I'm a real nigga, but I guess you figure, I was soft and she
thank me.[5]

Some people will say that the rappers are just entertainers. This
defense is suggested by the title cut of N.W.A.'s *Niggaz4life*:

Bitch this, bitch that, Nigger this, nigger that
In the meanwhile my pockets are gettin' fat
Gettin' paid to say this shit here
Makin' more in a week than a doctor makes in a year.[6]

Sounds like N.W.A. are saying that they are just using their lyrics
and skills to get rich. Another thing they might be saying is that
this is just entertainment: people are entertained by violent
movies, but the makers of violent movies aren't telling them to
go out and get violent.

But in "'Bout My Paper," Foxy Brown raps, "This is real, it's
not entertainment."[7] Foxy's point might be that the things rappers do and say could have serious consequences. If these lyrics
are harmful to women, then "I'm just an entertainer" might ring
hollow. Similarly, if your lyrics have harmful consequences, "I
just did it for the money" is hardly a defense: hit men don't have
it that easy.

## Dangerous Mouths: Causing Harm

One worry about the controversial lyrics is their relationship to
violence against women. If the only connection between hip-
hop lyrics and violence against women were that some hip-hop
lyrics are *about* violence against women, then it would be hard
to see how those lyrics were any worse for women than, say,
the nightly news, which is often about violence against women.
But there might be a tighter connection: maybe the controversial lyrics actually *cause* harm to women.

If the controversial lyrics actually cause harm to women,
then, according to the nineteenth century philosopher John
Stuart Mill (1806–1873), we have grounds for interfering with the

---

[5] N.W.A., *Niggaz4life* (Ruthless, 1991).
[6] N.W.A., "Niggaz4life," *Niggaz4life* (Ruthless, 1991).
[7] Foxy Brown, *Broken Silence* (Uptown/Universal, 2001).

freedom of expression of the rappers responsible for those harmful lyrics. Mill held:

> The only principle for which power can be rightfully exercised over any member of a civilized community, against his will, is to prevent harm to others.[8]

That is, the only legitimate reason for interfering with your freedom is to stop you from harming someone else. In the philosophical literature, this principle is called "the harm principle." The harm principle is Mill's answer to the question of how to balance individual freedom of expression with what he called "social control." If we were to ask Mill about hip hop, he would say that, for example, the fact that an artist's work is obscene is not a good enough reason to limit the artist's freedom of expression: the only reason good enough is that someone gets hurt.[9] For example, power could be rightfully exercised over an individual who yells "fire!" in a crowded theater when there is no fire; the panic that results could hurt people, and this provides legitimate grounds for punishment. But punishment could not, according to Mill's principle, be inflicted on an artist because his lyrics offend people. Unless the controversial lyrics actually harm people— as in the "fire!" example—the artist's freedom of expression should not be limited.

Let's look at some examples of lyrics that might cause harm to women by perpetuating or encouraging violence against them. Here's Ultramagnetic MC's: "Switch up, Change my pitch up / Smack my bitch up, like a pimp."[10] In hip-hop culture, rappers have authority about style, what you ought to have, and how you ought to act, and they often compare themselves to pimps (for instance Ice-T, Jay-Z, 50 Cent, Lil Jon, Twista) in order to establish this authority. Their lyrics— like the lyrics of "Give the Drummer Some"—seem to *endorse*

---

[8] John Stuart Mill, *On Liberty* (Indianapolis: Hackett, 1978), p. 9.

[9] For a concise and insightful discussion of the 1990 prosecution of 2 Live Crew on charges of obscenity, see Kimbarlé Crenshaw, "Beyond Racism and Misogyny: Black Feminism and 2 Live Crew," *Boston Review* 16 (1991).

[10] Ultramagnetic MC's, "Give the Drummer Some," *Critical Beatdown* (Next Plateau, 1988).

smacking your bitch up: it seems like they are saying that men are pimps, women are hos, and that if the ho is confused about this, you should hit her until she gets it.

These lyrics from "Can You Control Yo' Ho?" by Snoop Dogg (featuring Soopafly) also seem to say that you ought to keep a woman in line, and the way to do it is to hit her:

> You should have slapped her in her face
> I wanted to tell you but it wasn't my place
> I kept it on the low
> 'Cause I know you was gonna check that ho.[11]

These don't just describe a situation but recommend a way to act in a situation: if your ho gets out of line, you should beat her up.

But it's one thing to say that these lyrics seem to endorse being a pimp, or to tell you that you should act violently toward women; it's another to say that they actually *cause* that violence. In a recent *Vibe* article, "Love Hurts: Rap's Black Eye," Lisa Mendez Berry gives many examples in which hip-hop artists commit violence against women.[12] She also points out that murder by a romantic partner is a leading cause of death among African American women; that many young women think that when their partners beat them, that's an expression of care or that they deserve to be beaten. She says that many women who have spoken out against their abusers have gotten little or no support from the hip-hop community. For example, Liza Rios was allegedly beaten by her husband Big Pun. But when she spoke about it after his death, many people responded by saying that she had been unfaithful, and so deserved it.

Yet none of this shows that the controversial lyrics actually cause harm to women. Big Pun might have beat up Liza Rios, but to say that a rapper harmed Rios is not to say she was harmed by rap. Further, the Big Pun example is problematic. Big Pun was the author of violent lyrics, so it seems implausible that violent lyrics caused his alleged violent tendencies, rather than the other way around. If a case can be made that

---

[11] Snoop Dogg, *R&G (Rhythm & Gangsta): The Masterpiece* (Geffen, 2004).
[12] Lisa Mendez-Berry, "Love Hurts: Rap's Black Eye," *Vibe* (February 2005).

violent lyrics cause violence, then a better example would be a consumer, rather than a writer, of those lyrics. So our question remains: to what extent do hip-hop lyrics depicting violence cause real violence?

The claim that hip-hop lyrics cause violence against women is a *causal* claim, like the claim that smoking causes cancer. Causation has been a hot topic in philosophy since the ancient Greeks, but the person who has had the most influence on contemporary discussions is the eighteenth century Scottish philosopher David Hume (1711–1776). To say very much either about causation or about Hume's philosophy would take us away from our topic, but it will help to look at what Hume said about causation. In *An Enquiry Concerning Human Understanding* (1748), Hume offers this analysis of causation: one thing causes another *"where, if the first object had not been, the second never had existed."*[13] In other words, causation involves a relationship in which the effect depends on the cause: if the cause had not happened, the effect would not have happened. For example, consider the claim that Derek Fisher's shot caused the Lakers to win 74–73 against the Spurs in the 2004 Western Conference Finals. Hume would say that what makes that true is that if Fisher *hadn't* thrown the ball, the Lakers wouldn't have won.

Most philosophers today agree that Hume's analysis fails to provide a *necessary condition* for causation: they think that A could cause B even if B would have happened anyway. To see why, let's change our example slightly. Imagine that when Fisher shot the ball, there were still two seconds left on the clock, and that Shaq was perfectly positioned in the paint. So if Fisher had missed, Shaq would have slammed the rebound down (with one hand!) and the Lakers would have won, 74–73. In this case, it's still true that Fisher's shot caused the Lakers to win, even though, had he missed, they would've won anyway. So it seems pretty clear that one thing (like Fisher's shot) can cause another (like the victory), even though the second thing would still have happened had the first thing "missed."

---

[13] David Hume, *An Enquiry Concerning Human Understanding: A Critical Edition* (New York: Oxford University Press, 2000), Section VII, Part II.

Even though Hume's analysis doesn't provide a necessary condition for causation, we can still use it as a kind of first-pass test for causation: would, for example, Big Pun still have been abusive even if he hadn't been a rapper or a fan of hip-hop music? The answer is that we don't know. Of course violence toward women is not something that hip hop created. And while it's possible that controversial hip-hop lyrics contribute to violence against women, causal claims connecting the portrayal of violence toward women with actual violence toward women are difficult to establish. Furthermore, causal claims are *empirical* claims—claims that can't be settled by philosophizing, but can only be settled by an actual investigation into why particular acts of violence against women happen. It's not a question that we can settle *a priori*—just by engaging in philosophical analysis of concepts, or arguments, from the armchair.

## Wud U Say? Doing Things with Words

In connection with the question of hip hop and harm, it might be helpful to compare hip-hop lyrics to violent pornography. Some feminist philosophers think the graphic depiction of violence toward women in pictures and text may not just *cause* people to harm women, but actually *constitute* harm to women. But does that make sense? A picture of or story about a woman being physically harmed might *cause* someone to harm his girlfriend, but the picture is not *itself* a harm to his girlfriend. So what are the philosophers thinking?

They're thinking that words and pictures can *do* things. The twentieth century English philosopher J.L. Austin (1911–1960) is famous for paying attention to how language is used, and to the fact that words are tools we can use to perform a wide variety of *acts*. His book, *How to Do Things with Words*,[14] gives lots of examples: a priest who says, "I now pronounce you man and wife," in the right circumstances, doesn't just cause people to be married; his saying "I now pronounce you man and wife" *marries* them. When a cop says, "you're under

---

[14] J.L. Austin, *How to Do Things with Words* (Cambridge, Massachusetts: Harvard University Press, 1962).

arrest," he doesn't just cause you to be arrested, he *arrests* you.

Austin calls utterances that don't just cause things but also *do* things *illocutionary* acts. And some philosophers say that one of the things you can do with words—one of the illocutionary acts you can perform—is to subordinate someone. The philosopher Rae Langton gives the following example in her paper "Speech Acts and Unspeakable Acts": a Pretorian legislator makes it illegal for blacks to vote by saying "blacks are not permitted to vote." That utterance, she says, subordinates blacks.[15] Another example is the utterance "Whites only" uttered by a store owner; that too subordinates blacks.

Going back to pornography, Langton thinks that sexual violence against women is an aspect of their subordinate status in society. She says that just as the South African legislator ranks certain people as inferior and deprives them of rights, violent pornography ranks women as sex objects and legitimizes sexual violence against them.

But here's an objection to Langton's claim that pornography subordinates: certain illocutionary acts require authority. For example, in a game of cops and robbers, I could say "you're under arrest," but I'm not a cop, so I can't actually arrest you. In addition, uttering the sentence "blacks are not permitted to vote" only subordinates if uttered in the right context, by a person with the right kind of authority. Given this point about authority, it may seem like a bit of a stretch to claim that pornography subordinates. As Langton points out, whether it does depends on whether the pornographer has the right kind of authority; in particular on

> whether [pornography] is authoritative in the domain that counts—the domain of speech about sex—and whether it is authoritative for the hearers that count: people, men, boys, who in addition to wanting "entertainment," want to discover the right way to do things, want to know which moves in the sexual game are legitimate.[16]

---

[15] Rae Langton, "Speech Acts and Unspeakable Acts," *Philosophy and Public Affairs* 22 (1993), pp. 305–330.

[16] Langton, p. 303.

Many philosophers have thought that pornography does not subordinate women because pornographers don't have the authority to make women mere sex objects. Pornographers can, through pictures and words, make claims about what moves in the sexual game are legitimate, but they don't have the power to to legitimize those moves. For example, a pornographer could, through pictures or words, make the claim that raping a woman is a legitimate move in the sexual game. But he doesn't have the power to legitimize rape.

Back to the lyrics: arguably, rappers are more authoritative for their listeners than pornographers are for their viewers. There are many other areas concerning style, speech, lifestyle, and value in which they are authoritative. Further, rappers seem to play an authoritative role in defining male gender identity: Some young men or boys who want to emulate rappers will emulate pimps, because the rappers define their own gender identity in terms of pimping. Because rappers are authoritative in all of these domains, there is a *reason* to take them as authoritative about women: they are authoritative about other cultural matters and other cultural norms. By contrast, pornographers have few, if any, credentials in other domains.

Further, with respect to what pornographers say about women—that, for example, we want to be raped—there is an *independent fact of the matter*. We're sex objects, according to pornography, in part because all we really want is sex. But it just isn't true that all we really want is sex.

By contrast, hip hop's claims about women are more plausibly authoritative because the rapper is saying what is authentic or cool, and it is less clear that there is an independent fact of the matter about that. Rappers play an important role in *deciding* what's authentic or cool, so the rapper who says "smack up your bitch" might be able to make that the thing to do in the same way that he can make ice the thing to wear, or Cristal the beverage of choice.

Although there has been a lot of philosophical discussion about whether pornography subordinates women, as far as we know, there isn't any about whether there are aspects of hip-hop culture that subordinate women. But if Langton's argument is going to work against anything, it will work against aspects of hip-hop culture, because the rappers who rap in favor of violence against women are more authoritative than are pornographers. We leave it to you to think about whether the argument presented here, that some aspects of hip-hop culture subordinate women, is actually sound.

## Not Your Ho, Not Your Freak, and Tired of You Disrespecting Me

So far we have looked at two ways that controversial lyrics might be bad for women: by causing people to harm them, or, more directly, by constituting harm to them. Now we draw on the moral theory of Immanuel Kant (1722–1804) to explore a third idea: that the controversial lyrics are bad for women because they disrespect women.

You might think that there is something wrong with what the controversial lyrics say about women regardless of whether they cause harm to women or subordinate women. You might think: look, the lyrics we've been talking about *dis* women. Women are people, and people should be treated with respect, not with disrespect. We'll explore this complaint in a moment. But first, let's back up, and get familiar with some very broad distinctions in ethics.

In this track, we've been doing ethics: the part of philosophy that talks about right and wrong. One branch of ethics is applied ethics—the branch that addresses particular ethical questions: for example, is it wrong to have an abortion? Is it wrong to disconnect a feeding tube from a brain-damaged person who will die without it? Applied ethics can be contrasted with normative ethics, which addresses a more general question: what *makes* particular actions morally right or morally wrong? Mill and Kant gave very different answers to this question. Mill said that

> actions are right in proportion as they tend to promote happiness, wrong as they tend to produce the reverse of happiness.[17]

---

[17] John Stuart Mill, *Utilitarianism*, reprinted in *The Philosophy of Human Rights* (St. Paul: Paragon House, 2001).

This view is called utilitarianism. To clarify: when Mill says "to promote happiness," he doesn't just mean *your* happiness: he says, "as between his own happiness and that of others, utilitarianism requires [a person] to be as strictly impartial as a disinterested benevolent spectator"—meaning that what makes an action right or wrong is whether it promotes *general* happiness, that is, happiness for the greatest number. For example, suppose you have some extra money, and you could either use it to go on vacation or to help a local charity for inner-city kids. If giving it to the charity would make more people better off, then that's what you should do, even if it will make you less happy. Mill thinks morality is about happiness because he thinks happiness is what we desire *as an end in itself,* rather than as a *mere means.* In other words, we want happiness just because of what it is, not because it will help us get something else. Unlike money: you want money as a means to getting other stuff—like a ride, or a college education for your kids, or independence from your parents—not as an end in itself.

Yet many philosophers reject utilitarianism. Some object that utilitarianism is too demanding: asking you to always think of others is asking too much. Others object that if utilitarianism were true, we wouldn't know what we should do, because we don't know what would make the most people the best off. But the main objection—the most serious one— is this: if utilitarianism were true, then morality could sometimes require us to do things that are, clearly, just *wrong*. It could turn out, for example, that the way to make the most people happiest is to beat down a crackhead for a crime he didn't commit: if the angry mob is threatening to go on a violent rampage unless someone pays, then we could make the most people the best off by scapegoating someone who is regarded as useless anyway. Beating down an innocent man for a crime he didn't commit is clearly wrong, but utilitarianism says that sometimes it's the right thing—the morally right thing—to do. So utilitarianism doesn't seem to leave room for the fact that we could be made much happier as a result of some moral crime.

So maybe utilitarianism can't be the right story about morality. The main alternative is the Kantian theory, which says morality is all about respect. For Kant, respecting people basically means not *using* them. And you can see how someone who rejected utilitarianism for the reason just explained might be drawn to this alternative: ultimately, what's wrong with utilitarianism is that it tells us to respect people only when doing so maximizes happiness. But when we can maximize happiness by using someone—as in the case of the angry mob and the crackhead—utilitarianism tells us to go for it.

We already talked about the difference between means and ends, when we said we want happiness as an end in itself, whereas we want money as a means to getting something else. The Kantian says that you can't treat people like you treat money: you can't treat them as a mere means to getting something else. Here's one way Kant puts it:

> Kingdom of Ends: Act so that you treat people as ends, and never mere means.

That's not exactly right: after all, when you go to the movies, you use the ticket-taker to gain admission. You're not interested in the ticket-taker as an end in herself. And there's nothing wrong with that. But there is something wrong with using a friend for a ride, when the friend thinks you called because you like her. The difference is that the ticket-taker *consents* to being used in the way that you are using her, whereas the friend does not; she doesn't even realize she is being used. The idea, then, is that you can't use people in ways that they would not agree to being used, if they knew what was going on.

We've been asking whether some rappers are wrong to rap about women in the way that they do, and if so, why. When it comes to the question of what makes actions right and wrong, we said there are two main camps: the utilitarians, who say that whether an act is right or wrong depends on its consequences, and the Kantians, who say that whether an act is right or wrong depends on respect. According to the Kantians, if you're disrespecting people, then you're acting immorally.

Hip hop might be wrong on utilitarian grounds: if the empirical claim that hip-hop lyrics make women worse off than they would have been in the absence of those lyrics is true, then according to utilitarianism, writing and performing those lyrics is wrong. But from the Kantian perspective, we don't have to figure that out: we just have to figure out whether the lyrics disrespect women.

If any lyrics disrespect women, these from 50 Cent's "P.I.M.P" look like good candidates: "Man this ho, you can have her / When I'm done I ain't gon' keep her."[18] And these, from Lil Jon & the East Side Boyz:

> Back in the days I used to like bitches
> But I tell you now days bitches ain't shit (tell 'em) . . .
> I get so mad that I could slap her actin' like she Cleopatra
> Ain't no need to ask, she's a slave to the money and I'm the
> master.[19]

Women are referred to as bitches and slaves to the money worth no respect. They deserve to be treated like commodities you can use to get money, rather than as ends in themselves. It could be argued that rapping about women this way amounts to regarding them as outside the kingdom of ends.

Further, if rappers really do have authority in the hip-hop community and beyond, then if they regard women as mere means, this could influence the youth for whom rappers are authoritative: it could make them think that the right way to treat women is as mere means.

## Check Out Time

Back to our starting point: Is hip hop bad for women? Well, as we've established so far, it's complicated. Some lyrics protest the various ways in which women get dissed, or facilitate the development of feminine identity and sexuality, or otherwise put ladies' needs first. Other lyrics dis women, going so far as to endorse violence against them. In this case, hip hop could be one of the 99 problems a girrrrl's got. And the lyrics are just one part of hip-hop culture: in order to morally assess the

---

18 50 Cent, *Get Rich or Die Tryin'* (Shady/Aftermath, 2003).
19 Lil Jon & the East Side Boyz, "Bitches Ain't Shit," *Crunk Juice* (TVT, 2004).

complicated relationship between women and hip hop, one needs to recognize and understand its many elements, rather than generalize about the entire gender or genre. WORD.[20]

---

[20] Thanks to Alex Byrne, Jeff King, and Tommie Shelby for helpful comments and suggestions.

# 12

# "For All My Niggaz and Bitches": Ethics and Epithets

J. ANGELO CORLETT

Dave Chappelle infuses hip-hop music and culture into each episode of his successful TV program. Many people in the U.S. are repelled—even frightened—by what they and their children witness on MTV, BET, VH1, and other TV channels, which show young African Americans wearing glistening jewelry, scantily clad young black women gyrating to the beat of music in videos such as Nelly's "Tip Drill," and comedians such as Chappelle using terms such as "bitch" and "nigga" as if they were proper names. Some moral condemnations of hip-hop music videos and comedy might be explained by shallow and morally suspect puritanical influences (aversions to cursing, for instance), yet there are numerous philosophical issues raised by hip-hop music and comedy that deserve serious attention. On this track I'll put the spotlight on some of the ethical issues raised by the use of epithets such as "bitch" and "nigger," an especially controversial topic both outside and within the hip-hop community.

## The Ethics of Using "Bitch" and "Nigger"

Hip-hop lyrics and comedy are replete with words such as "bitch" and "nigger," which are normally considered pejoratives in U.S. society. And this prompts some critics to deem them morally perverse. Of course hip-hop music and comedy vary profoundly in how they present themselves to us. They don't always use what Too Short would call "cusswords." Yet what makes many people in U.S. society uncomfortable about some (often, prejudicially thought to amount to all) hip-hop music and comedy is that some of it involves linguistic usage that is normally considered morally wrong.

Moral philosophy can help us address the ethical issue of whether or not it is morally wrong for hip-hop artists and hip-hop inspired comics to use such words. Our primary concern in this track is to assess the view that the use of "bitch" and "nigger" in hip-hop comedy and music is morally problematic. But first we need a moral criterion for determining whether the use of these words is morally wrong as well as a perspective on what they mean.

The moral objection to using these words typically comes to this: it is morally wrong to include such verbiage in raps or comedy routines because it is harmful. Thus the idea of harm is used as the criterion for moral wrongness. Some hip-hop critics would object that the use of "nigger" is harmful to African Americans and that the use of "bitch" is harmful to women. The term "harm" can be defined in many ways but for now let's suppose that to harm means to set back a morally legitimate interest.[1] So, for example, if African Americans are harmed by the use of "nigger," then a morally legitimate interest of this group is set back. Likewise if women are harmed by the use of "bitch," then a morally legitimate interest of this group is set back. To fully develop this objection, these so-called morally legitimate interests would have to be identified and their moral legitimacy would have to be established. Moreover, we would have to determine whether these interests trump competing morally legitimate interests that license the use of these terms. For example, one could argue that a comedian's right to entertain his audience and their right to be entertained are competing morally legitimate interests that justify the use of terms such as "nigger" and "bitch" insofar as some people consider the use of these terms as an especially humorous aspect of hip-hop comedy.

Can this harm-based moral objection to hip hop be defended? If we don't attend to the meaning of these words—as used by hip-hop comics and artists—we might assign too

---

[1] For the seminal philosophical analysis on the nature of harms and how they differ from offences, see Joel Feinberg, *The Moral Limits of the Criminal Law*, four volumes (Oxford: Oxford University Press, 1984–88).

much weight to this moral objection. And attending to their meaning requires that we become mindful of the use-mention distinction in philosophy of language.[2] When I *use* a word or phrase, I intend to refer to a particular person or group. So if I use "bitch" or "nigger" and intend that those words refer to you, then I believe that you are indeed a bitch or a nigger. However, if I merely *mention* such terms, it is as if I place them in quotation marks, thereby referring to the word within the quotes rather than to the person or group. If I instruct my students to never use "bitch" or "nigger," I am mentioning the terms so as to encourage them not to use them. This is far different from my using the terms in reference to, say, a particular student by calling him a "nigger."

Many critics contend that the use of these terms is harmful because they are sexist and racist. African Americans have a morally legitimate interest in not being harmed or stigmatized by the use of "nigger," which has long been recognized as a way of denigrating them. Likewise women have a morally legitimate interest in not being harmed or stigmatized by the use of "bitch," which has a similar denigrating effect on them. Typically (though not always), it is use and not mention of pejoratives that is racist or sexist or otherwise morally wrong. But are all uses of "bitch" or "nigger" morally wrong because they are sexist or racist and therefore harmful to women or African Americans? If there is a clear case of uses of these terms that doesn't constitute sexist or racist usage, then this particular way of developing the harm objection cannot be sustained.[3] And hip-hop fans know that there is at least one such case.

## Chappelle's "Bitches" and "Niggers"

Dave Chappelle does not merely mention the terms "bitch" and "nigger," he uses them frequently, as when he refers affectionately to audience members as "bitches," and receives laughter in response. But does he do so wrongfully? Certainly U.S. society

---

[2] The following point about racist versus racial language is found in J. Angelo Corlett, *Race, Racism, and Reparations* (Ithaca: Cornell University Press, 2003).

[3] A similar objection to the use of such language can be posed in terms of significant offence rather than harm but it will not be pursued here.

has for the most part and out of a dubious sense of "political correctness" reached the point that it rejects the uses of such words as necessarily being cusswords. And of course we recall the great Richard Pryor's frequent (indeed, incessant!) mention and use of "nigger" throughout most of his career, only in the latter part of his career to retract his use and encourage others to follow suit. But is the "politically correct" view about language use sound? Does the balance of reason support the absolute moral condemnation of such words?

To investigate this matter philosophically we must consider the speaker's intended meaning. Let's begin with the use of "bitch." This term was once used to refer to females perceived to be mean and aggressive in undesirable ways, mostly by males and often by way of a double standard. And this use of "bitch" has been (and still is!) condemned largely because it singles out females in such ways. A male with the same characteristics would be considered an "asshole." So why are women singled out as "bitches"?

In contrast with the historical usage of the term "bitch," Chappelle uses "bitch" to refer to men as well as women. This consistent gender-neutral use of "bitch" seems to do well in evading the charge of sexism. But why are many people still bothered by Chappelle's use of the word? Keep in mind that Chappelle also uses "bitch" in reference to men and women as a term of endearment. Thus he has done to "bitch" what many African Americans (typically younger ones like Chappelle himself) have done to "nigger." Taking the term back and reconstituting its meaning, they have used it in ways such that the connotation would change with the change in intentions, thus losing its original sting (as a pejorative). In fact, Chappelle often uses "nigger" or "nigga" with multiple meanings in the same sentence, a kind of humorous equivocation.

In one skit, Chappelle refers to a white man, saying (with a grin), "Now that's a nigger who's one crazy nigger!" drawing laughter from his live audience. The context was Chappelle's parody of the kind of racism present in a TV program "Real World," wherein often one black person is sharing a house with several white folk who have serious dysfunctions. When the black person finally snaps because he or she cannot endure the pain of living with such pettiness, then it makes the black person seem anti-social. So Chappelle reverses the situation to what might happen when a white man is placed in a living situation with dysfunctional black folk. Predictably, Chappelle surmises, the white person breaks down. It is yet another lesson in the lengthy history of the morally questionable TV portrayal of blacks in the U.S.

Not much has changed since the beginnings of TV—blacks portrayed and set up as being bad or problematic! But Chappelle takes matters a step further: whether black or white, those in charge of TV programming make folk into niggers one way or another to boost TV ratings. Chappelle not only uses "nigger" in both a pejorative and endearing sense in the same sentence, but he uses the word to refer to anyone who is used as a mere means to an end by the TV business. This is quite a courageous move by someone whose TV program depends on the decisions of such bosses. No small wonder Chappelle begins some of his episodes with expressed surprise that his program remains on the air.

## Words that Wound and Mill's Harm Principle

Chappelle's comic uses of the terms "bitch" or "nigger" don't seem to be sexist or racist, in which case not all uses of these terms can be condemned as morally wrong because they are sexist or racist and therefore harmful to women or African Americans. (Of course, it is possible that such words might be harmful in non-racist or non-sexist ways.) It's hard to see how the mere use of "bitch" in gender inclusive or neutral ways is necessarily harmful to women as a group, just as it is unclear that the use of "nigger" by African Americans necessarily harms blacks as a group.

I am not aware of anyone who morally condemns Jeff Foxworthy (or other "blue-collar" comics), a self-described "redneck," for his comedy routine "You might be a redneck if . . ." And no Latino of whom I am aware condemns comedians George Lopez or Cheech Marin for their jokes about us Latinos. Perhaps herein lies the key to our understanding of such words and why they are morally wrong when they are. We can distinguish between rac*ial* humor and rac*ist* humor, and more generally between rac*ial* language and rac*ist* language. Whenever language is intended by the speaker or writer to be harmful in racist or sexist ways, it is rac*ist* or sex*ist* language and wrong because it harms or is intended to harm. Otherwise, it might be rac*ial* or *gendered* language, such as in the cases imagined by the comedians Chappelle, Foxworthy, Lopez and Marin. Perhaps in-group members enjoy a kind of linguistic privilege, though not absolutely, such that use of racial or gendered language such as "bitch," "nigger," "redneck," and "beaner" is not always racist or sexist. Furthermore, out-group members might acquire a kind of linguistic immunity, morally speaking, if their uses of such words are generalized to members of groups to which the terms are *not* typically applied.

So when Chappelle refers to men and women as "bitches" there seems to be no good reason to condemn it. By parity of reasoning and counterfactually, if an Anglo were to refer to *all* folk (not only some blacks) as "niggers," she would seem to be changing the meaning of the term to apply to a particular kind of person, regardless of race. I see no good reason to morally condemn this use of language outright, though the extent of the harmfulness of such usage would be a relevant consideration. But caution is in order, as with every use of words. Even if it's true that one has a moral right to do something, it is not always the best thing to exercise that right at will, without regard to persons, history, context, and circumstance. Wisdom should guide us in judging when it is better or worse to use such terms, especially when their socially accepted meanings are being changed. Apart from any harm that might result, the person might be morally blameworthy for arrogantly thinking that she can so easily change the meaning of such a powerful, historically complex, and insulting word.

The previous points concerning words and their intended meanings are directly relevant to how we know the meanings and how we ought to think about their moral statuses. And the law is helpful here. In U.S. law, words that merely offend are simply beyond the purview of the law due to First Amendment protection of freedom of expression. But words that wound (harm) are not protected by law, and may be prohibited. This standard can also be applied to morals. Hip-hop artists deserve the very same First Amendment protections as everyone else. To the extent that certain words wound (and are intended to wound), then they ought to be legally prohibited. If they do not harm but merely offend, then let them be.[4] John Stuart Mill's Harm Principle, which guards against legal paternalism, is important. It states that the only time that words ought to be prohibited by law is when they cause harm to others.[5] This principle implies that unless words indeed harm and not simply offend, it would be excessively paternalistic and an unjust limitation of human liberty to prohibit their use. And given that harm amounts to the wrongful setting back of a legitimate interest, we can begin to understand the fuller impact of Mill's Harm Principle as a legitimate liberty protecting one. Actions, inactions, and attempted actions and words that wrongfully harm others are to be legally prohibited but others are to be left alone.

This is all fine and well, one might argue. But what the law says about harmful words is not necessarily what the balance of human reason in ethics would say about harmful or offensive ones. Assuming that a proper understanding of Mill's Harm Principle is congruent with what the law ought to prohibit insofar as harmful speech is concerned, what about offensive language? As with harms, offenses can set back various kinds of interests. And I would follow the philosopher Joel Feinberg in arguing that to the extent that the use of language sets back a basic or welfare interest of a person, to that extent it would then threaten that person's right to something fundamental to her life. Under such conditions, the language ought to be prohibited. However, in each case, the particular interest that is set back must be weighed carefully against the language user's freedom of expression.[6] For example, if the KKK burns a cross outside of a black family's home (on the public street) leaving a sign in the

---

[4] For a philosophical discussion of the nature of racist hate speech and whether or not it ought to be prohibited in light of the First and Fourteenth Amendments to the U.S. Constitution, see J. Angelo Corlett, *Ethical Dimensions of Law,* forthcoming.

[5] John Stuart Mill, *On Liberty*, People's Edition (London: Longman's, 1865); Joel Feinberg, *Harm to Others* (Oxford: Oxford University Press, 1984). Feinberg copiously qualifies this general formulation of the Harm Principle in *Moral Limits.*

[6] What distinguishes my view from a traditionally politically liberal one on this issue is that, whereas liberalism grants *prima facie* moral weight to freedom (of expression, in this case), my view does not. Competing interests are to be weighed against one another, all things considered.

street reading: "niggers not welcome here!" this will surely serve to violently intimidate not only that black family, but all blacks who know about it, and in doing so it will set back the interests of every black person in being treated as an equal and without violence in a society that purports to guarantee its citizens peace and tranquility. Clearly, the interest of blacks to be treated as equals and without violence outweighs the KKK's interest in freedom of expression. After all, the KKK does not have a right to set back anyone else's interest—especially a fundamental interest.

On the other hand, the use of "nigger" in a black comedy club is not likely to threaten any except those overly sensitive to such language. And if it were wrong to express virtually anything that would merely offend others, then it would be wrong to express anything at all given the diversity of U.S. society and the world. If mere offensiveness is sufficient to warrant judgments of morally unjustified speech acts, we would then require an argument as to which person or group would qualify as being offended by certain language use. But then what might constitute morally justified language use in this society is likely to offend some person or some group globally. Even the kindest words uttered in a particular context by X might well offend Y. And it's absurd to think that such merely offensive speech is wrongful simply because some person is offended. What we would need is an account of the degrees and kinds of offensive speech that would rightfully qualify as being morally wrong. But *prima facie,* it seems rash to condemn merely offensive words without an account of the kinds and degrees of offensiveness that are morally problematic.[7]

## Epithets and the Fear of a Black Planet

Perhaps what many people in the U.S. fear is the reality of life often described by hip-hop artists. Whether it is the conditions of cyclical poverty, the emphasis on material possessions, or the sometimes graphic portrayals of everyday life in the "hood," including the physical abuse of women and children, drug and

---

[7] No doubt a stronger case can be made for the moral unjustifiedness of severely offensive language. But that is not a problem I can take up here.

alcohol abuse, what makes many feel uncomfortable ought in turn to instill in them a sense of moral responsibility that would lead to the dissolution of such conditions. For when folk are not constantly caught up in trying to "get over," they are then able to focus on higher aspirations and needs. But perhaps many U.S. citizens simply want to ignore such conditions, figuring somehow that they themselves have and want nothing to do with the root causes of the conditions that inspire much of hip-hop music.

Hip-hop comedy deals with conditions of the "hood." Chappelle frequently addresses issues of racism in his segments "Ask a Black Man" and "Frontline: Black KKK." In the latter he plays a blind African American Klansman whose loyal followers never know he is black until he removes his hood during his book signing to the total shock and confusion of the all white audience of Klanners. One point Chappelle is making is that racism—though groundless—is so alluring that a *blind* black man can engage in it as well as those who fail to examine racism beyond its surface. Chappelle exposes racial stereotypes and reduces them to laughable idiocies.

In another skit entitled "Reparations 2003" Chappelle plays an Anglo newscaster who announces that "reparations day" has come for African Americans. Fear and confusion is evident on the face of the white folk portrayed in the skit, and many blacks are portrayed as frivolous and irresponsible in their receipt of such reparations, which take the form of cash settlements. A controversial skit, it seeks to demonstrate both white and black attitudes (generally) toward the issue. One point in particular is that African Americans deserve reparations but cash settlements are likely to lead to frivolity and irresponsibility by many blacks receiving them. There is, of course, no portrayal of the millions of African Americans who would indeed receive and utilize the reparations "responsibly." But the skit doesn't deny this. In any case, Chappelle's courageous skit brings to the fore one of the most morally, politically, and economically important issues of our time. Knowing the meanings of his uses of "nigger" and "bitch," in the contexts of Chappelle's skits, enables us to appreciate his complex uses of such terms in trying to educate the public about the realities of racism and related problems.

Does the use of words like "nigger" or "bitch" really *harm* (wrongfully set back a morally legitimate interest) when used by in-group members? Or does it merely *offend* some folk? And if these words merely offend, is this a proper occasion for censorship, or is it rather a prime opportunity for each of us to learn from such artists, at least some of them, what is going on outside of our sheltered worlds and how we might be contributing to certain forms of immiseration?

## Final Skit: Paris's Field Nigga Boogie

My conclusion that uses of terms like "bitch" and "nigger" in hip-hop comedy such as Chappelle's, which aims to educate the public about racism, sexism, and other social ills, are not immoral can easily be extended to at least some hip-hop music as well. To be sure, rappers produce videos depicting scantily clad young women gyrating to the beat of lip-syncing, gold-chain wearing young men rapping lyrics the meanings of which typically pertain to "fucking hos," "bustin' caps in the asses" of other "hood rats," beating "bitches" and so forth. And this materialism and violence, sexual or otherwise, is what many people in American society tend to think of when they think of hip-hop music. But we must guard against premature moral condemnation of hip-hop lyrics before discerning their real meanings.

As with comedy, the moral status of hip-hop lyrics depends largely on whether or not such artists are using or mentioning the lyrics they employ. If they are simply mentioning most or all of their words, then they would be communicating to others how life is for many urban blacks and other urbanites who are part of the U.S. working (or non-working) poor. For example, when we consider Paris and other socially conscious rappers we discern that the deeper meaning of their music is politically progressive.[8] Paris challenges his listeners to consider a different way of understanding the world. Although his message is communicated in the language of rap, cusswords and all, the message is clearly progressive. One refrain in his song "Field Nigga Boogie" is "Unless you wanna live on your knees, then throw down!" This implies that those who do not exercise their right to change their government are in fact self-esteem-lacking, self-hating, free-riders who are content to reap the ben-

---

[8] See, for example, Paris, *Sonic Jihad* (Guerrilla Funk Recordings, 2003).

efits of U.S. society without working politically to make justice work for all.

Furthermore, in his cut "What Would You Do?" he offers a moral challenge to all U.S. citizens to place the government on notice that we will no longer allow it to commit evils around the world for *any* reason, much less for the benefit of a few wealthy individuals. Paris would charge that we are all "niggaz" for sitting back and being duped by such evildoers. An example of this, Paris urges in his track "AWOL," is how the U.S. uses the hope of a proud military career and its educational benefits to attract young and uncritical folk to fight a morally unjust war—and no "niggaz" even so much as wonder what the reasons are for fighting the war! Paris's challenge is reminiscent of Malcolm X's words about the Vietnam War (a clearly morally wrong war from the perspective of U.S. involvement); namely, his wonderment as to why he and other blacks ought to fight in it as no North Vietnamese ever wronged them.

In condemning the U.S. on moral grounds, Paris is urging us to make an epistemic paradigmatic shift in how we perceive the world. In this regard, his lyrics are much like Chappelle's comedy skits in that they enable us to perceive the world differently and more deeply than we otherwise would, which leads to moral perceptions that are critical to seeing reality for what it is. Moreover, these artists show us that at least some hip-hop comedy and music offer us important opportunities for moral and philosophical reflection.[9]

---

[9] Many thanks to Derrick Darby, Robert Francescotti, Bill E. Lawson, Rodney C. Roberts and Tommie Shelby for incisive comments on an earlier draft of this track. Thanks also to Darby and Shelby for suggesting that I turn to Snoop Dogg, *Doggystyle* (Death Row, 1993) for the track's provocative title.

# Disk 5

# Fight the Power: Political Philosophy 'n the Hood

# 13
# Microphone Commandos: Rap Music and Political Philosophy

BILL E. LAWSON

A number of commentators on hip-hop culture have noted that rap has important political dimensions.[1] Philosopher Tommy Lott, for example, has argued that, despite the widely held view among older, middle-class folk that rap is noise emanating from wild, young blacks, there is an element of cultural resistance in rap music.[2] Many black youths realize that they are trapped under American apartheid and have used rap as a way to resist the racial assault on their physical and mental well-being in particular and on the black community in general. In keeping with this idea, I will show that some rap music, if one listens closely, can be heard as challenging basic philosophical assumptions underlying the political order. In particular, some rap represents a fundamental challenge to liberal political philosophy.

In some hip-hop music we hear a call for blacks to reassess what it means to be an American citizen. By questioning the fundamental relationship between blacks and the state, this form

---

[1] Tricia Rose, *Black Noise: Rap Music and Black Culture in Contemporary America* (Middletown: Wesleyan University Press, 1994); Houston A. Baker Jr., *Black Studies, Rap, and the Academy* (Chicago: University of Chicago Press, 1995); William Eric Perkins, ed., *Droppin' Science: Critical Essays on Rap Music and Hip-Hop Culture* (Philadelphia: Temple University Press, 1995); Theresa A. Martinez, "Popular Culture as Oppositional Culture: Rap As Resistance," *Sociological Perspectives* 40 (1997), pp. 269–291; Alan Light, ed., *The Vibe History of Hip Hop* (New York: Three Rivers Press, 1999); and Imani Perry, *Prophets of the Hood: Politics and Poetics in Hip Hop* (Durham: Duke University Press, 2004).

of rap expresses a political philosophy of its own. In exploring this theme, I want to use the concept of the social contract as a philosophical backdrop, because the idea that the relationship between citizen and state is one of a contract has a long history in political philosophy. The social contract is thought to be a real or hypothetical agreement between free and autonomous individuals who come together to form a civil state. The state provides protection of one's life and property and affords individuals the opportunity to live a life of their own choosing; and citizens reciprocate by obeying the law and pledging their allegiance to the state. The state retains its moral authority as long as it fulfills its part of the contract. When the state fails to live up to its part of the contract, the contract is void and individuals are then free to protect themselves.[3]

Certain rap songs suggest that the social contract between blacks and the United States, if any ever existed, has been broken. This view has at least two important ramifications. First, it gives rise to the view that in the United States it's every person for himself or herself. In a country that puts so much emphasis on material possessions, without a strong positive relationship between marginalized people and the government, it can easily become "all about the Benjamins," as P Diddy says.[4]

Second, and most important for this track, some members of the hip-hop community know that the civil rights struggle for African Americans continues, though often in subtle ways. America has not lived up to its promise of full inclusion for all citizens, especially African Americans. Members of the hip-hop nation have an obligation to continue the struggle for the hearts and minds of the youth against what the philosopher Cornel West calls nihilism—"the lived experience of coping with a life of horrifying meaninglessness, hopelessness, and (most important) lovelessness."[5] Thus it is the role of conscious members of the hip-hop community to critique the proponents of material-

---

[2] Tommy Lott, 1992. "Marooned in America: Black Urban Youth Culture and Social Pathology," in Bill E. Lawson, ed., *The Underclass Question* (Philadelphia: Temple University Press, 1992), pp. 71–89.
[3] See Bill E. Lawson, "Crime, Minorities, and the Social Contract," *Criminal Justice Ethics* 9 (1990).
[4] Puff Daddy, *No Way Out* (Bad Boy, 1997)
[5] Cornel West, *Race Matters* (New York: Vintage, 1994), pp. 22–23.

ism and misogyny both in the hip-hop community and America more generally. Let's turn now to how this position calls into question the social contract between the U.S. government and African Americans.

## The Social Contract

The book that has had the greatest impact on American political philosophy is John Locke's *Second Treatise of Government* (1690). Locke argues that governments are established to protect the property rights of individuals. We should note that he has an expansive conception of "property," which includes one's body, life, liberty, and possessions. The role of the state is to protect our "property rights" in this broad sense. This protection can either be from outside invaders or from unsavory characters within the state.

According to Locke, prior to the establishment of government (a pre-political condition he calls the "state of nature"), not all were equally suited or equipped to defend their property claims against others. Some civil mechanism was needed to adjudicate property claims. Thus, free and equal individuals came together to form a compact in which they agreed to give up to the state certain rights they possessed as a matter of natural right. These rights included the right to be their own judge, jury, and executioner. By freely consenting to join with others in civil society, each is politically obligated to obey the dictates of the state.

The state is to ensure protection of their property by providing known laws, impartial judges, and swift and certain punishment for property violations. Individuals should then be able to live peaceful and secure lives with the knowledge that their property rights will be respected and protected. In this manner their chances of a life free of the inconveniences of the "state of nature" are ensured. The state then provides the social environment in which individuals have the right to decide how to order their lives.

## Hip-Hop Culture and Human Freedom

Important in discussions of the social contract is the principle of respect for personal autonomy. The liberal tradition in political philosophy rests on a moral commitment to individual freedom. It tries to give people the room to frame their own plans of life, develop their own talents, and act on their own preferences with as little external interference as possible. In short, liberalism tries to give individuals the space to be their own masters, to rule themselves as far as they are able.[6]

Hip-hop culture has been deeply impacted by the part of liberal social contract theory that emphasizes human freedom. It should not be surprising that young blacks would be drawn to this aspect of liberalism, as it was at the heart of the Civil Rights Movement. African Americans wanted to be able to express their individual autonomy unfettered by racism. Accordingly, the freedom to express individuality is an important aspect of hip-hop culture. This freedom means that one will likely find all sorts of ideologies expounded as part of hip-hop culture, many and sometimes conflicting views of what it is to be part of the hip-hop community.

I believe that those persons who claim to be part of hip-hop culture have the right to self-identify. Thus, there are many differing segments of hip-hop culture. This is why any attempt to view any one segment of the culture as defining the culture is generally regarded as not understanding the culture. Persons who look at the materialism often think that "the Benjamins" or the bling is all hip hop is about. Persons close to the culture will tell you that materialism is one view held by some in the community, but it does not define the culture. I want to focus on those members of the community who see hip-hop culture as a means to engender social change.

Early on there were rap artists who understood that the supposed principles of respect for individuals did not seem to apply to blacks. Black people, for all of their civil rights struggles, still had not overcome. The ideology of individual freedom still seemed like a distant goal. Many of the mainstream social leaders talked as if the "dream" had been realized, while for many urban blacks their life prospects seemed dim. Certain members of hip-hop culture expressed their dissatisfaction with the apparent hypocrisy of American culture. Such dissatisfaction is

---

[6] David Carroll Cochran, *The Color of Freedom: Race and Contemporary American Liberalism* (Albany: State University of New York Press, 1999), p. 6.

expressed in Grandmaster Flash's "The Message," 2Pac's "Trapped" (*2Pacalypse Now*), PE's "911 Is a Joke" (*Fear of a Black Planet*), Ras Kass's "The Nature of the Threat" (*Soul on Ice*), Kam's "Stereotype" (*Neva Again*), and many other songs or raps that speak to the racism, classism, and jingoism of the United States. Many rappers see hip hop as an oppositional culture. In particular, the treatment of blacks in the United States has led some socially conscious members of the hip-hop community to question the meaning of citizenship for the African in America. This segment of hip-hop culture often claims that black Americans do not have even formal freedom. Should Blacks question the value of their citizenship?

## The Idea of Citizenship

In the Lockean view of the state, autonomous persons are citizens in the full sense of the word. They identify with the state and see the state as the focal point of their social existence. Generally, citizenship is understood in a very broad sense to mark the status of an individual in an organized state with territorial sovereignty. The status of citizen provides us with a guide for the rights and responsibilities of the individual in such a state. Citizenship means being a full and equal member of a state, native or naturalized, who has responsibilities to the government of the state and who is entitled to certain protection and rights within it.

There are two important components of citizenship—the social and the political-legal. The social component suggests that one is a member of a specific political community. Citizenship encompasses a feeling of being a vital part of the state; it gives an individual a social reference point to gauge his or her place in history, world geography, and our global society. The individual feels that his or her actions are part of the history and development of the state and therefore feels loyalty to it. Citizenship is therefore a crucial aspect of an individual's identity. In rap music, we find challenges to the widely held belief that blacks are full citizens. These challenges can be seen in songs that assert that blacks are Africans first and foremost. We find this view articulated in the music of groups such as X-Clan (*To the East Blackwards*), Brand Nubian (*One for All*), and, more recently, Dead Prez: "I'm an African, never was an African-American / Blacker than black, I take it back to my origin."[7]

The second aspect of citizenship concerns the legal rights and political responsibilities that accrue to all official members of a society. Among these are government protection of one's life, liberty, and property; the right to acquire property; freedom of movement; due process; the right to vote; and the duty to pay taxes and to obey laws. There may be some residents of the state's territory whose status may be somewhat ambiguous, for example, undocumented workers, political refugees, and illegal aliens. Still, for most residents, these rights and responsibilities are relatively well defined. Yet, in rap music we find the claim that many of these basic rights are still denied to African Americans. If this is correct, then blacks are politically oppressed.

Political rappers contend that political oppression reduces or voids the political obligations of African Americans to the state. Some rappers have claimed that the oppression of blacks is total and hence there are no such obligations. Blacks, according to this position, are still in slavery, and the slave has no obligation or allegiance to the body politic of his master, for the slave is not even recognized as a citizen.

Although blacks were formally made citizens by the post-Civil War amendments to the Constitution, many persons still feel that they have been denied two of the most precious benefits of state membership—economic security and physical protection. The denial of these benefits has led many urban youths to view the U.S. government as working against blacks when it comes to economic advancement in America. The lack of economic protection constitutes a major charge against the United States. Discrimination in the economic sphere affects the amount of income one can earn and one's ability to secure the necessities of life. On his first solo album, Tupac noted that blacks are "trapped," living in neighborhoods with few job prospects and an oppressive police army watching them. Rappers understand how one's income will determine to a large measure how one is treated in other spheres of the society, for instance, within the criminal justice system, the political arena,

---

[7] Dead Prez, "I'm A African," *Let's Get Free* (Loud, 2000).

and informal social interactions with fellow citizens. Now old school, Naughty By Nature in "Everything Is Gonna Be All-Right" notes that people want black youth to be positive but questions whether they can be positive when they view the economic system as stacked against them:

> Say somethin' positive? Well positive ain't where I lived
> I lived right around a corner from west hell
> Two blocks from south shit, it was in a jail cell
> The sun never shone on my side of the street, see.[8]

In 2004, Jadakiss asks: Why? He answers: "They got me in the system."[9]

Closely related to economic discrimination is discrimination in education, since education is a means of economic advancement, whether directly through vocational training or indirectly through academic courses. Some rappers, for example, Dead Prez and KRS-One, argue that the educational system has miseducated blacks about their place in history and thus has undermined the self-respect that would come from accurate knowledge. Consider Dead Prez's "They Schools":

> They schools can't teach us shit
> My people need freedom, we tryin' to get all we can get
> All my high school teachers can suck my dick
> Tellin' me white man lies straight bullshit (echoes)
> They schools ain't teachin' us what we need to know to survive
> They schools don't educate, all they teach the people is lies.[10]

Receiving a bad or inferior education makes it difficult, if not impossible, to find meaningful employment, thus lowering one's economic prospects. And because one's economic condition is so basic to the amount of political power one has, economic discrimination is a threat to political self-determination. Lack of power to affect social policy can make one feel devalued. Thus, economic discrimination limits a group's ability to impact public debate and sway public policy.

---

[8] Naughty By Nature, "Everything Is Gonna Be All-Right," *Naughty by Nature* (Tommy Boy, 1991).

[9] Jadakiss, "Why?" *Kiss Of Death* (Ruff Ryder/Interscope, 2004).

[10] Dead Prez, "They Schools," *Let's Get Free*.

## "Who Protects Us from You?" The Police and Protection

As noted, one of the basic reasons for joining the state, according to social contract theory, is physical protection. But many rappers assert that the racist behavior of law enforcement officers clearly shows how the state has failed to protect blacks. In many urban areas, the residents believe that the efforts of the police are ineffective in protecting them from crime. These citizens complain that the police respond late or not at all to calls for assistance. As Public Enemy states bluntly, "911 is a joke." Many living in the inner city think that they are victims twice over. First, they have to contend with crime in their communities, and then they have to contend with lack of protection from the state coupled with police brutality when they try to protect themselves.

In Los Angeles, for example, the Nation of Islam has been active in the battle against drugs in black communities. Members of the Muslim group, who patrol communities unarmed, have had run-ins with the police. One such account of an altercation between thirteen young Muslims and twenty-four Los Angeles police officers is indicative of the problem:

> Although accounts differ, Nation of Islam spokesmen say the Muslims objected to being ordered to assume a prone position on the ground. "Why do you want us to bow down to you—bow in the streets, face down as though you were God?" a Farrakhan aide, Khallid Muhammad, said later. "You don't make the white folks of Beverly Hills bow down . . . We bow down to God and God alone." All thirteen of the Muslims were charged in the episode, and the controversy fueled mounting tensions in predominantly black south-central Los Angeles over what many residents see as harassment and the overuse of force by city police and sheriff's deputies.[11]

The actions of the state are crucial in residents' decisions about whether to regard their acts of self-protection as merely supplemental to police protection, or as replacing the police. The residents of this community believed they were justified in having patrols, because the police had abrogated their role as

---

[11] "Farrakhan's Mission," *Newsweek* (19th March, 1990), p. 25.

protectors. The political powers in many cities do admit that such patrols are necessary but nevertheless regard them as unjustified. However, when the state fails to allow citizens to protect their lives and property through what they regard as legally permissible actions, they will naturally doubt that the state takes their welfare seriously and they will tend to withdraw their allegiance to their government.[12]

In America, we consider sanctions in criminal law to be deterrents and look upon law enforcement agencies as protective agencies. I believe that the purpose of a legal system is to ensure that an individual may go peacefully about his or her business without coercive interference, which many African Americans living in urban areas cannot do. Blacks live in fear based on personal victimization or the victimization of friends, neighbors, or relatives. It's the same fear that has caused the residents of these areas to turn their houses into prisons in which they attempt to lock themselves in from crime. The majority of these citizens are not criminals, yet they find themselves often at the mercy of the criminal element. Members of these black communities cannot feel that the state is protecting them.

One might object that the problem is not too little police presence in black neighborhoods, but too much. The extraordinarily high arrest frequency and high incarceration rates of young, urban black men and women, coupled with anxiety about police brutality and racial profiling against blacks, suggest that law enforcement agents have great presence in black urban neighborhoods. Yet many urban residents think that the police are there to contain rather than to protect. It's no wonder that KRS-One asks about the role of the police: "Who protects us from you?"

If the government is to be viewed as legitimate, citizens have to believe that the state places equal importance on their lives as members of the state. When young blacks review their social history, they have grounds to doubt that the state will protect or value them equally. And if physical protection is one of the basic benefits of being a member of the social contract, then black urban residents have reason to question the value of contractual membership. The behavior of the police in inner cities

---

[12] Lawson, "Crime," p. 16

forces us to reassess our obligations to the state and our understanding of the legitimacy of the social order. For many urban
youths, the actions of the state indicate a broken contract and,
as a result, they conclude that not only is there no obligation on
the part of blacks to obey the law, but the police should be
regarded as enemy combatants in a state of war. Ice Cube
expresses this antagonism when he exclaims, "I wanna kill
[uncle] Sam":

> I wanna kill him, cause he tried to play me like the trick
> But you see, I'm the wrong nigga to fuck wit' . . .
> It seems like he got the whole country behind him
> So it's sort of hard to find him.
> But when I do, gotta put my gatt in his mouth
> Pump seventeen rounds, make his brains hang out.[13]

The enemy is all around us. We are at war. The war is a war
for the minds, hearts, and souls of black folks. This is the message of revolutionary rap and of the politically conscious in the
hip-hop community.

## Romanticizing Rap?

A number of objections could be raised against my interpretation of rap music and hip-hop culture. First, am I romanticizing
a criminal culture? Many middle-class blacks and whites think
that rap is the music of young black criminals. Why should we
think that the concept of the social contract is applicable to
them? I believe that the broad impact of rap music was clearly
shown in the aftermath of the Rodney King verdict. In surveys
of urban youth, rappers were seen as the only group that understood their plight and spoke the truth about conditions in
America. This suggests that the appeal of hip hop reaches far
beyond criminals.

It might be claimed: "It's only music!" Yet fans of rap view it
not only as music but as their communication network, a kind
of black CNN, as Chuck D has dubbed it. When blacks are vic-
timized in the United States, the event is retold in rap songs,
spreading the "news." A related objection is that rap and hip-
hop culture are simply fads. But rap is now more than twenty-

---

[13] Ice Cube, "I Wanna Kill Sam," *Death Certificate* (Priority, 1991).

five years old and has spread from U.S. urban centers like New York and L.A. to countries all around the world. There are now rappers in Africa, Russia, China, and France, and they use the art form to express their dissatisfaction with the "powers that be" in their own countries. It's beyond the fad stage.

However, it might still be asked, why should we look for some political philosophy underpinning hip-hop attitudes? And why the social contract in particular? The social contract idea is an important philosophical element of our conception of political authority. One aspect of this philosophy is the role of the state in protecting the lives of its citizens. Hip-hop artists, like many Americans, understand the relationship between the state and its members as one of reciprocal obligations. Many political rappers maintain that the United States has never lived up to its obligations to ensure justice for African Americans. Indeed, some seem to agree with philosopher Charles Mills that the social contract was never meant to include blacks.[14] Mills contends there was a social contract but it was a "racial" contract, one that was constructed to maintain white supremacy. It is this state-against-black-America perception that defines this political stance. This position is articulated in the music of Talib Kweli (*Quality*), David Banner (*MTA2: Baptized in Dirty Water*), Dilated Peoples (*Expansion Team*), Paris (*Sonic Jihad*), The Coup (*Steal This Double Album*), and others. These rappers have a political philosophy, and from Grandmaster Flash's "The Message" to Mos Def's "War" (*The New Danger*) this message has been increasingly negative about the treatment of blacks in America and beyond.

For many young urban dwellers, rap has become their way to get their message across despite continuing racial discrimination. In this regard, rap music serves a political function and is perhaps the best method to get news and information to other urban communities. The one message that comes across very clearly is that black urban neighborhoods are under siege. Whites in power direct the attack and the goal is to destroy the black race. As Gang Starr notes (*Daily Operations*), the condition of blacks in America is not an accident, there is a white conspiracy.

---

[14] Charles W. Mills, *The Racial Contract* (Ithaca: Cornell University Press, 1997); also see Bill Lawson, "Locke and the Legal Obligations of Black Americans," *Public Affairs Quarterly* 49 (1989).

## Post-Civil Rights Music

Martin Kilson has argued that scholars of hip hop such as Todd Boyd and Michael Eric Dyson uncritically endorse the "hedonistic, materialistic, nihilistic, sadistic, and misogynistic ideas and values propagated by most hip-hop entertainers."[15] This criticism has merit, but it is one-sided. There are members of the hip-hop community who see their music as a continuation of the civil rights struggle, as post-civil rights music. These are young people who grew up in the United States and are a product of our collective history. Hip-hop culture comes out of that history. There is an important relationship between hip-hop culture and the historical struggle of Africans in America. Rap music and hip-hop culture have roots in the slave songs, freedom songs, and artists such as The Last Poets, Watts Prophets, and Gil Scott-Heron. Yet, rap represents a break with these forms of sonic expression in that it is the sound of young people who came of age in a period of great racial change in the social and political texture of the United States.

Hip-hop culture does have its roots in the political struggles of blacks. But hip hop has developed in a cultural context that is infused with post-modern critiques. It should not be surprising that young blacks have different views about life in the United States. Such young persons were never denied entrance to places of public accommodation, they have seen more black images on television and in the movies than at any other time in American history, and they can make more money in a few years than my family has made since we have been in America. It may seem strange to think that these youths could have any frustrations about their life in America. However, their frustration with America is simply a different type of frustration than that of previous generations of African Americans. Many urban youths see themselves in a battle for the social and political life of African peoples in a manner that older Americans, black and white, do not and cannot see. This may explain why old-school messages of social responsibility and civil protest are not effective in reaching many young urban black teenagers. Hip-hop culture, at least the political segment, speaks to the unfinished business of social justice but in a post-civil rights voice.

---

[15] Martin Kilson, "The Pretense of Hip-Hop Black Leadership," *The Black Commentator,* http://www.blackcommentator.com/50/50_kilson.html.

# 14

# Halfway Revolution: From That Gangsta Hobbes to Radical Liberals

## LIONEL K. McPHERSON

Rappers and rap commentators have claimed there's revolution in the music. They suggest not simply that rap is revolutionary in form—lyrics spoken rather than sung, sound driven by distilled beats rather than melody. No, they also suggest that rap is *politically* revolutionary. Exhibit A is Public Enemy and much of the hype surrounding this greatest of rap groups.[1]

Anyone who hasn't heard Nelly or, back in the day, MC Hammer or the Sugar Hill Gang might assume that rap is by nature music of urban anger and protest. It isn't, of course. Still, politically-oriented rap—which speaks to black life under conditions of adversity—has been a defining strain of the music. If you doubt there's room for political themes in this era dominated by pop-rap, listen to Dead Prez or The Coup.[2]

Ironically, most political rap has not been politically revolutionary. I say this not as a criticism, only as an observation. While political rap does represent a culture of resistance, it's not true that such rap "represents a fundamental challenge to liberal political philosophy."[3] This view gets at least two things wrong:

---

[1] See, for example, Public Enemy, "Revolutionary Generation," *Fear of a Black Planet* (Def Jam, 1990). Music critic Stephen Thomas Erlewine writes that PE "pioneered a variation of hardcore rap that was musically and politically revolutionary." Biography of Public Enemy, *AMG Allmusic*, http://www.allmusic.com (5th February, 2005).

[2] See, for example, Dead Prez, *RBG: Revolutionary But Gangsta* (Columbia, 2004); and The Coup, *Steal This Double Album* (Foad, 1998).

[3] Track 13 in this volume, p. 161.

1) the range of resistance politics expressed in rap, and 2) the progressive potential of political liberalism.

Few rappers have seriously advocated political revolution—a transformation of society that would produce government and social arrangements that are fundamentally different from the established ones. "We are hip hop / Me, you, everybody, we are hip hop / So hip hop is goin where we goin," Mos Def tells us.[4] And most of us aren't politically revolutionary. Rap's political visions have mainly been amoral, Afrocentric, or liberal. They find support in prominent theories in political philosophy.

## The Hood and America as a State of Nature

A few hundred years ago, Thomas Hobbes observed that life is "solitary, poor, nasty, brutish, and short."[5] This was supposed to be the typical condition of persons in "a state of nature"—a world where individuals ultimately must fend for themselves in conflict with others. As Nas succinctly updates this theme, "life's a bitch and then you die."[6] Only the strongest, cleverest, or luckiest could hope to enjoy secure and full lives in a state of nature. Most persons would do better in civilized society.

Hobbes was imagining the situation we'd be in without a government, especially its ability to impose law and order. This represents a version of what philosophers call "social contract theory." If we're rational, according to Hobbes, we would consent to be governed in the interest of our mutual benefit. The crucial part of this bargain for Hobbes is our willingness to submit to a government's coercive authority and power: each of us must agree not to pursue our own desires through force, or else we'll slide back to a "war of every one against every one."[7] In return we're to get peace and security as members of society.

From the perspective of hardcore rappers, however, the world looks an awful lot like a state of nature. So Mobb Deep's Prodigy raps in "Survival of the Fittest":

---

[4] "Fear Not of Man," *Black on Both Sides* (Rawkus Entertainment, 1999).
[5] Thomas Hobbes, *Leviathan* (Harmondsworth: Penguin, 1968 [1651]), Chapter 13.
[6] "Life's a Bitch," *Illmatic* (Columbia, 1994).
[7] Hobbes, *Leviathan*, Chapter 13.

There's a war goin' on outside, no man is safe from
You could run but you can't hide forever . . .
It's similar to Vietnam
Now we all grown up and old and beyond the cop's control . . .
My goal's to stay alive
Survival of the fit, only the strong survive.[8]

Viewing society as a system of mutual benefit is apparently at odds with reality in urban America. The government fails to provide the security necessary for trust and co-operation. In fact, the police are seen as a major part of the problem, hardly less of a danger to life and liberty than rival gangstas—a point N.W.A. bluntly makes on "Fuck tha Police." Add to this the government's failure to address overwhelming black poverty and miserable black schools. Such neglect spurs an underground economy of drug dealing, thieving, and pimping.

No surprise, then, that many young black men, concentrated in ghettos across the country, tend to view the hood and American society in general as a state of nature. Hardcore rap lays bare the truth that no social contract has ever existed between blacks and the United States. The mere promise of a social contract extending to blacks was broken long ago, epitomized in the "forty acres and a mule" that freed slaves never got.

The gangsta ethic fits Hobbes's social contract theory. This might distress critics of the antisocial attitude sometimes voiced in rap. For Hobbes, though, justification for the government rests solely on assumptions about how rational, self-interested individuals would respond to mutual distrust and aggressive competition for resources. Contested beliefs about morality, a god's commands, or the good life play no role in this justification. When individuals have reason to believe they're not better off submitting to the authority and power of the government, they would have no reason to comply with its laws.

Hobbes's morality-free justification for the government is not entirely plausible. In order for a society to be stable, persons need to be committed to social co-operation. Otherwise, allegiance to

---

[8] *The Infamous* (RCA, 1995).

the society is always provisional, dependent on whether individuals are unable to get away with pursuing their own interests by any means necessary. Desirable stability requires that persons acquire a sense of fairness—that they will co-operate with others because this is the right and reasonable thing to do and not simply because of the threat of punishment. Yet if groups of persons do not see the society as working for them, the society cannot expect their allegiance.

Thus the gangsta ethic not only leads some rappers to chronicle ghetto life but also often to celebrate its amoral dimensions. The message is that only fools, frauds, or cowards—suckas— would comply with the society's rules when these rules are likely to leave black folks disrespected, broke, in jail, or prematurely dead. An anti-black, market capitalist society that approximates for many a state of nature can expect the credo 50 Cent adopts: "get rich or die tryin'."

## An Afrocentric Community

Social contract theories focus on the basic interests of individuals. By contrast, communitarian theories emphasize the ideal of community, which can involve shared nationality, culture, language, or religion. Contemporary communitarian philosophers such as Alasdair MacIntyre, Michael Sandel, Charles Taylor, and Michael Walzer argue that persons can't have an adequate conception of themselves—let alone adequate conceptions of morality, justice, and the good life—independently of their community.[9] On this view, the value of community is at least as important as liberty and equality for individuals.

The ideal of community is familiar in rap that espouses Afrocentrism. We can roughly distinguish two types of Afrocentrism in rap: nationalist and Native Tongues. Nationalist Afrocentrism has its roots in the "Back to Africa" movement of Marcus Garvey and in the Nation of Islam. It advocates separa-

---

[9] See, for example, Alasdair MacIntyre, *After Virtue*, second edition (Notre Dame: University of Notre Dame Press, 1984); Michael Sandel, *Liberalism and the Limits of Justice*, second edition (Cambridge: Cambridge University Press, 1998); Charles Taylor, *Hegel and Modern Society* (Cambridge: Cambridge University Press, 1979); and Michael Walzer, *Spheres of Justice* (New York: Basic Books, 1983).

tion from whites as a defense against persistent white supremacy and urges social and economic empowerment through group self-help. Afrocentric rappers of the late Eighties and early Nineties—for example, Brand Nubian, Paris, X-Clan—mainly were nationalist. This trend has been revived by Dead Prez, who proclaim: "I'm an African, never was an African American / Blacker than black, I take it back to my origin."[10]

Presumably, few white communitarian philosophers would be comfortable with this kind of pro-black stance, though they'd have to admit that the ideal of community is evident in such lyrics. Communitarians believe that personal identity, moral life, and political rights should be determined within a community. They object to forms of individualism that ignore history. Nationalist Afrocentric rappers might well agree.

Native Tongues Afrocentrism takes a different pro-black line. The "Native Tongues" designation comes from the New York-based collective that included the Jungle Brothers, Queen Latifah, De La Soul, A Tribe Called Quest, and Mos Def. The Afrocentrism of this rap isn't dedicated to racial separation or a reconstructed African identity. Its attention is on promoting black self- and group-esteem and on raising consciousness of issues—especially violence, drug abuse, and sexism—afflicting "the black community." Native Tongues Afrocentrism tends to be more cosmopolitan, drawing on influences that aren't typically identified with black youth culture. Musically, this has meant incorporating pop, rock, and jazz elements into the mix, De La Soul's *3 Feet High and Rising* (1989) being a classic case. Lyrically, this has meant lauding rap's potential for universal appeal, in the manner of A Tribe Called Quest: "We on award tour with Muhammad my man / Goin' each and every place with the mic in their hand / Chinatown, Spokane, London, Tokyo."[11]

A cosmopolitan, Native Tongues-type Afrocentrism is better able to respond to objections to communitarianism. Many African Americans recognize that "race" is the most significant feature of their social identity in the U.S. Yet they recognize that gender, class, and sexual orientation also constitute who they

---

[10] "I'm a African," *Let's Get Free* (Loud, 2000).
[11] "Award Tour," *Midnight Marauders* (Zomba, 1993).

are. Like members of other groups, African Americans have complex social identities, and the strength of their identification with the black community can depend on political contingencies and their own personal concerns.

Communitarianism obscures this fact by implying a proper, unified self shaped by the community. Similarly, nationalist Afrocentrism suggests that African Americans are essentially black or African, in biological or spiritual terms, and calls out as Uncle Toms those brothers and sisters perceived not to be down with the cause. However, we can acknowledge the importance of solidarity in a community without accepting a "politics of the common good" that would impose on individuals the dominant conception of a community's "way of life."[12]

A communitarian approach to minority groups is also troubling. Minorities often practice ways of life—through culture, language, or religion—that diverge from mainstream norms. Official policies designed to advance the majority community's values risk licensing or encouraging hostility toward minority groups. Some U.S. public schools, for instance, have prohibited students from wearing baggy pants or religious headdress. Generally, communitarianism might not express enough tolerance for the ways of life of marginalized groups and individuals, be they African Americans, women, Muslims, homosexuals, and so forth.

This has practical implications for rap. According to historian Tricia Rose, laws that restricted where and how jazz could be played "were attached to moral anxieties regarding black cultural effects and were in part intended to protect white patrons from jazz's 'immoral influences'."[13] She connects those laws to the attitudes of arena owners and insurance companies, whose exaggerated fears about black violence fuel resistance to booking rap shows. The bottom line is that communitarian politics—even in the form of nationalist Afrocentrism—are risky for

---

[12] See Will Kymlicka, *Contemporary Political Philosophy*, second edition (New York: Oxford University Press, 2002), p. 220. For an account of African American solidarity in particular, see Lionel K. McPherson and Tommie Shelby, "Blackness and Blood: Interpreting African American Identity," *Philosophy and Public Affairs* 32 (2004), pp. 171–192.

[13] Tricia Rose, *Black Noise: Rap Music and Black Culture in Contemporary America* (Hanover: Wesleyan University Press, 1994), p. 133.

African Americans, given their minority status and relatively weak economic and political power in the U.S.

The rapper Paris, overtly nationalist though he is, seems to get this: "Not idiot crossover songs / That appeal to all and make you sing along, no / This one is for the chosen few / Who want to build and upflift my people too."[14] His reference to "the chosen few" is ambiguous, open to involving whites and anyone else who cares about the progress of "my people," black people. A community bound by such a commitment need be neither racially or culturally exclusionary nor skeptical of individualism.

## Radical Liberals

Political philosophers distinguish between ideal and non-ideal theory. Ideal theory looks for principles that any just society must embody and assumes that everyone would follow these principles. Non-ideal theory looks for principles that can handle injustice in a society. For example, non-ideal theory might allow race-based affirmative action given a history of racial injustice. If a society were racially just, taking race into account in hiring or school admissions would be unnecessary and unfair, since there would be no racial injustice to correct.

The most influential and criticized contemporary political philosopher has been John Rawls. His ideal theory of justice doesn't say much about racism. So when Chuck D. of Public Enemy asks, "What's a smilin' face / When the whole state's racist?", Rawls might seem to have no answer, like much of the social contract tradition.[15] Yet Rawls's vision of political liberalism is more down with PE's agenda than we might think.

Rawls proposes the idea of "the original position," which represents a hypothetical situation where persons agree on fair terms of social co-operation.[16] These persons are free, equal, and reasonable citizens in a democratic society. Despite their diverse

---

[14] "Ebony," *The Devil Made Me Do It* (Tommy Boy, 1990).
[15] "By the Time I Get to Arizona," *Apocalypse 91 . . . The Enemy Strikes Black* (Def Jam, 1991).
[18] See John Rawls, *A Theory of Justice*, revised edition (Cambridge, Massachusetts: Harvard University Press, 1999); and Erin Kelly, ed., *Justice as Fairness: A Restatement* (Cambridge, Massachusett.: Harvard University Press, 2001).

moral outlooks, they seek principles of justice that regulate society's basic structure and that serve their mutual advantage. Rawls wants to figure out what principles such persons *would* agree to, even if actual agreement in a society never happens.

In the real world we're at different levels of wealth and privilege; we're born men or women; we belong to different racial and ethnic groups; we don't share all the same values; and we have different natural abilities. For agreement on the principles of justice to be fair, Rawls argues, such contingent facts about persons shouldn't be allowed to bias their choice of the principles. We should imagine deliberating behind a "veil of ignorance" that limits knowledge of our own bargaining advantages. Although we'd discover our circumstances in society once the veil is lifted, we would have committed to following the principles we agreed to behind the veil.

Rawls believes that persons in the original position would choose two principles of justice. The first principle, which has priority, holds that everyone must have equal basic liberties— for example, freedom of thought, the right to vote, and equality under the law. The second principle holds that social and economic inequalities must be consistent with fair equality of opportunity and of greatest benefit to the disadvantaged.[17] Some persons could make more money than others not because they deserve to but only as an incentive to do work that above all would improve the lives of society's least well-off members. Playing the system for maximum, personal advantage is disallowed. This idea seems radical in these times of growing inequality.

Critics of Rawls have questioned how we could respond strongly to racism if we're thinking about justice from behind a veil of ignorance. After all, race is supposed to be out of the picture in the original position. The liberal ideal of equal moral status threatens to leave African Americans without a platform for combating racial injustice. Chuck D. essentially makes this point when he declares: "People, people we are the same / No we're not the same / 'Cause we don't know the game / What we need is awareness, we can't get careless."[18] The mere rhetoric of

---

[17] Rawls, *Justice as Fairness*, pp. 42–43.
[18] Public Enemy, "Fight the Power," *Fear of a Black Planet*.

equality won't do much to change the realities of race and racism.

But Rawls's theory isn't done once there's agreement on the principles of justice. We're to apply the principles using our general knowledge about the society, including the prevalence and effects of racism in it.[19] Rawls doesn't put up practical barriers to remedying racial injustice by insisting on absolute "color-blindness"—that is, treating everyone without considering race, even when racism helps to explain inequality. Further, since African Americans as a group don't enjoy equal opportunity and are disproportionately poor or struggling, the second principle of justice—which requires a roughly equal distribution of resources—would in effect greatly benefit them.

Chuck D. provocatively calls out the U.S. government as "an anti-nigger machine" organized by "a swarm of devils," who run the criminal justice system as "a form of slavery."[20] Yet beneath PE's lyrically and sonically confrontational approach is a commitment to setting the historical record straight and to demanding justice and respect for African Americans as equal members of society. If PE had truly given up on white America, Chuck D. wouldn't have bothered "waitin' for the date" for politicians to honor Martin Luther King, Jr. with a national holiday.[21] Nor would Chuck D. express disappointment with whites "who never repented / For the sins within that killed my kin."[22]

Thus Public Enemy's "pro-Black radical mix" seems fundamentally liberal in its opposition to white supremacy.[23] Not much of substance separates PE and Rawls regarding a political response to racial injustice. Of course, they have very different *styles*. PE gives shout outs to the Nation of Islam—without advocating nationalist separatism or a literal view of whites as morally hopeless evildoers. Rawls philosophizes at an abstract level and never deploys figurative violence—though he's undeniably motivated by awareness of how race affects opportunities

---

[19] See Tommie Shelby, "Race and Social Justice: Rawlsian Considerations," *Fordham Law Review* 72 (2004), pp. 1706–08.

[20] Public Enemy, "Black Steel in the Hour of Chaos," *It Takes a Nation of Millions to Hold Us Back* (Def Jam, 1988).

[21] "By the Time I Get to Arizona."

[22] Public Enemy, "Who Stole the Soul?", *Fear of a Black Planet*.

[23] "Party for Your Right to Fight," *It Takes a Nation of Millions to Hold Us Back*.

and outcomes in American life. So Chuck D. needn't target him in rapping: "Yeah, he appear to be fair / The cracker over there / He try to keep it yesteryear / The good ol' days / The same ol' ways."[24] Rawls's ideal theory of justice—unlike fake colorblind ideology—supports taking reasonable means necessary to bringing about justice, including racial justice, in a non-ideal world.

## Reality versus Revolution

I've argued that political rap hasn't been politically revolutionary. The amoral gangsta ethic favors individual self-interest or the collective interest of gang or crew. Afrocentric rap focuses on black group- and self-empowerment, not on a broader transformation of society. The few references to socialism Dead Prez drops are more about show than content. Radically liberal rap endorses the idea of society as a fair system of social cooperation but hardly questions whether this is ultimately compatible with capitalism. Accepting a kinder, gentler market-driven economy isn't the stuff of political revolution.

I'm not saying that "niggers are scared of revolution," as The Last Poets charged back in 1970. My point is that black politics, like hip hop, is going where we're going. As the music writer Nelson George observes, hip hop's central values—its materialism, anti-intellectualism, aggression, and spirit of rebellion—"are very much by-products of the larger American culture."[25] The revolution will not be televised for the simple reason that there's no real desire among African Americans for political revolution. Black folk do have a real desire, however, for racial progress.

Political rap is the soundtrack to the hip-hop generation's disaffection over being left out of the American dream.[26] Not all African Americans dig the soundtrack. Still, most would look forward to the day they had a truly equal opportunity for the kinder, gentler, and fairer version of the dream to pay off.[27]

---

[24] "By the Time I Get to Arizona."

[25] Nelson George, *Hip Hop America* (New York: Penguin, 1999), pp. xiii, 155.

[26] The hip-hop generation is said to cover African Americans born between 1965 and 1984. See Bakari Kitwana, *The Hip Hop Generation* (New York: Basic Civitas Books, 2002), p. xiii.

[27] In transcribing many of the lyrics quoted, I have consulted *The Original Hip-Hop Lyrics Archive*, http://www.ohhla.com.

# 15

# Criminal-Justice Minded: Retribution, Punishment, and Authority

ERIN I. KELLY

The payback attitude heard in gangsta rap sounds like a call for retribution. As 50 cent puts it, "Nigga you play around, I lay you down / That's how it's goin' down."[1] Justice as retribution echoes the feeling that vengeance is sweet, redeeming those who've suffered the humiliation of being wronged. This appeals to many people. It fact, it seems to express the attitude many law-abiding citizens would direct at gangstas themselves. Yet the desire for retribution that some rappers express isn't proposed as a legitimate basis for a system of punishment. To begin with, the situations they portray are sometimes way outside of the law, as Nas depicts in "Every Ghetto": "Circle the block where the beef's at / And park in front of my enemy's eyes / They see that it's war we life-stealers, hollow-tip lead busters."[2]

Behind rappers' desire to settle the score often lies a firm belief that the law does not, and doesn't aim to, protect them. If the law doesn't protect you and won't deliver justice, you may have to protect your own honor and reputation by seeking vengeance against your enemies. In Dr. Dre's words, "And if motherfuckers come at me wrong / I straight put my .44 Desert Eagle to his motherfuckin' dome / and show him why they call me the notorious one."[3]

---

[1] 50 Cent, "Rotten Apple," *Guess Who's Back* (Full Clip, 2002).
[2] Nas, "Every Ghetto," *Stillmatic* (Sony, 2001).
[3] Dr. Dre, "Nigga Witta Gun," *The Chronic* (Priority, 1992).

Many rappers are skeptical about justice in America and alarmed by our system of punishment. They suggest that racial bias in our criminal justice institutions—police, courts, and prisons—undermines the notion that criminals are getting their "just deserts." Rappers also call into question whether the massive effort to incarcerate black men serves the purpose of public safety. The rhetoric of both retribution and the public good seem to them to be a front for unjust forms of social control that help to maintain a system of racial privilege for whites. I will discuss "retributivist" and "consequentialist" philosophies of punishment and how rap music aims to snatch the disguise from the ugly face of the system.

## Punishment as Retribution

Retribution as a justification for the state-sanctioned, legal practice of punishment has become popular. Punishment as retribution is based on the idea that criminal wrongdoing calls for punishment—quite apart from the consequences of punishment, such as incapacitating or deterring offenders. The demand for retribution would be considered justified even at substantial economic and social cost. The point is that justice is done only when wrongdoers suffer. This punishment is imposed through the formal procedures of the law, where punishment takes place well after the crime and for reasons other than self-defense.

In lawless circumstances, by contrast, the line between retribution and self-defense gets blurred. Retaliation and even preemptive action might seem necessary to defend person and property. "Ready to rhyme / Standin' my ground / Never back down," says OutKast, "Willin' to rob, steal, and kill any thang that threatens mine."[4] But advocates of retribution (a.k.a. retributivists) are not interested in retaliation as a means to personal safety or as a reaction to a threat. They advocate retaliation for wrongdoing as a matter of justice. This has led famous retributivists, the philosophers Immanuel Kant (1724–1804) and, in our time, Robert Nozick (1938–2002), to stress differences between vengeance and retribution. Vengeance is emotional, personal,

---

[4] OutKast, "Return of the 'G,'" *Aquemini* (La Face, 1998).

reckless, and often disproportionate to the wrong. Retribution is impartially applied by a dispassionate and legitimate authority, and carefully calculated to fit the crime. In a civilized society, these philosophers claim, retribution should replace vengeance. This does not mean that retribution will be less violent or brutal. The death penalty and maximum-security prisons are hardly gentler alternatives to vigilante vengeance—as the French philosopher Michel Foucault (1926–1984) emphasizes in *Discipline and Punish: The Birth of the Prison* (1975).

Yet the ideal of retribution carries with it more than a trace of vengeance. Indeed, some recent books, such as Peter French's *The Virtues of Vengeance* and Jeffrie Murphy's *Getting Even*, urge us to embrace the emotional, personal, and expressive value of punishment as retribution. These philosophers accept continuity between vengeance and the justification of punishment. French offers four conditions that vengeance must meet if it's to count as justice:

1. *Communication.* The penalty must effectively communicate that what the offender did was wrong.
2. *Desert.* The penalty must be deserved.
3. *Proportionality.* The penalty must fit the crime.
4. *Authority.* Someone with legitimate authority must administer the penalty.

When these conditions are met, vengeance guides us to justice, or so it is claimed.

## Doubts about the Justice of Retribution

Rappers tell a cautionary tale—the retributivist's conditions for justice aren't met. Here is Public Enemy's angle on political authority:

> I got a letter from the government
> The other day
> I opened and read it
> It said they were suckers
> They wanted me for their army or whatever
> Picture me givin' a damn—I said never
> Here is a land that never gave a damn

About a brother like me and myself
Because they never did
I wasn't wit' it, but just that very minute . . .
It occurred to me
The suckers had authority.[5]

PE's Chuck D implies that the authority of a government that doesn't care about some of its people can't be legitimate. A legitimate government serves the interests of all of its people, including minority groups. A government that fails to do this exercises only power, not legitimate authority—might, not right.

The most basic rights associated with our criminal justice system, guaranteed by the U.S. Constitution, are these: people should not be subjected to unreasonable searches and seizures (Fourth Amendment); people are innocent until proven guilty through due process of the law (Fifth Amendment); people should not be subjected to cruel or unusual punishment (Eighth Amendment); people should be equally protected by the law (Fourteenth Amendment). Many rap artists point to violations of these basic constitutional rights—police and prosecutorial misconduct, lack of access to legal counsel, unfair sentencing policy, and inhumane prison conditions. These are well-documented problems that disproportionately affect African Americans and Latinos.

Consider, for example, racial profiling. As Mos Def describes it, "The po-po stop him and show no respect / 'Is there a problem officer?' / Damn straight, it's called race."[6] Racial profiling is a policing strategy that is strongly correlated with the excessive use of force and with disproportionate incarceration of minorities.[7] Problems such as these threaten not only U.S. Constitutional rights but also internationally recognized human rights. They give us reason to doubt whether many punishments have been justly imposed.

But grounds for doubt about punishment as retribution may extend beyond worries about racial bias in its application. How

---

[5] Public Enemy, "Black Steel in the Hour of Chaos," *It Takes a Nation of Millions to Hold Us Back* (Def Jam, 1988).

[6]Mos Def, "Mr. Nigga," *Black on Both Sides* (Rawkus, 1999).

[7]See Amnesty International's report, *Threat and Humiliation: Racial Profiling, Domestic Security, and Human Rights in the United States* (New York: Amnesty International USA, 2004).

could we know whether the desert condition or the proportionality condition for justice as retribution has been satisfied? Consider this discussion about fitting the punishment to the crime:

> Tailoring the fit appears to depend on the moral sensitivity or intuitions of the punisher(s). When is the fit 'just right'? When does a suit of clothes fit? When it feels right? Yes, but also when it looks right to the wearer and to others. . . . Morality is an art, not a science.[8]

Statements such as this should worry if not alarm us. The lack of a cohesive moral community and a shared basis for moral judgment in multicultural, multiethnic, multireligious America dooms this justification of punishment. We simply don't agree about who deserves what. The haphazard nature of desert judgments cannot justify the high-stakes social policy of criminal punishment. Our system of punishment costs us almost 60 billion dollars per year;[9] it disrupts families and communities; and it deprives offenders of their most basic liberty, sometimes for a very long time. Metaphorical and biblical references to cosmic balance, the scales of justice, "an eye for an eye," or the art of morality are inadequate as rational and public justifications for a system of punishment. We must look elsewhere for a more plausible rationale.

## Punishment as Social Control

The main alternative rationale for punishment is about social control, not desert. Many rappers know this all too well through personal experience. The standard philosophical theories of punishment as social control come from a tradition influenced by the work of Jeremy Bentham (1748–1832). Bentham and other "consequentialist" philosophers have argued that punishment can only be justified when it has good consequences for society. In particular, punishment can be justified by considerations of deterrence, rehabilitation, or incapacitation.

---

[8] Peter French, *The Virtues of Vengeance* (Lawrence: University Press of Kansas, 2001), p. 227.
[9] Unless otherwise specified, the statistics in this essay come from the Bureau of Justice Statistics, United States Government.

Deterrence is achieved when, by punishing offenders, criminals or potential criminals are effectively discouraged from committing crimes. Rehabilitation is achieved when an offender's desire to re-offend is extinguished and replaced by respect for the law. Incapacitation is achieved when the guilty are rendered incapable of re-offending because they're locked up. Rappers express skepticism about whether anything but incapacitation is achieved by punishment.

We have seen that the moral authority of the criminal justice system is precarious when the rights of members of minority groups are not protected. This makes it hard to secure respect for the law, which dims the prospects for rehabilitating criminals. A deterrence rationale is also on unsteady ground, since deterrence is ineffective when the conditions outside prison are like the "jungle" that Melle Mel describes in "The Message":

> Broken glass everywhere
> People pissin' on the stairs
> You know they just don't care
> I can't take the smell, can't take the noise
> Got no money to move out, I guess I got no choice
> Rats in the front room, roaches in the back
> Junkies in the alley with a baseball bat
> I tried to get away but I couldn't get far
> 'Cause a man with a tow truck repossessed my car.[10]

When people are poor, unemployed, without hope, and subject to street violence and police abuse, prison may seem a lot less like something to fear, as Dead Prez makes clear in "Behind Enemy Lines":

> You ain't gotta be locked up to be in prison
> Look how we livin'
> 30,000 niggas a day, up in the bing, standin' routine
> They put us in a box, just like our life on the block.[11]

Of course, prison is in many ways worse than "life on the block." The point is that people in difficult social circumstances

---

[10] Grandmaster Flash and the Furious Five, "The Message," *The Message* (Sugarhill, 1982).
[11] Dead Prez, "Behind Enemy Lines," *Let's Get Free* (Loud, 2000).

are more willing to take risks, especially when they're angry or desperate. This fact, which might be called "the ghetto factor," substantially weakens the effectiveness of punishment as a deterrent.

We're left with incapacitation, and herein lies a deeper story. It begins with an agonizing recognition of the prospects facing many people who get caught up in the system: "They're scared of us, rather beware than dare to trust / Always in jail, million dollar bail, left there to rust."[12] Incapacitation could be a legitimate rationale for punishment only if the aim is public safety. But rappers charge that the long sentences that many African Americans face often serve interests that reach beyond the safety of the public.

For instance, federal sentences for cocaine possession and distribution are much harsher for the drug in crack form as compared to powder form. Possession of five grams of crack triggers a five-year mandatory minimum sentence, whereas it takes five hundred grams of powder cocaine to trigger the same sentence. Although evidence indicates there are far more white crack users and dealers than black ones, 84 percent of crack defendants are African American.[13] By contrast, only 31 percent of powder cocaine defendants are African American. The racial disparity may be explained by a concentration of drug law enforcement in urban, minority communities in which crack, the cheaper form of cocaine, is more prevalent than powder cocaine. The media also hyped the "evils" of crack as the government launched its "war on drugs" in the 1980s. The result is what Human Rights Watch has described as "an indefensible sentencing differential [that] becomes unconscionable in light of its racial impact."[14]

The idea that our criminal justice system punishes not only crime but also race comes up time and again in rap tracks. In the words of Ice Cube: "I think back to when I was robbin' my own kind / The police didn't pay it no mind / But when I start

---

[12] Big Punisher, "Capital Punishment," *Capital Punishment* (Loud, 1998).

[13] U.S. Sentencing Commission, 2000 Sourcebook of Federal Sentencing Statistics.

[14] Human Rights Watch Presentation to the United States Sentencing Commission (25th February, 2002).

robbin' the white folks / Now I'm in the pen wit' the soap-on-a-rope."[15]

## Prison/Ghetto

Let's further probe the relationship between prison and ghetto. Here's Goodie Mob's "Cell Therapy": "Loc up folks they in the hood, got an eye on every move / I make open your face to info you ain't know / 'Cause it's kept low how the new world plan / Reeks the planet without the black man."[16] The ambiguity of the line, "Loc up folks they in the hood, got an eye on every move," implies that both prison and ghetto serve to control and to segregate African Americans, especially young men.

Similarities between prison and ghetto have caught the attention of sociologists. The ghetto is a physical space that segregates, stigmatizes, coerces, and makes people vulnerable to economic exploitation.[17] Ghettos have worked this way, in apartheid South Africa, the Jim Crow American South, Chicago, and New York City. The racial profile of the U.S. prison population—65 percent of the prison population is non-white—suggests that prison too contributes to racial segregation. No doubt it also stigmatizes. And further, private companies are making big money marketing products and services. Telephone companies, for instance, are reaping hundreds of millions of dollars on unregulated phone rates for calls from prisons, some as high as $2.20 per minute.[18]

Greater racial integration in American society achieved by the civil rights movement of the 1960s has been followed by a massive increase in the incarceration rate. The total U.S. prison population has shot up, incredibly, from less than 200,000 to almost 1.4 million today—about seven times. In addition, close to 700,000 people are held in local jails. This brings us to a grand total of 2.1 million people behind bars in America today.

---

[15] Ice Cube, "AmeriKKKa's Most Wanted," *AmeriKKKa's Most Wanted* (Priority, 1990).
[16] Goodie Mob, "Cell Therapy," *Soul Food* (La Face, 1995).
[17] See Loïc Wacquant, "From Slavery to Mass Incarceration," *New Left Review* 13 (2002), pp. 49–54.
[18] Kim Curtis and Bob Porterfield, "California Inmates' Calls Home Prove Costly to Families, Friends." *The Boston Globe* (6th September, 2004).

At the current rate, about 1 in 3 black men will do time at some point in their lives. Sociologist Loïc Wacquant remarks on the post-civil rights era: "As the walls of the ghetto shook and threatened to crumble, the walls of the prison were correspondingly extended, enlarged and fortified, and 'confinement of differentiation,' aimed at keeping a group apart . . . gained primacy over 'confinement of safety'."[19] Wacquant draws a contrast here between incarceration as a way to make society safer and incarceration as a way to stigmatize and ostracize a despised group. His point is that our prison system has increasingly functioned to stigmatize and to ostracize African Americans; the advancement of public safety cannot plausibly be characterized as its primary aim. Some rappers, like Nas, seem to be making the same point:

> My country shitted on me (My country)
> She wants to get rid of me (Naw, never)
> 'Cause the things I seen (We know too much)
> 'Cause the things I seen (We seen too much).[20]

Rappers challenge us to be more aware and critical of the systematic abuse, exclusion, and marginalization of the black urban poor. They protest the endless cycling of black men between ghetto and prison. Their strategy is aggressively provocative—by being provocatively aggressive. Ice-T's "Cop Killer" is an early example that prompted a censorship debate in the 1990s. The lines I quoted from OutKast are more subtle. We don't know whether "standin' my ground, never back down" is a matter of rhyming or something more threatening. We often find rappers playing on words, or signifying, in order to drive home a deeper message. Think of KRS-One's play on the similarity between the words "officer" and "overseer" to draw a parallel between the control and violence that people in each role have exercised over the lives of African Americans.[22] An aim in the music here, as elsewhere, is to destabilize our perceptions of state legitimacy and criminal justice.

---

[19] Wacquant, "From Slavery to Mass Incarceration," p. 52.
[20] Nas, "My Country," *Stillmatic* (Sony, 2001).
[21] See KRS-One, "Sound of Da Police," *Return of the Boom Bap* (Jive, 1993).

Criminal "justice" in an unjust society is suspect. The burden on those who shoulder it is heavy. Despite the materialistic, consumerist values frequently found in rap tracks, sometimes a simpler, deeper, and more soulful plea can be heard, as in Dead Prez's cry for freedom:

> Yo, this world is oh so cold, I think about my ancestors
> Being sold, and it make me wanna break the mold . . .
>
> I don't wanna be no movie star
> I don't wanna drive no fancy car
> I just wanna be free, to live my life, to live my own life.[22]

---

[22] Dead Prez, "We Want Freedom," *Let's Get Free* (Loud, 2000).

# 16

# Gettin' Dis'd and Gettin' Paid: Rectifying Injustice

RODNEY C. ROBERTS

The slave trade and its progeny of racial injustice are excellent examples of far-reaching, unresolved, and massive injustices. Although the U.S. didn't, much of the global community acknowledged these injustices in 2001 following the United Nations World Conference Against Racism, Racial Discrimination, Xenophobia and Related Intolerance (WCAR), held in Durban, South Africa. The participants acknowledged that "slavery and the slave trade are a crime against humanity . . . and are among the major sources and manifestations of racism, racial discrimination, xenophobia and related intolerance, and that Africans and people of African descent, Asians and people of Asian descent, and indigenous peoples were victims of these acts and continue to be victims of their consequences." Moreover, it was strongly reaffirmed that "as a pressing requirement of justice, that victims of human rights violations" such as these, be assured of "the right to seek just and adequate reparation."[1]

The importance of these issues to hip hop is reflected in the words of Chuck D. Performing "Down to Now" with The Last Poets (*Time Has Come*), he describes how we came from Africa in ships, with most of us dying along the way. He asks what the tax would be on the horrors of the Middle Passage, and what

---

[1] Report of the World Conference Against Racism, Racial Discrimination, Xenophobia, and Related Intolerance, Durban, South Africa (31st August–8th September, 2001), U.N. Doc. A/CONF. 189/12 (2002), http://www.unhchr.ch/html/racism/index.htm, pp. 11, 24.

this country has really done for us since then. In "Kill Em Live" he raps about just wanting to get paid back for uncompensated slave labor, slavery's progeny of Jim Crow, and other racial injustices.[2]

This sentiment is reflected in the art of Hulbert Waldroup, whose mural at 168th Street and Broadway in New York City representing the fight for black reparations was photographed for the *New York Amsterdam News* in November 2002. Waldroup was not only trying to inform people of the reparations struggle, but also to get them to think about this important issue. The Russell Simmons' Phat Farm ad that ran in *Black Enterprise* magazine had an even greater aim. The ad featured Rev. Run of Run-DMC, and proclaimed the power of hip hop to impact society. The point of Simmons's campaign was to inform, inspire, and ensure support for this serious issue. He went even further and donated a percentage of the money from the sale of his Phat Classic toward getting the word out, and toward more research. Donating some of the cash from the sale of these kicks to inform others and to enhance our understanding of this important issue is consistent with KRS-One's "Edutainment" music style. He reminds us that hip hop is not rap. Unlike rap, hip hop is not just something that you do; it is something that you live. So if you're serious about livin' hip hop, you oughta be thinking seriously about injustice and what should be done about it.

The best way to start thinking seriously about injustice and rectification is to get an understanding of fundamental ideas like compensation, reparation, punishment, and apology, and how they relate to one another. This track will get us started.

## Just Us in Western Philosophy

Western philosophy has historically been dominated by white males, and has paid relatively little attention to questions concerning injustice and the need to address it. Although the ancient Greek philosopher Aristotle begins the discussion of relevant issues in his *Nicomachean Ethics*, the amount of scholarship since then pales in comparison to other areas of justice. Most contemporary justice theorists have focused on questions

---

[2] Public Enemy, *Bulworth: The Soundtrack* (Interscope, 1998).

of retribution (punishment), and, to a greater extent recently, on distribution (the distribution of rights and duties in society). In particular, questions concerning private property and individual liberty have been thought to be among the most important. Unfortunately, these questions concerning distribution have been addressed using ideal theory.

In ideal theory it is assumed that everyone acts justly. So ideal theory does not have to consider injustice, or even the possibility that there may be a requirement in justice to rectify it. Moreover, contemporary critics of traditional Western philosophy have shown that ideal theory includes a set of assumptions that reflect the experience of the privileged.[3] By clouding social reality, ideal theory serves to enhance the interests of the privileged, and contribute to their continued group advantage. Consequently, the traditional Western approach to justice has favored a privileged perspective on justice, one that limits our reflection on justice, and helps to ensure that the concerns of victims of injustice, including those who are systematically oppressed in democracies like the United States, have almost no place in our deliberations about justice. This is a serious problem. Ideal theory facilitates the marginalization of women and other subordinated groups by excluding their reality from consideration. Chuck D. and Flavor Flav acknowledge this exclusion in their classic call-and-response "Brothers Gonna Work It Out" (*Fear of a Black Planet*). Chuck is delivering a message to all of the Brothers: there should be no mystery to history, and Black America's experience is a real part of history. Flav responds: not *his* story. For Chuck, workin' this thing out includes gettin' paid—or as Eric B. and Rakim would say, gettin' paid *in full*.

## Blowin' Up the Spot

Progressive political philosophers began to produce scholarship in the 1960s and 1970s that challenged traditional Western political theory. So while this period never saw black folk take to the streets in a unified revolutionary action, this challenge to

---

[3] See Charles W. Mills, "'Ideal Theory' as Ideology," in Peggy DesAutels and Margaret Urban Walker, eds., *Moral Psychology: Feminist Ethics and Social Theory*, (Lanham: Rowman and Littlefield, 2004).

philosophy was something of a revolution. For centuries Western philosophy had been virtually oblivious to any political concerns that were not those of privileged white males. Bringing concerns about gender and racial justice into the mix forced a radical change in how philosophy was done. A great deal of the motivation for the emergence of contemporary injustice scholarship came from the Black Civil Rights Movement. Affirmative action in particular became a much-debated topic among philosophers. Maybe more than any other, this topic has helped the rise of injustice theory. Just as Gil Scott-Heron reminded us back-in-the-day that the revolution would be live and not televised, progressive theorists keep political philosophy "live" by forcing it to include the lived reality of those who are not advantaged in society in its analyses of justice.

## Gettin' Dis'd

It should be obvious that the Atlantic slave trade and slavery in the Americas are important parts of the lived reality in what is now the United States of America. These crimes against humanity are also paradigm injustices, injustices created by countless rights violations. This is real disrespect, and real disrespect only happens when rights are violated. But what exactly are rights anyway?

When we say that we have a "right," we are saying that we have a certain kind of justification, a kind of justification that provides good reasons for interfering with someone else's freedom, and for determining how that person should act.[4] Take babies for example. Because we think that they are totally innocent, and that their innocence (among other things) is a good reason for them not to be harmed, we think that everyone's freedom should be interfered with insofar as harming babies is concerned—you shouldn't do it. Consequently, when we say that all babies have a right not to be harmed, we are also saying that everyone has a duty to *respect* that right. So we are limiting freedom, and determining how folks should act.

We typically ascribe the right not be harmed to innocent adults as well. When a twenty-two-year-old Guinean immigrant

---

[4] H.L.A. Hart, "Are There Any Natural Rights?" *Philosophical Review* 64 (1955), pp. 175–191.

named Amadou Diallo was hit nineteen times in a hail of bullets fired into the doorway of his house by New York City cops on the same street in the Bronx where I grew up, it was an obvious violation of his rights. But whether rights are violated in a lethal or non-lethal way, or in a racist or non-racist way, real disrespect is of serious concern to hip hop. In addition to the flowers and signs that adorned the bullet ridden building where Diallo was gunned down, there was a mural commemorating the tragedy painted on the wall of a flower shop just down the block from where he was killed. The mural, another piece of art by Hulbert Waldroup, depicted the four cops who shot Diallo dressed in police uniforms with KKK hoods. Not surprisingly, police brutality was among the issues that inspired the National Hip Hop Political Convention that was recently held in Newark, New Jersey. Student delegates at the convention worked long hours to draft an agenda that, among other things, demanded human rights reform.

We must be careful, however; careful not to confuse morally legitimate cases of being dis'd with those that are not. Recognizing this distinction is particularly important because, although trivial kinds of being dis'd are not injustices, they can sometimes prompt a violent response. Take for example the scene in *Boyz n the Hood* where Ricky and Tre are kickin' it up on Crenshaw. When the dude in the Chicago Bulls hat bumps into Ricky, Ricky naturally feels dis'd. This leads to a heated verbal exchange between the two of them. But because Ricky publicly challenged him, the dude felt as if *he* had been dis'd. This feeling was so strong that he finds Ricky later in the movie and has him blasted with a gauge, ending any future Ricky may have had as a student-athlete at USC. All that really happens in that scene is a very minor accident, or perhaps a minor provocation; but the egos of both characters caused things to get way out of hand. Because the dude was embarrassed, he felt that Ricky had to be paid back for what he had done.

## Payback

When injustices do occur, one obvious and natural response is payback—revenge. This is the kind of response the Notorious B.I.G. has in mind after he gets the 411 on his boy C-Rock in "Somebody's Gotta Die" (*Life After Death*). When Biggie's late-night visitor tells him that C-Rock has just been hit, he immediately wonders if his boy is in critical condition. Whether he is or is not, B.I.G. makes it clear that he intends a forceful retaliatory response to the shooting of his friend. But while revenge may be a natural response, the general view in our society is that revenge-killing is a criminal act—at least when we do it ourselves.

In spite of claiming that he wrote the Declaration of Independence without any reference to other authors, Thomas Jefferson suggested the same sense of political society, and the same sense of our having certain natural, inalienable rights, that British philosopher John Locke had written about in the seventeenth century.[5] Locke saw society primarily as a mechanism to preserve private property, or as custodian of everyone's natural right to punish anyone who violates the rights of someone else and does them harm. The justification for the interference with one's freedom is now *legal,* and the state documents the duties that accompany this right by establishing laws. In this case, laws against killing which sometimes include a penalty of death for failing to obey them.

So what makes revenge by Biggie "criminal" is the violation of the law against killing in this situation. It is up to society to provide punishment for gross violations of rights such as homicide. When people are dis'd in this way, it is up to the government to punish the perpetrator of the injustice. One good reason for thinking that such perpetrators should be punished is that they deserve it. Wrongdoers deserve to be punished for what they have done. Part of what we may need to do in order to rectify an injustice, to set it right, is to punish the wrongdoer.


## Gettin' Paid

But in order to rectify an injustice we have to consider more than just the perpetrator, we also have to consider the victim. So rectification provides for compensation, or a counterbalancing of the unjust loss or harm with something else of value (this is generally what is meant by reparation). In contrast to punishment, where the concern is what the perpetrator may deserve,

---

[5] John Locke, *Two Treatises of Government* (Cambridge: Cambridge University Press, 1988).

compensation is concerned with what the *victim* of the injustice may deserve as part of an attempt to set the situation right. Justice may require that the victim *get paid*.

As noted by the participants of the WCAR, compensation for unjust losses or harms is not only relevant to injustices in the distant past, but also to contemporary injustices. This statement suggests some linkage between the injustices of the past and those of the present. KRS-One makes this connection by way of the overseers on America's slave plantations, and the police officers on America's streets. In "Sound of Da Police" he argues for an analogy between the way overseers dis'd slaves and the way blacks continue to be dis'd by Five-O.[6] Like the overseers on the plantation, the police ride around and can stop black folk seemingly at will (obviously Walking While Black was a concern long before Driving While Black was even thought of). Like the overseer's right to get ill with the slaves under his control, and if necessary, kill them if they fought back, the cops have a right to arrest, and if you fight back they can wet you up without fear of reprisal (like the cops who killed Diallo, and then got off). Of course, black men don't have to be fighting back to get shot by the cops. Speaking the truth about this kind of injustice is exactly what Ice Cube has in mind on the *Straight Outta Compton* track "F*** Tha Police." Cube rejects the unjust racist treatment by police in South Central Los Angeles. He cites his skin color as sufficient to give police the idea that they are authorized to kill him. But Cube ain't down for that, nor is he down for being beaten and thrown in jail. Rather, he is ready to go to blows with any cop who would dis him like that.

It should be clear that the kind of gettin' paid we are concerned with here is not the kind of gettin' paid that happens as the result of a J-O-B. In the Spike Lee Joint, *Do The Right Thing*, Mookie (played by Spike) tells Sal, the owner of the pizzeria where he works, "Sal, start countin' my money tonight, 'cause I gots ta get paid." True, this is an example of compensation. The money is something of value that is meant to counterbalance the labor Mookie has provided to Sal. Also, expending labor seems like a loss, since we give something up in at least two ways while working: the labor itself, and the freedom to do something

---

[6] KRS-ONE, *A Retrospective* (Zomba, 2000).

else during working hours. But even if this is a loss that deserves compensation, since the loss is incurred voluntarily, as part of an agreement to exchange labor for money, it can't be an unjust loss. So the compensation in this kind of case is not rectificatory compensation.

## Forty Acres and a Mule

One form of compensation that is not monetary, and which has come to be symbolic of the movement for the rectification of the injustices perpetrated against blacks in America, is the idea of "forty acres and a mule." This idea prompted Representative John Conyers of Michigan to designate as H.R. 40 his Commission to Study Reparation Proposals for African-Americans Act. The act would "acknowledge the fundamental injustice, cruelty, brutality, and inhumanity of slavery in the United States and the thirteen American colonies between 1619 and 1865" and "establish a commission to examine the institution of slavery, subsequent *de jure* and *de facto* racial and economic discrimination against African-Americans, and the impact of these forces on living African-Americans, to make recommendations to the Congress on appropriate remedies, and for other purposes."[7] Unfortunately, any value that might be attached to this form of compensation relies on the assumption that the aim of forty acres and a mule was to aid blacks in their transition from slavery *and* to compensate them for slavery. But the aim of forty acres and a mule was not to provide rectificatory compensation for the injustices of slavery. In any event, the bill that would have provided forty acres to each family of newly freed slaves never made it into law—it was vetoed by President Andrew Jackson.[8]

Chuck D. tells of how blacks were fooled by the forty acres and a mule proposal. In "Who Stole the Soul?" he notes that there has been no repentance for the injustice of slavery and its

---

[7] Commission to Study Reparation Proposals for African-Americans Act, U.S. Congress, 107th Congress, 1st Session, January 3, 2001, H.R. 40 IH.

[8] For a more detailed discussion of forty acres and a mule, see Rodney C. Roberts, "Rectificatory Justice and the Philosophy of W.E.B. Du Bois," in Mary Keller *et al.*, eds., *Recognizing W.E.B. Du Bois in the Twenty-First Century* (Macon: Mercer University Press, 2006).

progeny that killed his ancestors, and that, because of the forced separation of family members that was an essential part of "assimilating" Africans in America, he'll never know exactly who all of his relatives are. Playing on the classic nursery rhyme, he asks:

> Jack was nimble, Jack was quick.
> Forty acres and a mule Jack.
> Where is it why'd you try to fool the Black

Then, almost as if anticipating one of the standard objections to rectifying the injustices perpetrated against blacks in America ("*I never owned any slaves*"), he notes:

> It wasn't you, but you pledge allegiance
> To the red, white and blue
> Sucker that stole the soul![9]

Chuck D. understands that more is at issue here than merely compensation. He recognizes that in addition to the harm to families over many generations, there is also the failure to repent or apologize for slavery and its progeny of racial injustice. Even if forty acres and a mule had been provided, since there is no sense of acknowledgment or remembrance of the injustice, nor any show of respect for the newly-emancipated Americans of African decent, it fails even as an earnest symbolic gesture of rectification. Rectification calls for an apology because this coupled with some substantive degree of compensation serves to acknowledge an injustice and to reaffirm the moral standing of those who have been dis'd.

### Even if Ya'll Got Paid, Ya'll Wouldn't Know What to Do With It

Some people might object to attempting to rectify the injustices perpetrated against blacks in America, because they object to the idea of providing compensation. They think 'cause we're waitin' for that big payback, that we won't know how to act. No doubt many people envision the kind of result portrayed by

---

[9] Public Enemy, *Fear of a Black Planet* (Def Jam, 1990).

comedian Dave Chappelle in a skit he called "Reparations 2003." On Chappelle's Show, all the black folks in America got paid. Everybody had mad loot, and went crazy spendin' it on all kinds of bling-bling. Folks was drivin' around in new custom Escalades, sportin' big diamond rings, you name it, we bought it. But this objection is wack for at least two reasons. First, for those at the vanguard of the legal battle for compensation, it isn't even about individual checks. Rather, as the Reparations Coordinating Committee tells us, the point would be to relieve the condition of African Americans who continue to suffer the most from the history of racial injustice in America.[10] Second, even if it was about individual checks, providing compensation in this, or any other way, is irrelevant to the *justification* for the compensation itself. The reasons for thinking that rectifying the injustices perpetrated against blacks in America is justified don't have anything to do with the way in which recipients get paid, or what each person will do with that compensation once it is paid. Nor does the likelihood or unlikelihood of actually getting paid necessarily weigh against arguments claiming that compensation *ought* to be paid.

## Not Just a Black Thing

Some people might think that since I have focused mostly on bringing the philosophical enterprise to bear on the black experience, injustice theory is a black thing. But remember that those who participated in the Durban conference were concerned not only with Africans and the African Diaspora, but Asians, people of Asian descent, and indigenous peoples as well. Contemporary injustice theory naturally includes a concern for justice and all people. This seems to be the case in hip hop as well. Take Native Americans, for example. In "Straight Up Nigga" (*O. G. Original Gangster*), Ice-T characterizes himself as a nigga in America 'cause when he sees what he wants, he just takes it. Similarly, the "settlers" who came to this continent saw what they wanted and just took it from the Indians. That was a straight-up nigga move according to Ice-T. Another example that ought to be of concern

---

[10] Charles J. Ogletree, "Reparations for the Children of Slaves: Litigating the Issues," *University of Memphis Law Review* 33 (2003), pp. 245–264.

to American citizens is the perpetuation of injustice against the Kanaka Maoli, the indigenous people of the Hawaiian Islands. Although America formally apologized for the overthrow of the Hawaiian Kingdom, without any restoration of lands, compensation, or even any serious discussion about sovereignty, these injustices are a long way from being rectified.[11] Certainly in cases where indigenous peoples are concerned, and where no real attempt at rectification is made, KRS-One is right: we can never really have justice on stolen land.

---

[11] 107 Stat. 1510 Public Law 103-150—Nov. 23, 1993, on the 100th anniversary of the overthrow of the Hawaiian Kingdom.

# After . . . Word!

# The Philosophy of the Hip-Hop Battle

MARCYLIENA MORGAN

As the essays in this volume demonstrate, hip hop not only invokes many ideas and arguments from the Western philosophical tradition, it is rooted in its own classic battles of philosophy. Although hip-hop philosophy developed from many influences, I first became aware of its importance in the 1980s. It did not come to me in the form of lyrical competition, displays of unfathomable skills, or demonstrations of devotion to the power of *The Word*. Instead, it came to me in the form of kung-fu movies. On Saturdays from 12:00 p.m. to 6:00 p.m., the local television station presented a series of Hong Kong films they aptly named Kung Fu Saturday. I was treated to six hours of uninterrupted battles of will, martial arts skills, betrayal, revenge, and lessons of honor and integrity! I learned about styles of fighting and that some styles, though lethal, have subtlety and wit, while others are simply brutal, blunt, and deadly. Battle or fighting styles were associated with different houses or crews. Each house was guided by sets of philosophical principles that had to do with the individual, the inner self, the mind, the body, desire and much more.

I watched warriors involved in endless philosophical teachings and contests coupled with practice sessions, with crouching, kicking, swooshing sounds and arms waving and momentary breaks when the "master" would query the novice about the philosophical lesson of the day. Those working under different philosophical schools/houses/crews and masters practiced against imaginary foes and battled for the future of humanity.

Often warriors from honorable houses used their bodies and embodied stereotypes to subvert and confront power with a style that recognized the opponents every move. I was not prepared for the power shown by women in these films. They often first appeared demure and "traditional"—serving men and accepting their indifference and abuse. But when trouble developed in the form of intruders, they would channel Audre Lorde's "power of the erotic" and throw their (always) long hair back, or put in a bun, jump over any object in their way, and kick some serious butt![1]

In the midst of my education, I attended a Kung Fu movie festival in Chinatown. The line to the movie theater was a block long. It was composed of a variety of teenage males representing virtually every ethnicity; and many wore clothing representing the latest hip-hop style. As they waited to enter, they practiced rhymes and dance moves and gathered in circles/ciphers, incorporating style/house/crew battle and philosophy within their own sense of place, representation, identity, and culture. Their assessments and critiques of skills were ruthless and righteous. While everybody was kung fu fighting, they channeled the words of Wu-Tang: "Take in my energy, breath and know the rest. 'Cause the good die young and the hard die best."[2] They prepared for battles that were not simply about winning, but based on principles and philosophies about contestations: what these battles mean, what causes them, when it is time to engage in them, why one loses, why one wins, and how one wins.

In the late 1970s, when the elements of hip hop—MC rhyming, b-boying, graffiti art, and deejaying—congealed in the South Bronx, youth brought back home something bigger than hip hop. Youth of color in urban communities suddenly enjoyed a renaissance of ideas and exchanges about their lives, their communities, their neighborhoods and about those who wanted to control them and held them in disdain. Much more than CNN, hip hop brought back the search for reality and truth within a

---

[1] Audre Lorde, "Uses of the Erotic: The Erotic as Power," in Katie Conboy, Nadia Medina, and Sarah Stanbury, eds., *Writing on the Body: Female Embodiment and Feminist Theory* (New York: Columbia University Press, 1997), pp. 277–282.

[2] Wu-Tang Clan "A Better Tomorrow," *Wu-Tang Forever* (Loud, 1997).

modern, highly advanced world of ideas, technology and modes of communication. For many youth, hip hop conducts its real business in the counterpublic where it is actualized through a central edict that is constantly repeated and reframed: *represent, recognize,* and *come correct.*

Hip hop did not begin in the Bronx, but in the ritual expression of a particular generation at a particular time reflecting the same state of crisis emerging from their neighborhoods. The development of hip-hop culture is an instance of what Victor Turner considers a passage through a threshold state into a ritual world that embodies crisis. The threshold state is a power ritual where there is structure and anti-structure—official positions and local positions.[3] In retrospect, the South Bronx was the perfect location for the birth of a hip-hop nation, for in popular and dominant culture it was considered a wasteland and described as full of death rather than life, despair rather than hope, hate rather than love.[4] In fact, the youth of the South Bronx were determined to salvage themselves from their crisis state. From its threshold beginnings, hip hop was an artistic and cultural phenomenon that wrote the most rejected and despised youth back into public and popular culture with an unforeseen script. Hip hop not only had something to say, it did it in such a way that it achieved the Brechtian ideal of art as politics as it thrived on the tension between the mirror and description of society and the events and the dynamic depiction of its contradictions and injustices.[5] Without formal training, urban youth created a new visual, poetic, and dance aesthetic, raised philosophical questions, introduced new technologies and remolded old ones into a powerful 'workforce' of art.

---

[3] Victor Turner, *The Ritual Process: Structure and Anti-Structure* (New York: Aldine De Gruyter, 1969). See also discussions of liminality in Arnold van Gennep, *The Rites of Passage* (Chicago: University of Chicago Press, 1960).

[4] The Bronx Historical Society online lists this description in their timeline: "1977—President Jimmy Carter visits The Bronx, followed by television and newspaper cameramen recording widespread devastation and destruction of the urban surroundings. This projects a powerful negative image of The Bronx across the nation and around the world." See www.bronxhistoricalsociety.org.

[5] Bertolt Brecht, *Brecht on Theatre: The Development of an Aesthetic* (New York: Hill and Wang, 1964); and Darko Suvin, "The Mirror and the Dynamo: On Brecht's Aesthetic Point of View," *The Drama Review* 12 (1967), pp. 56–67.

Though the refrain *represent, recognize, come correct* may suggest essentialist notions of cultural membership and proof of citizenship, it is seldom the case because identity and unity in hip hop are the result of what is referred to as 'flow'. In their introduction to this volume, Tommie Shelby and Derrick Darby emphasize the importance of flow through their riff on the Raekwon quote "That shit ain't easy." Flow in hip hop refers to consciously moving within a chaotic context of fragmentation, dislocation, disruption, and contradiction to create balance, unity, and collective identity. One enters the chaos, battle, cipher in order to represent, recognize, and come correct. A collaborative relationship is created where the artist serves as the audience's envoy, representing its intentions, consciousness, and pleasure. In this respect, the artist embodies the signifier sign and the signified one, the form and the concept. Yet, as artists work to identify, define, and refine their conception of truth and the real, they do so through often highly politicized contestations and confrontations about how to talk about and represent reality and the truth.[6] Once the "real" and socially critical context is established, artists may enter what Csikszentmihalyi calls *flow state* as they reach contentment and are fully absorbed in the activity.[7] It's in this sense that hip hop's ritual of respect and collaboration undermines and mines the status quo by not only exposing hegemony, but recklessly teasing it as well. On the surface, artists appear to stalk, boast, and deride. In reality, they are arguing for inclusion on their terms. Hip hop, and its often-epic quest for what is real, is part of Foucault's technology of power and a battlefield where symbols, histories, politics, art, life, and all aspects of the social system are contested. It is not an endless Nietzschean search for truth, but a determination to expose it and creatively represent all of its manifestations.

As the philosophers in this volume have shown, to *represent* in hip hop is not simply to identify with a city, neighborhood, school, and so on. It is also a discursive turn—it is the symbols, memory, participants, objects, and details that together produce

---

[6] See Marta Savigliano, *Tango and the Political Economy of Passion* (Boulder: Westview, 1995).

[7] Mihaly Csikszentmihalyi, *Beyond Boredom and Anxiety* (San Francisco: Jossey-Bass, 1975); and *Flow: The Psychology of Optimal Experience* (New York: Harper, 1991).

art of the space and time. Hip hop not only disrupts many classical disciplines and approaches to knowledge, but challenges theories of modernity by publicly holding them in contempt. This level of representation is accomplished through a fantastical and complex system of indexicality—literally pointing to and shouting out places, people and events when an interaction is framed around important referential symbols and contexts. In this case, shout outs index and remind us of contextual layers that then invoke related contexts and ideologies. In the end, only those who know the reference can manage to understand what is being said in the present and in the refurbished framework of the hip-hop world.[8] Through this system of representation, hip hop endorses its cultural insiders and the particular set of interpretative beliefs and practices that are in play.

To *recognize* what is hip hop challenges the participants to both contribute their skills and analyses within this value system. It is also to acknowledge that there is a dominant method of evaluation that is hostile to and suspicious of hip hop's system of fair play as well. Similarly, to *come correct* requires constant artistic and personal development, study, analysis, and evaluation. The motives are subversive, the purpose is to reset the world for possibilities and openness.[9]

The survival of hip hop depends on a counterpublic sphere and counterlanguage that, to paraphrase the political scientist Michael Dawson, is a product of *both* the historically imposed separation of the working class, women, blacks, and other minorities from whites throughout most of American history and the embracing of the autonomy of each group as both an institutional principle and an ideological orientation.[10] Hip-hop, artistic expression is not to be valued according to the level of appreciation exhibited by those outside of the cultural framework but within hip hop itself. In that respect, the art is

---

[8] Charles S. Peirce, "Logic as Semiotic: The Theory of Signs," in J. Buchler, ed., *Philosophical Writings of Peirce* (New York: Dover, 1955), pp. 98–119; and Benjamin Lee, *Talking Heads: Language, Metalanguage, and the Semiotics of Subjectivity* (Durham: Duke University of Press, 1997).

[9] Turner, *The Ritual Process*.

[10] Michael C. Dawson, *Black Visions: The Roots of Contemporary African-American Political Ideologies* (Chicago: University of Chicago Press, 2001), p. 27.

not outside of day-to-day experience. Consequently, the critic, scholar, and especially the *academic philosopher* are always under suspicion.

However, the enduring emphasis on "keeping it real" is not necessarily evidence of a modernist sensibility. In fact, hip hop identities are not fractured or always intended as resistant—though they may be interpreted as such. Indeed, adolescent identities are often impulsive and not readily identifiable in relation to personal, social, cultural and political motivation. That is, youth identities are framed within a consistent set of core characteristics and standards that are simultaneously sensitive to the complexities of place, time, and generation.[11] These characteristics include socialization into hip-hop values, beliefs, and attitudes; knowledge of local, personal, and foundational hip-hop history; a common language, mode of interaction, and discourse style; and shared beliefs about representation and evaluation of ability. It's in this sense that hip-hop culture aggressively confronts what Cornel West calls the "ignoble paradox of modernity [that] has yielded deep black allegiance to the promises of American democracy."[12] Hip hop calls into being—through words, sounds, and style of discourse—a matrix of tropes that connect and reframe cultural, historical, social, and political contexts that reintroduce not only events, but narratives about activities and attitudes that existed as part of the past event. Artists express agency, constantly undergo change, and inevitably express the right of all youth who participate in hip-hop culture to assert identities that incorporate race, gender, social class, location, and philosophy. So instead of being fixed, hip hop identities are resolute. Instead of being fluid, they flow.

The introduction of hip hop brought to light the visceral sense of pleasure and power experienced by listeners and fans when artists perform at the highest level of artistic skill. In turn, each hip-hop era is marked by philosophical battles over the

---

[11] Murray Forman, *The 'Hood Comes First: Race, Space, and Place in Rap and Hip-Hop*, (Middletown: Wesleyan University Press, 2002); Tricia Rose, *Black Noise: Rap Music and Black Culture in Contemporary America* (Hanover: Wesleyan University Press, 1994); and Nelson George, *Hip Hop America* (New York: Viking, 1998).

[12] Cornel West, *The Cornel West Reader* (New York: Basic Civitas Books. 1999). p. 53.

nature of representing and identity, the notion of recognizing and truth and sense and reference, and the notion of comin' correct and intentionality and power. Similarly, the hip-hop mantra "keepin' it real" represents the quest for the coalescence and interface of ever-shifting art, politics, representation, performance and individual accountability that reflects all aspects of youth experience.

Hip-hop youth battle through the theoretical houses of Michel Foucault, Mikhail Bakhtin, Judith Butler, Antonio Gramsci, Jürgen Habermas, and more, "shouting out," testing, and challenging theories and philosophies, trying to bring it back to their young bodies in motion, trying to keep theory real. Instead of Descartes's split, they spit rhymes as they reason about their existence. They channel classic old school questions like those presented by Marvin Gaye and Tammi Terrell as they explain "Ain't Nothing Like the Real Thing" and by Nick Ashford and Valerie Simpson as they check their flow and demand, "Is it Still Good to You?" Hip hop is a battle. It is a philosophical fight exploding with overwhelming expectation, opportunity, and challenges that affect real lives. In this battle, there is no such thing as a dead philosopher—just one that has not been resurrected yet to make sure they pay their dues to the flow of hip hop.

# Beats & Rhymes!

# A Selected Discography

Afrika Bambaataa. *Looking for the Perfect Beat* (Tommy Boy, 1982).

Beastie Boys. *Ill Communication* (Capitol, 1994).

Big Punisher. *Capital Punishment* (Loud, 1998).

Biz Markie. *The Biz Never Sleeps* (Cold Chillin', 1989).

Black Eyed Peas. *Elephunk* (Interscope, 2003).

Black Star. *Mos Def and Talib Kweli Are Black Star* (Rawkus, 2002).

Bloodhound Gang. *One Fierce Beer Coaster* (UMG, 1996).

Body Count. *Body Count* (Warner Brothers, 1992).

Boogie Down Productions., *Criminal Minded* (Sugar Hill, 1987).

———. *By All Means Necessary* (Jive/Novus, 1988).

———. *Ghetto Music: The Blueprint of Hip Hop* (Jive, 1989).

———. *Edutainment* (Jive, 1990).

Brand Nubian., *One for All* (Elektra, 1990).

———. *In God We Trust* (Elektra, 1992).

Common. *Like Water for Chocolate* (MCA 2000).

The Coup. *Steal This Double Album* (Foad, 2002).

David Banner. *MTA2: Baptized in Dirty Water* (Universal, 2004).

De La Soul. *3 Feet High and Rising* (Tommy Boy, 1989).

Dead Prez. *Let's Get Free* (Loud, 2000).

———. *RBG: Revolutionary But Gangsta* (Columbia, 2004).

Dilated Peoples., *Expansion Team* (Capitol, 2001).

Dr. Dre. *The Chronic* (Interscope, 1992).

———. *2001* (Aftermath, 1999).

Eminem. *The Marshall Mathers LP* (Interscope, 2000).

———. *The Eminem Show* (Interscope, 2002);

———. *8 Mile* (Interscope, 2002).

Eric B. and Rakim. *Paid in Full* (Fourth & Broadway, 1987).

50 Cent. *Guess Who's Back* (Full Clip, 2002).

———. *Get Rich or Die Tryin'* (Shady/Aftermath/Interscope, 2003).

Foxy Brown. *Broken Silence* (Uptown/Universal, 2001).

The Game. *The Documentary* (Aftermath, 2005).

Gang Starr. *Daily Operations* (Capitol, 1992)

Goodie Mob. *Soul Food* (La Face, 1995).

Gorillaz featuring Del tha Funkee Homosapien. *Gorillaz* (Virgin, 2001).

Grandmaster Flash. *Message from Beat Street: Best of Grandmaster Flash* (Rhino, 1994).

Guru. *Jazzmatazz, Vol. 2: The New Reality* (Capitol Records, 1995).

Ice Cube. *AmeriKKKa's Most Wanted* (Priority, 1990).

———. *Death Certificate* (Priority, 1991).

Ice-T., *O.G. Original Gangster,* (Sire, 1991).

———. *Return of the Real* (Priority, 1996).

Ja Rule. *The Last Temptation* (Def Jam, 2002).

Jadakiss. *Kiss of Death* (Ruff Ryder/Interscope, 2004).

Jay-Z. *Reasonable Doubt* (Roc-A-Fella, 1996).

———. *Volume 3: Life and Times of S. Carter* (Rock-A-Fella/Def Jam, 1999).

———. *Blueprint* (Roc-A-Fella, 2001).

———. *The Black Album* (Roc-A-Fella, 2003).

Jay-Z and Linkin Park. *Collision Course* (Warner, 2004).

Jeru the Damaja. *The Sun Rises in the East* (Payday, 1994).

Kam. *Neva Again* (Atlantic, 1993).

Kelis. *Tasty* (Arista, 2003).

KRS-One. *Return of the Boom Bap* (Jive, 1993).

———. *KRS-ONE A Retrospective* (Zomba, 2000).

———. *The Sneak Attack* (Koch, 2001).

———. *Keep Right* (Grit, 2004).

Kurtis Blow. *The Best of Kurtis Blow* (Mercury, 1994).

The Last Poets. *Time Has Come* (Mercury, 1997).

Lauryn Hill. *The Miseducation of Lauryn Hill* (Ruffhouse, 1998).

Lil Jon and the East Side Boyz. *Crunk Juice* (TVT, 2004).

Lil' Flip. *The Leprechaun* (Sony, 2002).

Lil' Kim. *Hard Core* (Undeas/Big Beat, 1996).

———. *Notorious KIM* (Atlantic, 2000).

LL Cool J. *Bigger and Deffer* (Def Jam, 1987).

Missy Elliott. *Miss E . . . So Addictive* (Goldmind/Elektra, 2001).

Mobb Deep. *The Infamous* (RCA, 1995).

———. *Murda Muzik* (Loud, 1999).

Mos Def. *Black on Both Sides* (Rawkus, 1999).

———. *The New Danger* (Geffen, 2004).

Ms. Dynamite. *A Little Deeper* (Polydor, 2002).

Nas. *Illmatic* (Columbia, 1994).

———. *Nastradamus* (Columbia, 1999).

———. *Stillmatic* (Sony, 2001).

———. *God's Son* (Columbia, 2002).

———. *Street's Disciple* (Sony, 2004).

Naughty By Nature. *Naughty by Nature* (Tommy Boy, 1991).

Me'Shell NdegéOcello. *Plantation Lullabies* (Maverick, 1993).

————. *Bitter* (Warner, 1999).

————. *Cookie: The Anthropological Mixtape* (Maverick, 2002).

Nelly. *Nellyville* (Universal, 2002).

————. *Da Derrty Versions: The Reinvention* (Universal, 2003).

Notorious B.I.G. *Ready to Die* (Bad Boy, 1994).

————. *Life after Death* (Bad Boy, 1997).

N.W.A. *Straight Outta Compton* (Priority, 1988).

————. *Niggaz4life* (Ruthless, 1991).

OutKast. *Aquemini* (La Face, 1998).

————. *Speakerboxxx/The Love Below* (Arista, 2003).

Paris. *The Devil Made Me Do It* (Tommy Boy, 1990).

————. *Sonic Jihad* (Guerrilla Funk, 2003).

Public Enemy. *It Takes a Nation of Millions to Hold Us Back* (Def Jam, 1988).

————. *Fear of a Black Planet* (Def Jam, 1990).

————. *Apocalypse 91 . . . The Enemy Strikes Black* (Def Jam, 1991).

————. *He Got Game* (Def Jam, 1998).

————. *Bulworth: The Soundtrack* (Interscope, 1998).

Puff Daddy. *No Way Out* (Bad Boy, 1997).

Queen Latifah. *All Hail the Queen* (Tommy Boy, 1989).

Rakim. *The 18th Letter* (Universal, 1997).

Ras Kass. *Soul on Ice* (Priority Records, 1996).

The Roots. *Things Fall Apart* (MCA, 1999).

Run-D.M.C. *Run-D.M.C.* (Arista, 1984).

————. *King of Rock* (Profile, 1985).

Salt-N-Pepa. *Very Necessary* (UMG, 1993).

Sir Mix-A-Lot. *Mack Daddy* (American, 1992).

Shyne. *Godfather Buried Alive* (Gangland, 2004).

Spearhead. *Home* (Capitol, 1994).

Snoop Dogg. *Doggystyle* (Death Row, 1993).

————. *R&G (Rhythm & Gangsta): The Masterpiece* (Geffen, 2004).

Angie Stone. *Mahogany Soul* (J-Records, 2001).

Talib Kweli. *Quality* (Rawkus, 2002).

Thug Life. *Thug Life Volume I* (Interscope, 1994).

A Tribe Called Quest. *Midnight Marauders* (Zomba, 1993).

2Pac. *Pacalypse Now* (Interscope, 1991).

————. *Me Against the World* (Interscope, 1995).

————. *All Eyez On Me* (Death Row, 1996).

————. *Until the End of Time* (Amaru/Interscope, 2001).

Ultramagnetic MC's. *Critical Beatdown* (Next Plateau, 1988).

U.T.F.O. *U.T.F.O.* (Select, 1985).

Various Artists. *Lyricists Lounge,* Vol. I (Priority, 1998).

————. *The Hip Hop Box* (Hip-O, 2004).

Kanye West. *The College Dropout* (Roc-A-Fella, 2004).

Whodini. *Back in Black* (Jive, 1986).

Wu-Tang Clan. *Enter the Wu-Tang (36 Chambers)* (Loud, 1993).

———. *Wu-Tang Forever* (Loud, 1997).

X-Clan. *To the East, Blackwards* (Fourth & Bway/Pgd, 1990).

# The Crew

**J. Angelo Corlett** is Professor of Philosophy and Ethics at San Diego State University, and the author of the books: *Analyzing Social Knowledge*; *Responsibility and Punishment*; *Race, Racism, and Reparations*; *Terrorism: A Philosophical Analysis*; *Interpreting Plato's Dialogues*, as well as over seventy-five articles in various philosophy and other scholarly journals. He is the Editor-in-Chief of *The Journal of Ethics: An International Philosophical Review*; and editor of *Equality and Liberty: Analyzing Rawls and Nozick*.

**Derrick Darby** was born in the South Bronx and raised in the Queensbridge Housing Projects, NYC. After graduating from MLK Jr. High in Manhattan, he received his B.A. in philosophy from Colgate University and his Ph.D. in philosophy from the University of Pittsburgh. He is Associate Professor of Philosophy and Humanities at Texas A&M University, College Station, Texas. His areas of research and teaching include social and political philosophy, ethics, and African American philosophy with a focus on questions concerning the nature and value of rights. He is currently writing a book on rights entitled *At the Hands of Community: Rights, Race, and Recognition*.

**Kathryn T. Gines** is Assistant Professor of African American and Diaspora Studies and Philosophy at Vanderbilt University. Her areas of research and teaching interests include: African American Philosophy, Social and Political Philosophy, Continental Philosophy, Diaspora Studies, and Race and Gender Theory.

**Lewis R. Gordon** is a Laura H. Carnell University Professor of Philosophy at Temple University, where he also is director of the Institute for the Study of Race and Social Thought and the Center for Afro-Jewish Studies. He also is President of the Caribbean Philosophical Association. He is the author of several influential books, including the award-winning *Her Majesty's Other Children: Sketches of Racism from a Neocolonial Age*.

**Mitchell Green** received his Ph.D. in Philosophy from the University of Pittsburgh. He is now Associate Professor of Philosophy at the

University of Virginia. He has held fellowships from the Andrew Mellon Foundation, the American Council of Learned Societies, and the Center for Contemplative Mind in Society. His research concerns the Philosophy of Language, Aesthetics, and the Philosophy of Mind. His books *Self-Expression,* and *Moore's Paradox* (the latter edited with John Williams) are forthcoming with Oxford University Press. His *Engaging Philosophy: A Topical Introduction,* is forthcoming.

**JOY JAMES** is the John B. and John T. McCoy Presidential Professor of Africana Studies and College Professor in Political Science at Williams College, where she chairs its African-American Studies program. She is the author of a number of publications including *Resisting State Violence* (1996); *Transcending the Talented Tenth* (1997); *Shadowboxing: Representations of Black Feminist Politics* (1999); and *Memory, Shame, and Rage: The Central Park Case, 1989–2002* (2006). James's edited collections on prisons and policing include *States of Confinement* (2000); *Imprisoned Intellectuals* (2003); *The New Abolitionists: (Neo)Slave Narratives and Contemporary Prison Writing* (2005); and *Warfare: Prison and the American Homeland* (2006).

**BILL E. LAWSON** is Distinguished Professor of Philosophy at the University of Memphis. He has published articles on the urban under-class, John Locke's theory of political obligation, social contract theory and African Americans, jazz, and urban environmental philosophy. He is the author (with Howard McGary) of *Between Slavery and Freedom* (1992), editor of *The Underclass Question* (1992), co-editor (with Frank Kirkland) of *Frederick Douglass: A Critical Reader* (1999), co-editor (with Laura Westra) of *Faces of Environmental Racism* (2001), and co-editor (with Donald Koch) of *Pragmatism and the Problem of Race* (2004).

**ERIN I. KELLY** is Associate Professor of Philosophy at Tufts University. She received her Ph.D. from Harvard University. Her research interests are in ethics, political philosophy, and the philosophy of law, with a focus on questions about justice, moral responsibility, and theories of punishment. Her publications include, "Doing Without Desert" (2002) and "The Burdens of Collective Liability" (2002).

**MARCYLIENA MORGAN** is Associate Professor of Communications at Stanford University. She is the director of Stanford's Hip Hop Archive, which she founded at Harvard University's W.E.B. Du Bois Institute in 2002 while on the faculty in African and African American Studies. Her research focuses on youth, gender, language, culture and identity, soci-olinguistics, discourse, and interaction. She is the author of *Language,*

*Discourse, and Power in African American Culture* (2002) and editor of *Language and the Social Construction of Identity in Creole Situations* (1994). Her other publications include articles and chapters on gender and women's speech, language ideology, discourse and interaction among Caribbean women in London and Jamaica, urban youth language and interaction, hip hop culture, and language education planning and policy. She is currently completing a book on hip-hop culture entitled: *The Real Hip Hop: Battling for Knowledge, Power, and Respect in the Underground.*

**SARAH MCGRATH** is an assistant professor of philosophy at Brandeis University. She received her Ph.D. from MIT in 2002, and taught at the College of the Holy Cross in Worcester, Massachusetts, from 2002 to 2005. Her research interests include metaphysics and ethics, and the connections between the two.

**LIONEL K. MCPHERSON** received his Ph.D. in philosophy from Harvard University. He is currently an assistant professor of philosophy at Tufts University. His published articles in moral, political, and social philosophy include "Innocence and Responsibility in War" (2004) and "The Moral Insignificance of 'Bare' Reasons" (2002). Prior to his academic career, he worked as a music and media critic. He was named, for all of three hours, *The Source*'s first managing editor.

**JOHN P. PITTMAN** teaches philosophy and justice studies at John Jay College of Criminal Justice, CUNY. His research interests include Africana philosophy, nineteenth-century German philosophy, and contemporary social theory. In addition to authoring numerous essays, he is the editor of *African-American Perspectives and Philosophical Traditions* (1997) and co-editor (with Tommy L. Lott) of *A Companion to African-American Philosophy* (2003). His sons, Isaiah and Jackson, do what they can to keep him honest.

**RODNEY C. ROBERTS** is a descendant of the African peoples who were enslaved at the Somerset Place plantation in Creswell, North Carolina. He grew up in the Soundview area of the Bronx, New York, and attended the High School of Performing Arts and James Monroe High School. Following ten years of service in the U.S. Navy as a submariner, scuba diver, and electronics instructor, he completed his associates and bachelor's degrees, and earned his M.A. and Ph.D. in philosophy from the University of Wisconsin, Madison. Dr. Roberts is currently assistant professor of philosophy at East Carolina University where he teaches social and political philosophy, ethics, and Africana philosophy. In 2005–06 he will be a Fulbright Lecture and Research

Scholar in the Department of Philosophy, University of Cape Town, South Africa. He is the editor of *Injustice and Rectification*.

**TOMMIE SHELBY** earned his Ph.D. in philosophy from the University of Pittsburgh. He is currently the John L. Loeb Associate Professor of the Social Sciences at Harvard University, where he teaches in the Department of African and African American Studies and in the Committee on Degrees in Social Studies. In addition to publishing several articles on African American philosophy, political philosophy, and social theory, he is the author of *We Who Are Dark: The Philosophical Foundations of Black Solidarity* (2005).

**RICHARD SHUSTERMAN** is Dorothy F. Schmidt Eminent Scholar Chair in the Humanities and Professor of Philosophy at Florida Atlantic University, Boca Raton. A recipient of senior NEH and Fulbright Research Fellowships, he is author of *The Object of Literary Criticism* (1984), *T.S. Eliot and the Philosophy of Criticism* (1988), *Pragmatist Aesthetics* (1992, now in its second edition, 2000, and translated into twelve languages), *Practicing Philosophy* (1997), *Performing Live* (2000), and *Surface and Depth* (2002). From 1992 to 1994 he wrote rap criticism for the North Philly rap fanzine *JOR* (Journal of Rap) under the moniker "Rich Frosted."

**PAUL C. TAYLOR** received his bachelor's degree in philosophy from Morehouse College and his Ph.D. in philosophy from Rutgers University. He has numerous publications in the areas of aesthetics, race theory, Africana philosophy, and social philosophy, including the book *Race: A Philosophical Introduction* (2004). Taylor is an associate professor of philosophy at Temple University, Associate Director of Temple's Institute for the Study of Race and Social Thought, a fellow of the Jamestown Project at Yale, and a co-editor of *The Africana Review*, an online journal.

**STEPHEN LESTER THOMPSON** is Assistant Professor of Philosophy at William Paterson University in Wayne, New Jersey. He has written a number of papers in the philosophy of language and logic, and is currently writing a book on the grammar of black English. He lives in New York City.

**LIDET TILAHUN** is the Director of World Hip Hop. She's currently conducting research at the W.E.B. Du Bois Institute for African and African American Research at Harvard University on Hip Hop's influence in African youth culture. She received her B.A. in Political Science from Emmanuel College and M.A. in International Relations from

Northeastern University. Her research interests include the ways African youth have used—and continue to use—hip hop as a powerful agent for social and political change; a platform of self-expression; a subversive means of critiquing corruption and tradition; a measure of national self-reflection; and a tool for education, HIV/AIDS prevention, and access to health care.

**CORNEL WEST** has authored many groundbreaking and thought-provoking books that have changed the course of discussion of race, justice, and democracy. His best-selling *Race Matters* (1993), a collection of profoundly moral essays, served as a call to social action and has become a contemporary classic. In his follow-up, *Democracy Matters* (2004), Dr. West continues his impassioned argument, this time aimed at the raging debate about democracy and America's role in today's troubled world. Dr. West continues to explore new avenues for teaching and communicating. He has appeared in the *Matrix* trilogy and served as the philosophical foundation for the films. His CDs, *Sketches of My Culture* and *Street Knowledge*, highlight his belief that growing divisions in our society foster the despair and distrust that undermine our democratic process. By working to create an ongoing dialogue between the myriad of voices in our culture, Dr. West is vigilant in his efforts to restore hope to America.

# The Hip-Hop Head Index